Supervisory Relationships

Exploring the Human Element

Tamara L. Kaiser
University of St. Thomas

BROOKS/COLE
CENGAGE Learning

Australia • Brazil • Japan • Korea • Mexico • Singapore • Spain • United Kingdom • United States

BROOKS/COLE
CENGAGE Learning

Supervisory Relationships:
Exploring the Human Element
Tamara L. Kaiser

Sponsoring Editor: Lisa Gebo

Editorial Assistant: Terry Thomas

Production Editor: Tessa A. McGlasson

Manuscript Editor: Barbara Kimmel

Permissions Editor: Carline Haga

Marketing Team: Jean Thompson and Deborah Petit

Marketing Representative: Jon Holloway

Interior Design: Vernon T. Boe

Art Editor: Lisa Torri

Interior Illustration: Kathy Joneson

Cover Design: Sharon Kinghan

Indexer: James Minkin

Typesetting: Susan Rogin Benoit

For product information and technology assistance, contact us at **Cengage Learning Customer & Sales Support, 1-800-354-9706**

For permission to use material from this text or product, submit all requests online at **cengage.com/permissions** Further permissions questions can be emailed to **permissionrequest@cengage.com**

Library of Congress Control Number: 96-9680

ISBN-13: 978-0-534-34559-4

ISBN-10: 0-534-34559-X

Brooks/Cole
511 Forest Lodge Road
Pacific Grove, CA 93950
USA

Cengage Learning is a leading provider of customized learning solutions with office locations around the globe, including Singapore, the United Kingdom, Australia, Mexico, Brazil, and Japan. Locate your local office at: **international.cengage.com/region**

Cengage Learning products are represented in Canada by Nelson Education, Ltd.

For your course and learning solutions, visit **academic.cengage.com**

Purchase any of our products at your local college store or at our preferred online store **www.ichapters.com**

Printed in the United States of America
8 9 10 11 12   14 13 12 11 10

ED216

Contents

Chapter Five

Trust   130

Preface

What really goes on in the relationship between supervisor and supervisee? Most texts talk about the "how to's" of supervision without really attending to the human element, which both underlies and adds excitement and challenge to the task. In teaching classes on supervision, it became clear to me and my students that we needed a vivid picture of what happens in this relationship. This book will give the reader a unique inside look at the complex dynamics that characterize the supervisory relationship. I introduce a conceptual model, which lists three elements of supervision: the goal of competent service to clients, the process of accountability, and the context of the supervisory relationship. The model also illustrates that supervision takes place within the larger context of both the organization and outside forces, such as funding sources and licensure bodies. The three key aspects of the supervisory relationship that are explored are:

- the use of power and authority
- the development of shared meaning
- the development of trust between supervisor and supervisee

The model shows the interrelationships among all these aspects.

The first chapter introduces the notion of the importance of relationship in supervision and gives an overview of the conceptual model. Chapters 2 and 3 discuss topics related to power and authority. Chapter 4 focuses on the development of shared meaning, and Chapter 5 on the development of trust. The theoretical material is brought to life by the many stories shared by supervisees and supervisors alike about their experiences in this relationship. The stories give readers exposure to a wide range of experiences in supervision, many of which they may not have yet lived themselves. They can draw from these experiences to understand a variety of ways to handle issues and a variety of potential reactions from both supervisors and supervisees. A recurrent theme is that it is important to look at this relationship through the lens of ethical principles. Therefore, the process of supervision is discussed in ethical as well as practical terms, applying concepts developed by several authors on relational ethics. Each chapter ends with a series of questions, many of which refer to specific examples within the text. The questions can serve as a basis for classroom discussion and activities or conversations between supervisors and supervisees, or as a means for helping the individual reader respond to the material.

My training and background is in social work and marriage and family therapy, and much of the theoretical material and supporting literature is grounded in the principles that guide these two professions. However, many of the people whose stories I have collected were trained in different professions, such as psychology and counselor education, and others had very little professional training. In my opinion, the material offered here is equally applicable to those supervisory relationships.

This book is intended primarily for courses on supervision. Its most common use would be as a supplement to a more comprehensive core text. Students in programs with an emphasis on clinical practice will benefit from this illumination of the broader issues. In addition, faculty and students will find the book useful for understanding some of the dynamics at play in the internship and practicum situation; several of the examples are specifically about students in the field. Finally, it is my hope that, for both supervisors and supervisees currently in practice, this book will provide insight into the interpersonal issues that either impede or enhance effective supervision.

ACKNOWLEDGMENTS

This book has been in the making for the past nine years, and many people have helped me bring it alive. Peg Thompson taught me first-hand the powerfully positive impact of a good supervisory relationship. In addition, it was she who encouraged me to embark on the initial project that led to this book. Bill Doherty, my most valued mentor during my graduate studies, helped me immeasurably with the conceptualization and implementation of the initial project and offered important feedback and support for this project. His most recent book, *Soul Searching: Why Psychotherapists Must Promote Moral Responsibility*, helped deepen the quality of this text. I have spent many hours discussing the intricacies of ethical and competent supervision with my friend and colleague Marilyn Peterson. Her work as a teacher, supervisor, clinician, and author has profoundly influenced my own. Angeline Barretta-Herman and I have taught supervision both to students in our social work program at the College of St. Catherine and the University of St. Thomas and to practicing supervisors through the CSC/UST

Supervision Institute. Our relationship has been a constant source of learning, inspiration, and support for me. Lisa Gebo, my editor, believed in this project when I was losing faith, and offered consistent, enthusiastic encouragement and useful feedback whenever I needed them.

In addition to these five individuals, several other colleagues and friends served as readers and valuable critics of the drafts of this book. I would like to thank Linda Budd, Susan Cochrane, Denise D'Aurora, Diane Dovenberg, Ann Romanczuk, Barbara Shank, and Erik Storlie for their important input. Barbara, who is dean of our school of social work, deserves an extra thanks for making the time available for me to write. The following individuals served as reviewers for Brooks/Cole: Janice Adams, Indiana Wesleyan University; Joan DeGiulio, Youngstown State University; Alberta Dooley, University of Oklahoma; Bart Grossman, University of California, Berkeley; Mary Hayes, University of St. Thomas; William Hershey, University of Washington; Carlton Munson, University of Maryland at Baltimore; Carolyn Saari, Loyola University Chicago; Federico Souflée, University of Texas; and Barbara Thomlison, University of Calgary. I thank them for their significant contribution to the development of this book. Joan McDonald, my research assistant, acted as my legs and eyes in the library, finding relevant articles and books. In addition, both she and Lois Stevenson spent countless hours transcribing the interviews that served as source material for the stories. My student, Karen Matts, performed a study on communication in cross-cultural supervision. Her findings were extremely useful and interesting, and, with permission from her subjects, she shared the transcripts of her own interviews with me, some portions of which appear here as stories. Finally, the book could not exist without the dozens of supervisors and supervisees who were willing to openly share with me the peaks and valleys of their own experiences.

I would like to offer a special thank you to my children, Ghita and Mark Levenstein; my parents, Dr. Paula Kaiser and the late Henry Kaiser; and my sister, Rebecca Kaiser, all of whom supported me in this endeavor, both through their words of encouragement and through sacrifices of their own.

Tamara L. Kaiser

Chapter One

The Importance
of Relationship

I began my career as a social worker more than 20 years ago. I was young, insecure, and naive about the enormity of the task I had taken on. As do many people in the helping professions, I entered the field with my own personal issues, which, along with my lack of experience, contributed to my doubts about whether I had anything to offer those who came to me for help. A few years after receiving my M.S.W., I encountered a supervisor whose style of supervision only added to my already shaky professional identity. She believed, as I do, that one's personal issues affect one's work. Her approach was to focus primarily on investigating these issues in a forceful and penetrating way, leaving me with a feeling of vulnerability and self-doubt. During a discussion about a client, she would inevitably turn the discussion toward a look at my deficiencies, with comments such as, "Tamara, you have a deep personal wound, which, if not addressed, will seriously hinder your ability as a professional." If I tried to claim my strength, she defined the effort as one of resistance to supervision or as a reflection of my discomfort with her as a powerful woman. Although several members of our work group had some difficulty with her style, she framed each of the relationships as ones in which the worker's personal problems were the cause of the difficulty. She also appeared to use her administrative power to punish those who did not get along with her.

After a few years, I found myself at a professional crossroads. Although by now I had been a social worker for several years, I felt completely ineffective in my work and wondered whether I should make a career change. I decided that before doing so, I would put considerable effort and resources into my professional development. To that end, I went outside the agency and hired a consultant to help me with my work. This relationship proved to be the most profoundly positive influence in my adult life. As had the previous supervisor, she challenged me to address my personal issues so that I could more effectively use myself in my work with clients. However, she consistently communicated a message of belief in me and in my ability. She also taught me many frameworks and techniques for working with clients. Finally, when there was conflict between us, she was willing to discuss our differences in a respectful manner and to acknowledge her part in the difficulty, as well as expecting me to acknowledge mine. Because of my trust in her and of hers in me, I could tell her in a deeply honest way the full story of what I had done with a client—what I did well and where I thought I had made mistakes. She challenged me to examine the mistakes I had made and to do what was necessary to right them. She challenged me, as well, to take the risk to try new approaches with my clients. And she enabled me to build on the strength I brought to my work.

The most important thing I learned from her was that I could be both vulnerable and competent at the same time. I blossomed under her tutelage. I became alive in my work with clients, able to help them confront the challenges in their lives and to make important and useful changes. I left that relationship with a new and solid sense of competence and creativity and, since then, have accomplished much as a social worker and as a teacher to others entering the field. I left, as well, with a personal knowledge of the enormous power of the supervisory relationship.

These experiences in supervision led to my writing this book about the supervisory relationship, a relationship that has received little attention in the literature on supervision. In the past several years, I have spoken to many people from various human service fields who have been in the position of supervisor, supervisee, or both. I have been a supervisor and have had the opportunity to teach others about supervision. All this work has underscored for me the importance of my own lesson as a supervisee—that this relationship has a profound influence on the quality of the practitioner's work with clients.

A great deal has been written about supervision in human services. Supervision is commonly viewed as a primary avenue through which new practitioners learn the tools of the trade. Kadushin (1992) noted that, especially in the early years of social work, many came to agencies with little academic background and therefore had to be educated about the field of social work on the job. He described supervision as consisting of supportive, educational and administrative functions, and provided a comprehensive discussion about the skills and tasks involved in each. The other two primary authors on the topic in social work (Munson, 1993; Shulman, 1982, 1993) agree with Kadushin's general framework but have elaborated on different aspects of the process of supervision. Munson described a variety of techniques and skills necessary to perform the evaluative, educational, and supportive functions, focusing primarily on educational techniques. He also introduced the concept of supervisory styles. Shulman proposed an interactional model of supervision and described the functions and issues pertinent to the tasks of supervision during the beginning, middle, and end phases. In addition, he discussed specific, concrete interactional skills the supervisor needs to successfully accomplish the tasks.

In marriage and family therapy and in psychology, supervision is primarily discussed as a vehicle for teaching practitioners or students. The focus therefore is mostly on educational issues (for example, Wiffen & Byng-Hall, 1982; Stoltenberg & Delworth, 1987; Liddle, Bruenlin, & Schwartz, 1988; Bernard & Goodyear, 1992). In more recent years, there has been increased attention to ethical and legal issues in supervision (for example, Upchurch, 1985; Ryder & Hepworth, 1990; Sherry, 1991; Kaiser, 1992; Goldberg, 1993; Peterson, 1993a, 1993b). As compared to social work, in these professions there is less discussion of the administrative aspects of most agency supervisors' jobs.

In all professions, and especially in social work (for example, Perlman, 1979), the relationship between client and worker is seen as the medium through which change occurs. Sometimes this relationship receives major attention. For example, psychodynamic approaches overtly address issues of transference and countertransference and consider the therapeutic relationship a "corrective experience" that enables the client to heal old wounds. In other modalities—for example, behavioral and strategic approaches—little direct attention is paid to the quality of that relationship in the course of the work. However, a positive relationship between client and practitioner is considered necessary for treatment to be effective.

Similarly, most would agree that a positive relationship between supervisor and supervisee is important if the supervision is to be effective. Although the tasks of supervision appear to follow common sense, those who have been either supervisors or supervisees observe that these tasks are often quite complicated in the real world. Two major blocks to the effective and smooth functioning of supervision are contextual issues, such as agency mission and funding restrictions, and relational issues.

The premise of this book is that the supervisory relationship is the medium through which supervision occurs. This premise is supported in the literature by the concepts of parallel process (Eckstein & Wallerstein, 1958; Doehrman, 1976; Shulman, 1982, 1993) and isomorphism (Cade & Seligman, 1982; Liddle, 1988; Mazza, 1988; Frankel & Piercy, 1990). The concept of *parallel process* was introduced by Eckstein and Wallerstein (1958), who noted that the supervisee's behaviors frequently parallel those the client is manifesting in treatment. Given this phenomenon, those behaviors can be addressed in the supervisory relationship, thus freeing up the practitioner and providing the practitioner with a model for addressing the same issues with the client. Others (for example, Doehrman, 1976; Abroms, 1978; Kahn, 1979; Shulman, 1982; Peterson, 1986; Springman, 1989; Sigman, 1989; Alpher, 1991; Kadushin, 1992) have elaborated on the notion that an intricate interplay exists between the therapeutic and supervisory relationships.

The concept of *isomorphism* is discussed primarily in the field of marriage and family therapy. Kadushin (1992) maintains that this term is a general one, meaning that patterns tend to repeat themselves across systems. Often the literature on supervision in this field refers to an isomorphic relationship between the model of therapy being taught and the approach to supervision being used. For example, a supervisor teaching a Bowenian approach to family therapy might have supervisees present a genogram of their own families of origin (Papero, 1988).

Sometimes the term isomorphism, like the concept of parallel process, is used to describe a connection between the supervisory and treatment relationships. Frankel and Piercy (1990) sought to discover whether the degree of isomorphism between supervisor and supervisee behaviors was related to subsequent client change. They collected data from videotapes of live supervision sessions in which phone-ins were audiotaped and dubbed in where they occurred. The tapes were coded with regard to client resistance, therapist behavior, and supervisor behavior. The researchers studied therapists' and supervisors' "support" behaviors, which reflect relationship skills, and their "teach" behaviors, which reflect structuring skills.

From the results of the study, Frankel and Piercy distinguished between all examples of supervisor "teach" and "support" behaviors and those behaviors that both supervisors and supervisees thought were most effective. The investigators found no significant change in the supervisees' post–phone-in "support" and "teach" behaviors made in response to the simple engagement of those behaviors by the supervisors. By contrast, there was a significant change in the supervisees' behaviors after an effective intervention by the supervisors.

The researchers also examined clients' degree of cooperation to determine whether a significant change occurred when there was isomorphism between the behavior of the supervisor and that of the supervisee. When both supervisors and supervisees exhibited effective "support" behaviors, both individual members and entire families increased their cooperative behavior. When supervisors and supervisees exhibited effective "teach" behaviors, individual family members' cooperation increased, but the cooperativeness of the family as a whole did not change significantly. Thus it appeared that "support" behaviors had a more powerful impact than did "teach" behaviors. The authors noted that this finding is consistent with research suggesting that the most important predictors of positive client outcomes are: first, therapists' relationship skills; and second, therapist's structuring skills (Alexander, Barton, Schiavo, & Parsons, 1976; Gurman, Kniskern, & Pinsoff, 1986).

Frankel and Piercy's work provides empirical support for the notion that there is an isomorphic relationship between supervisor and supervisee behaviors, as well as a connection between these behaviors and subsequent changes in client behaviors. The study further supports the contention that an effective relationship between supervisor and supervisee is an essential ingredient for effective treatment. Therefore, the supervisory relationship is not just something that needs to be operating well for treatment skills to be taught; rather, it interacts in a dynamic way with the teaching of those skills.

In fact, my first supervisor had many valuable lessons to teach. But because I put so much energy into defending myself against what I perceived was an attack, I was not open to learning from her. I was reluctant to discuss any doubts I had about my work or to ask for guidance. As a result, I often became stuck in my work with clients, unclear about what direction to take that would be useful. By contrast, I was a willing learner with my second supervisor. As I grew, so did my clients. I was able to challenge my clients, as I was challenged, to enter unfamiliar or threatening territory. Certainly supervision is not the only arena in which people find support to do their work; many practitioners benefit greatly from input from their peers or other professionals. However, the function of supervision is a multifaceted one, involving a complex process of accountability that hopefully leads to the ensurance of competent work with clients. As the many stories in this book will illustrate, problems in the supervisory relationship often lead to difficulties with the larger processes of supervision. Conversely, a positive supervisory relationship creates an environment in which the processes of supervision can operate so that clients are ultimately better served.

In the last half of this chapter, I introduce a model that describes four basic aspects of supervision: greater context (agency, funding sources, political environment), immediate context (supervisory relationship), process (accountability), and goal (competent service to clients). The model also depicts how these aspects of the process interact with one another in a dynamic fashion, each affecting the other.

In Chapters 2, 3, 4, and 5, I will address in detail the three core elements of the relationship between supervisor and supervisee: power and authority, shared meaning, and trust. I will offer theoretical discussion and stories from supervisors and supervisees to give the reader an "inside" look at the complicated relational dynamics that are operating. With regard to power, for example, I will address issues such as attitudes toward the power differential in supervision, the power of both supervisor and supervisee in the relationship, and the dynamics of power that underlie the frequent and often inevitable dual roles in the supervisory relationship.

The discussion of shared meaning will include the development of mutual understanding and mutual agreement about both what will occur in the supervision and what constitutes effective treatment. The concept of trust will be elaborated beyond the common statement that supervision operates most effectively in an atmosphere of safety and trust. It will include such topics as how honesty is demonstrated and communicated in the supervisory relationship and how a supervisor's treatment of the supervisee's feelings of vulnerability relates to the creation (or destruction) of trust. It will become evident by the discussion that all these elements affect and are affected by one another and are an integral part of the process of supervision as a whole.

A word about the stories: I gathered the stories over the past several years through numerous interviews with supervisors and supervisees, as well as through my own experiences as a supervisee, a supervisor, a consultant, a faculty liaison for students in clinical internships, a teacher, and a trainer of supervisors. Because I have lived and worked in Minnesota for the past 26 years, most of the stories are from people in that part of the world. Although the stories are true, I have changed information that would identify the people involved in them. The experiences take place in a number of settings, ranging from supervision in large agencies to consultation with a private practitioner. Included in the discussion is extensive application of the material to cross-cultural relationships. My effort was to engage in a frank, sensitive, and balanced discussion about what is, for many, a controversial topic. Throughout the book, I have offered my own interpretation of the events that occurred, as well as my best understanding of the perceptions of those who shared their stories with me.

I believe that many of the issues that arise in relationships in general and in the supervisory relationship in particular are paradoxical, and therefore complicated, in nature. For example, it is essential that we understand that all behaviors and belief systems are developed in cultural contexts and that "truth" is not absolute (Sue, Allen, & Pederson, 1996). It is equally important that supervisors and clinicians take a stand on the side of core moral or ethical values (Doherty, 1995) and against behavior that is harmful to self or others.

To be effective supervisors and clinicians, we must be sensitive to and respectful of the enormous importance of others' cultural contexts and life experiences; and we must recognize that what is helpful for one client or one supervisee may be entirely counterproductive for another. Furthermore, a lack of such sensitivity and respect can lead, either wittingly or unwittingly, to the perpetuation of serious misunderstandings and of destructive negative stereotypes. Still, we have come to understand that we cannot and ought not operate in a value-less vacuum. Each time we take a stand—for example, on the side of safety for a battered woman or a physically abused child—we are supporting a value that is not universally held. As will be demonstrated through the stories, it is frequently unclear where or how to take a stand and where or how to support behavior and values that may be quite different from our own.

The questions to promote critical thinking offered at the end of each chapter are designed to help the reader further analyze the material. Although many of the stories are presented from only one person's point of view, at times I have speculated on the point of view of others involved. Readers are encouraged to do the same, both on their own and through the aid of the critical thinking questions. My hope is that readers will engage in discussion with others in a search for deeper understanding of the complex issues raised here.

A distinction is made in the literature between supervision and consultation (Bernard & Goodyear, 1992; NASW, 1994). *Supervision* is described as an involuntary relationship in which the supervisor is imbued with the power to make decisions or take actions that affect such things as hiring and firing, promotion, salaries, or, in the case of a student, passing or failing. *Consultation* is a voluntary relationship in which the supervisee asks for help on a particular or a type of case and is free to accept or reject the consultant's advice. The consultant has no line authority over the supervisee. Often the division between these two relationships becomes somewhat less clear. For example, a worker may go outside the agency to receive supervision to meet requirements for licensure or to receive accreditation for admission to a particular organization, such as the American Association of Marriage and Family Therapy. In these situations, the supervisor has the power to approve or not approve the supervisee's accreditation, but the supervisee can also decide to find a different supervisor. Although these relationships are all somewhat different with regard to the level of accountability between supervisor and supervisee, there is much common ground. Therefore, although the focus of this book is on the supervisory relationship, the principles and some of the examples will apply to consultative relationships as well.

In today's society, there is an increasing concern with ethical behavior. Although much of the attention has been on legal issues, there is also a renewed interest in the level of integrity that characterizes human interaction. Because of the power and importance of the relationship between practitioner and client, the ethical implications of that relationship are becoming a significant area of study and discussion (Miller, 1990; Doherty & Boss, 1991; Peterson, 1992; Gartrell, 1994; Doherty, 1995). Peterson (1992), for example, maintains that professionals—including therapists—are imbued by society with a spiritual sanction to guide and care for their clients. To be helped, she argues, clients must put faith in the professional relationship and make themselves vulnerable to be touched by those from whom they seek assistance. Because professionals are given this level of power to influence, it is incumbent on them to use that power with utmost care.

If practitioners are to treat their clients with the deepest possible integrity, they must have a place to go where they can carefully and honestly examine their own behavior. That place, ideally, is the supervisory relationship. Discussing the supervisory relationship without attending to its ethical dimension would ignore a crucial aspect both of the relationship itself and of the function of supervision (Levy, 1973, 1982; Cohen, 1987; Upchurch, 1985; Jacobs, 1991; Sherry, 1991;

Kaiser, 1992; Peterson, 1993a, 1993b; Storm, Peterson, & Tomm, 1997). In the discussion of the conceptual model, I define the process of supervision as one of accountability and the goal as competent service to clients. Given the concepts of parallel process and isomorphism, we can assume that if that relationship is not one that is itself guided by ethical principles, supervisees will be unable to use it as a resource for this dimension of their practice.

The theoretical base of this book will come, therefore, not only from the literature on supervision; it will also come from concepts developed by several authors whose work is grounded in relational ethics. Ivan Boszormenyi-Nagy is a psychiatrist and family therapist who developed the practice of contextual family therapy. An important and unique dimension of his framework is the emphasis on issues pertaining to fairness in relationships—primarily between family members, but also between the family and the therapist. Nell Noddings is a philosopher and educator who integrates feminist and ethical thinking into a theory of relational ethics. As an educator, she offers a perspective on the teacher/student relationship, a relationship that is similar to that between supervisor and supervisee. Marilyn Peterson is a social worker, marriage and family therapist, educator, supervisor, and consultant. Her work on the nature and impact of boundary violations in professional relationships provides important guidance for understanding and operating ethically in relationships that carry an inherent power differential. William Doherty is a professor of marriage and family therapy, family therapist, supervisor, and consultant. His recent book (Doherty, 1995) encourages clinicians to challenge both themselves and their clients to operate from a set of principles that includes responsible treatment of others. His discussion draws extensively on the work of the other three authors. Although only Peterson has applied her ideas specifically to supervision (Peterson, 1984, 1986, 1993a, 1993b; Thompson, Shapiro, Nielson, & Peterson, 1989; Storm et al., 1997), all these authors offer concepts that are useful for our understanding of the supervisory relationship.

Recently, as agencies experience financial and time restrictions, increased demand for paper accountability, and larger caseloads, many have dispensed with the educational or clinical aspects of supervision and sometimes even the supportive functions, focusing primarily on administrative tasks (Munson, 1989). Particularly given the rise in concern about ethical violations in treatment, many sanctioning bodies have noted the need for more effective clinical supervision. Therefore, the focus of the model and of the theoretical discussion in this book will be on clinical supervision.

Although the emphasis in the training of practitioners will differ, depending on whether the training is in social work, marriage and family therapy, psychology, or counselor education, actual clinical practice in the four fields probably has more commonalties than differences. The following definition of clinical social work was developed by the Board of Directors of the National Association of Social Work National Council on the Practice of Clinical Social Work (Northern, 1989) and will serve as a general framework for what is meant in this book by clinical work:

> Clinical social work practice is the professional application of social work theory and methods to the treatment and prevention of psychosocial dysfunction, disability, or impairment, including emotional and mental disorders. It is based on knowledge and theory of psychosocial development, behavior, psychopathology, unconscious motivation, interpersonal relationships, environmental stress, social systems and cultural diversity with particular attention to person-in-environment. It shares with all social work practice the goal of enhancement and maintenance of psychosocial functioning of individuals, families and small groups.
>
> Clinical social work encompasses interventions directed to interpersonal interactions, intrapsychic dynamics, and life support and management issues. It includes, but is not limited to individual, marital, family and group psychotherapy. Clinical social work services consist of assessment; diagnosis; treatment, including psychotherapy and counseling; client-centered advocacy; consultation and evaluation.
>
> The process of clinical social work is undertaken within the objectives of social work and the principles and values contained in codes of ethics of the professional social work organizations. (p. 1)

THE CONCEPTUAL MODEL OF SUPERVISION

The professions of both social work and marriage and family therapy use a systemic approach as a basis for understanding and intervening on clients' behalf. The premise of systems theory—that both individuals and relationships exist in and interact with a larger context—is relevant to a discussion about supervision. Although the focus of this book is the supervisory relationship, that relationship interacts with all aspects of supervision, including the context within which the supervision occurs. In the following discussion, I present a model that describes the elements of supervision and their interaction. As will become evident, a challenging feature of the model is its complexity, which, in my opinion, reflects the complicated nature of the supervisory process itself. At this point, the discussion will be primarily theoretical. The following four chapters will include in-depth discussions of power, shared meaning, and trust, along with applications of the material to concrete examples.

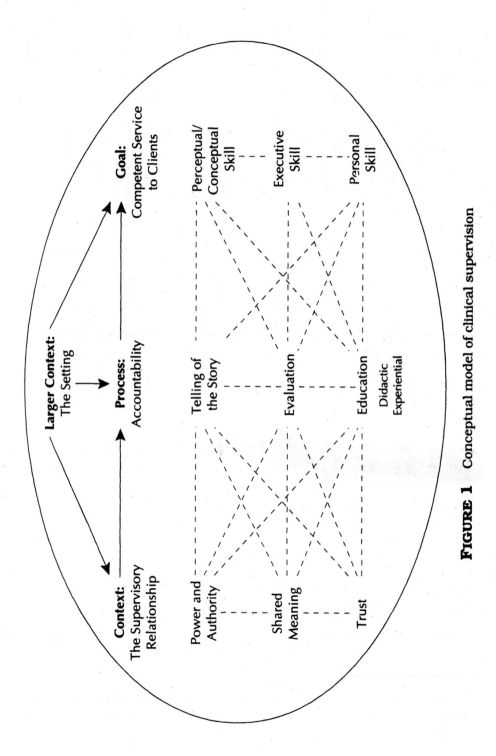

FIGURE 1 Conceptual model of clinical supervision

Figure 1 is a picture of the model. The solid lines demonstrate the general flow of activity, and the dashed lines illustrate the dynamic quality of supervision, in which each part is affected by the others. The circle around the outside of the model is labeled "The Larger Context," indicating that supervision takes place within a particular setting, such as a public agency or a university department. That setting is influenced by the immediate and larger community within which it exists and that it serves. Reading from left to right, we see that supervision occurs in the immediate context of the supervisory relationship, under which are listed the elements of the relationship: power and authority, shared meaning, and trust. The center label refers to the overall process of supervision as one of accountability, and the steps of the process include the telling of the story, evaluation, and education. The goal of supervision, pictured on the right of the model, is competent service to clients, demonstrated by the practitioner's perceptual/conceptual, executive, and personal skills. An elaboration of the model is more clearly understood if its components are discussed in reverse order, from right to left. Therefore we will begin with a discussion of the goal of supervision, move to the process, go on to the supervisory relationship, and, finally, address the larger context.

The Goal: Competent Service to Clients

The goal of competent service to clients is achieved through the development of perceptual, conceptual, executive, and personal skills (Tomm & Wright, 1979). *Perceptual skill* is the ability to observe what is happening with the client, and *conceptual skill* is the ability to interpret those observations. Because what we perceive is intricately connected to what we think, these two skills are difficult to separate. Conceptual skills include those in three general categories: (1) knowledge and application of theoretical approaches, (2) diagnosis and assessment, and (3) identification of the subjective experiences of both client and practitioner.

Executive skill is the ability to intervene effectively in the treatment. Tomm and Wright (1979) provided an outline of perceptual/conceptual skills and the executive skills that would accompany them. For example, a perceptual/conceptual skill is the ability to notice the positive effect that deliberate acknowledgment of each member has on the entire family. The accompanying executive skill is to interact directly with every individual in a way that both recognizes them and gives them status.

To some extent, the specific skills that practitioners use reflect their theoretical orientation. For example, those operating from a cognitive/

behavioral approach might use techniques such as thought stopping or reattribution (Beck & Emmery, 1985); a gestalt therapist might use the empty chair technique (Fantz, 1991); and a strategic family therapist might invoke paradoxical injunctions (Nichols & Schwartz, 1995). However, a study comparing different approaches to family therapy demonstrated that although there is a great deal of divergence in theoretical approaches, those differences are much less obvious when one observes practitioners' actual in-session behaviors (Green & Kolvezon, 1982). Woods and Hollis (1990), whose psychosocial approach incorporates many compatible theoretical orientations, described a list of procedures they consider core to treatment. They maintained that all practitioners, including those whose jobs are not defined specifically or narrowly as "therapy," use some combination of these procedures, depending on the needs of the client.

Personal skill is the practitioner's ability to develop increased self-awareness, and it includes a commitment to personal growth. Of the elements in the goal, the most controversial is whether to focus in supervision on the self-awareness and personal growth of the supervisee. There is a widely held concern regarding how to identify and properly draw the line between therapy and supervision (Rubinstein, 1992). In my experience, with which this chapter began, both supervisors considered the practitioner's use of self to be an important focus of the supervision, and I agreed. However, I thought the first supervisor crossed the line from supervision to therapy in her nearly exclusive focus on personal issues and in her intrusive manner.

To some extent, the answer to the question about how and where to draw the line is related to the type of approach the practitioner is using, as well as to the nature of the job. For example, family therapists who use the strategic approach often believe that the personal issues of the practitioner should not be a topic for discussion in supervision (Haley, 1988; Pirotta & Cecchin, 1988; Hass, Alexander, & Mas, 1988). On the other hand, those who use a psychodynamic approach tend to view the need for practitioners to identify and work through their own issues as of paramount importance (Abroms, 1978; Schneider, 1992). Practitioners whose jobs are more task-oriented or educational in nature may need to pay less attention to their personal responses than do those who become more deeply involved with their clients' psychological processes. The current need of the supervisee is another variable that affects the degree of attention paid to personal awareness. For example, a supervisee might already have gained a great deal of personal awareness and might currently be needing supervision focused on learning a particular theoretical approach or set of skills. Wherever one stands on this issue, most agree that personal awareness of the practitioner's responses to and impact on clients is important.

The Process: Accountability

Society mandates that the human services professions provide competent service to clients, and the professions are increasingly being asked for an account of that service (Munson, 1989; Kadushin, 1992). Funding bodies are asking for a more detailed account of and explanation for what happens in the treatment. Expanded awareness of practitioners' maltreatment of clients has led to legislation defining qualifications for licensure and parameters for acceptable practice, and has led as well to litigation against those who have harmed clients. State licensing boards and most professional organizations have codes of ethical conduct and procedures for reporting and sanctioning those who breach the codes. All these measures are in place with the hope of ensuring that practitioners will act with integrity toward their clients and will take appropriate corrective action if they have not.

The person most directly responsible for ensuring the ethical and competent practice of a given worker is that individual's supervisor. Supervisors are increasingly being considered legally liable for the actions of those under them (NASW, 1994). One could also argue that even if they are not legally accountable for the supervisee's failure on the job, they are ethically obligated to do everything possible to help the supervisee succeed and to ensure that the supervisee does not harm clients (Levy, 1973, 1982; Sherry, 1991).

Loganbill, Hardy, and Delworth (1982) define supervision as a relationship in which the supervisor is designated to facilitate the supervisee's therapeutic competence. They list four functions of supervision, two of which relate directly to accountability. The first is the assurance, above all else, of clients' welfare. The second is the evaluation of the supervisee. A primary distinction between supervision and therapy is the fact that supervisees are held accountable for their behavior through evaluation connected to raises, hiring, firing, or accreditation (Bernard & Goodyear, 1992).

In discussing another dimension of accountability, Peterson (1984) contends that, to do their work, practitioners must let themselves be "touched" deeply by their clients. This makes them more vulnerable to losing their objectivity and potentially losing their ability to act in the clients' best interests. It is the job of the supervisor, viewing the situation from a more detached position, to help the clinician regain that ability. Although the idea that the supervisor is more removed and therefore more objective is frequently stated (for example, Berger & Dammann, 1982; Rabanowitz, 1987; Fox, 1989), Peterson was the first to describe this phenomenon as one of accountability.

Like Peterson (1984) and others (such as NASW, 1994), I consider the overall process of supervision as one of accountability. My definition of accountability includes a definition offered by Boszormenyi-Nagy and Krasner (1986) and one provided by *Webster's New World Dictionary* (Neufeldt & Guralnik, 1988). Boszormenyi-Nagy and Krasner contend that, regardless of our intentions, we are responsible for the consequences of how we behave or fail to behave. They maintain further that authentic relationships are those in which participants are committed to taking into consideration the needs and rights of others and to treating others in a genuinely equitable manner. Behaving in this manner increases each individual's sense of personal worth, in addition to making a positive contribution to the relationship. It requires a level of self-awareness that includes the recognition that one's relationships contribute to the development of personal identity. True autonomy, therefore, involves understanding both one's own interests and those of the other. Webster's dictionary defines the verb *account* as "to provide a reckoning," "to give satisfactory reasons or an explanation for," and "to make satisfactory amends for" (p. 9).

I see accountability as the process of taking responsibility for one's behavior and for the impact of that behavior on self and others. First, it is a *commitment to tell the truth* about oneself to the best of one's ability. This requires supplying the facts about what one has done, thought, and felt in a given situation. Accomplishing this task calls both for self-knowledge and for the willingness to share this knowledge. It requires, as well, taking responsibility for one's intended and unintended impact on another. Second, accountability is a *commitment to take responsible action* by making amends or correcting an injustice and by treating others with integrity, understanding both their needs and one's own. Within the context of supervision, the supervisor's job is to help supervisees arrive at and maintain this level of integrity about their work.

The following is a description of steps in the process of accountability, assuming it is working effectively. The steps are not necessarily sequential, as the process is a dynamic one.

The Telling of the Story

Supervisees provide an account of their work in the form of a written or verbal report, an audio- or videotape, or some sort of live supervision. In addition, they give an explanation, to the best of their ability, of what was behind their actions. This explanation includes their personal feelings and reactions and the theoretical frameworks that guided their thinking about the case. Using my definition of accountability, this step is the supervisee's first effort at "telling the truth." Part of the supervisor's job, at this point, is to help the supervisee give as complete an account as possible, so that both parties can arrive at an understanding of what has happened in the treatment.

Evaluation

The second part of the supervisory process is that of evaluation. Evaluation involves making judgments regarding the quality of the practitioner's work. This means determining such things as whether the supervisee is doing competent work and whether the supervisee knows and is staying within the parameters of the ethical code of the profession. It also means assessing what the practitioner needs to learn in order to work more effectively.

Education

Education includes both that which is didactic and that which is experiential in nature. Didactic education includes teaching the worker the larger theoretical concepts within which a specific situation can be understood. It also includes providing concrete suggestions about actions that could be taken in the treatment. Experiential education relates to the phenomena of parallel process and isomorphism.

In addition to conscious use of parallel process and isomorphism to address clinical issues, the way the supervisor treats a supervisee about things that are not directly client-related may be repeated in the client/worker relationship. For example, a supervisee whose request for an emergency meeting with a supervisor is refused may in turn refuse such a request from a client (Kadushin, 1992). The ethical climate of the supervisory relationship may also influence that of the treatment relationship. In their discussion of accountability, Boszormenyi-Nagy and Krasner (1986) stress the need for practitioners to hold both their clients and themselves accountable for ethical behavior in their relationships. It follows that if supervisors assume responsibility for their own contribution to problems in the supervision and demonstrate a willingness and ability to make appropriate amends, their supervisees will experience a role model for their own behavior with clients. They will be encouraged to operate ethically with clients and to challenge their clients to do the same in their relationships with family members and with others.

As a result of the evaluation and education processes, the supervisee has tools to work more effectively and therefore to meet the goal of competent service to clients. Using the above definition of accountability, effective work constitutes responsible action. If the practitioner has made an error or has chosen an ineffective path, this action may include a corrective move. More often, it will simply involve a next step in the treatment.

The evaluation and education processes also add to supervisees' level of perceptual/conceptual, executive, and personal skill, thus enabling them to more fully "tell the story" about their work in future supervisory sessions.

The Context:
The Supervisory Relationship

Supervision takes place in the context of the relationship between supervisor and supervisee. The three major components of this relationship are the use of power and authority, the creation of shared meaning, and the creation of trust.

Power and Authority

This model presumes that the most salient element in the supervisory relationship is the dynamics of power and authority. A distinction can be made between the terms *power* and *authority*, with power being the ability to influence or control others and authority being the right to do so (Kadushin, 1992). Some supervisors' authority may be sabotaged, or supervisors may be unable to exercise their power because of characteristics of their own or of their supervisees. However, although a supervisory relationship can indeed exist without either shared meaning or trust, it has, by definition, a built-in power differential. This differential is a result of the functions of the process of accountability. Supervisors have power over practitioners primarily because they need to evaluate the quality of supervisees' work. In addition, the supervisor's role as educator presumes, at least in the case of new practitioners, the need to know more than the supervisee. Supervisors are often unaware that many supervisees experience this differential quite intensely and are therefore more deeply affected by exchanges in supervision than the supervisor intended them to be (Kadushin, 1974; Doehrman, 1976).

However, although supervisors have more power in the relationship, supervisees are not completely powerless. They can avoid supervision both by sharing a minimum of information about their work (telling less of their story) and by refusing to accept the supervisor's guidance. If supervisees behave in this manner, their supervisors can punish them but cannot have much positive impact on the quality of the supervisees' work. To be effectively supervised, practitioners need to fully participate in the process. As I have already mentioned, primarily because I experienced my first supervisor as quite powerful, I withheld information from her and was not open to her guidance and feedback. I therefore learned little of value from her, although she potentially had something of value to offer.

Although there is general acknowledgment in the literature of the supervisor's greater power and authority, there is disagreement—depending on both philosophy and approach to treatment—about whether the hierarchical nature of the supervisory relationship should be emphasized or minimized (McDaniel, Webber, & McKeever, 1983; Wheeler, Avis, Miller, & Chaney, 1986; Haas et al., 1988; Nichols, 1988;

Liddle, 1988; Kadushin, 1992; Munson, 1993). This debate includes discussions about whether the supervisor should take more charge in decision making or should invite participation and input from the supervisee. The debate also includes discussions about how much the supervisee should be encouraged to act autonomously versus depending on the supervisor for guidance.

Perhaps a more important question to address, however, is not where on the continua of hierarchy/egalitarianism or dependency/autonomy one falls, but rather how the issue of power is addressed, no matter what the degree of emphasis. An assumption underlying this discussion is that responsible use of authority in supervision involves a balance, in which the supervisor is neither using that power in an arbitrary or destructive way (Horner, 1988; Jacobs, 1991) nor abdicating that power, failing to acknowledge its inherent existence in the relationship (Thompson et al., 1989). Perhaps the most significant difference between my first and second supervisors was my experience of their use of the power in the relationship. In my opinion, the first supervisor used her power to be overly intrusive and to reward and punish those with whom she did or did not get along. Because my second supervisor was a consultant rather than an actual supervisor, she did not have the same type of administrative power. However, she was quite clear about her greater power in the relationship and took appropriate charge of the supervision, while treating me fairly and with respect.

The concept of reciprocity (Noddings, 1984; Boszormenyi-Nagy & Spark, 1984) is useful for understanding issues related to appropriate use of power. According to Noddings and Boszormenyi-Nagy and Spark, a fair and genuinely caring relationship is characterized by mutual give and take. Even when relationships are on the same hierarchical level—for example, between spouses, siblings, or friends—a person's sense of equality is based on subtle factors that cannot be objectively determined.

Measuring reciprocity becomes more complicated in an unequal relationship, such as the supervisory one. Noddings (1984) named the participants in such a relationship the "one-caring" and the "cared-for." It is incumbent on the one-caring, as the person with greater power, to give without expectation of a particular response from the cared-for and to see the world through both her or his own eyes and those of the cared-for. This same idea is expressed by Boszormenyi-Nagy, who contends that parents behave in a trustworthy fashion with their children by taking care of them without expectation (Boszormenyi-Nagy & Spark, 1984; Boszormenyi-Nagy & Krasner, 1986; Boszormenyi-Nagy, 1988). The cared-for in an unequal relationship may, on occasion, give back in the same manner. In fact, children have both a right and a need to give in a developmentally appropriate fashion to each parent, such as by offering comfort when a parent is sad (Goldenthal, 1993).

Others in hierarchically uneven relationships frequently also have these same rights and needs.

Clearly the nature of the cared-for's response affects the relationship. It is much easier to give to those who give back by taking what is offered, using it fully, and sharing their internal processes and accomplishments. However, the one-caring cannot demand this sort of responsiveness; to do so would be to treat the cared-for as an object, existing for the gratification of the one-caring's own needs. Children placed in the position of having to respond in a certain way become parentified. That is, they become more concerned with the needs of the parents than with their own and are consequently robbed of the experience of being a child (Boszormenyi-Nagy & Spark, 1984). Peterson (1992) considered this sort of role reversal in the relationship between professional and client a significant characteristic of a boundary violation. In her framework, problems occur when the needs of the professional become more important than those of the client. Clients then no longer feel safe or free to attend to the issues that originally brought them to the professional.

As the one in charge, the supervisor is responsible for setting appropriate limits and boundaries with respect to such issues as the structure of the supervisory hour, the parameters of acceptable professional behavior, and the focus on the supervisee's rather than the supervisor's needs. This appropriate use of power connects to the issue of trust, in that setting the boundaries creates a safe space for supervisees to share their work (Peterson, 1984, 1992).

The concept of reciprocity is useful in understanding the power of the supervisee as well as that of the supervisor. As I stated above, the less powerful participant wants and needs to give back to the more powerful one, and the nature of that gift affects the relationship (Noddings, 1984; Boszormenyi-Nagy & Spark, 1984; Boszormenyi-Nagy & Krasner, 1986; Boszormenyi-Nagy, 1988). An important source of a supervisee's power is the ability to accept or reject the role of learner. The good student certainly gives more by way of appreciation of and satisfaction to the teacher.

Both supervisor and supervisee come to the relationship with preconceived notions of what it means to be an authority (Shulman, 1982, 1993; Peterson, 1992). Therefore an important part of the supervisory process is to continually address this theme. This action helps both to clarify the issue in supervision and to enable supervisees to use their position of power with clients in a more effective manner.

Shared Meaning

Shared meaning relates to mutual understanding and agreement between supervisor and supervisee. To the extent that both understanding and agreement occur in the relationship, the supervision will probably operate more effectively. Clear communication is the mechanism by which understanding is achieved. Although ensuring that the message sent is the message received is challenging in many relationships, the challenge increases when differences between the participants are greater. In cross-cultural supervision, factors such as nonverbal cues, values, norms, culturally specific meanings, and false assumptions can potentially lead to a great deal of both misunderstanding and disagreement, particularly if these factors are not addressed.

For the supervision to proceed most smoothly, several major issues require a basic understanding and agreement between supervisor and supervisee. These issues fall under two general categories: the supervisory contract and the approach to treatment.

Contract   The need to establish a clear contract for supervision is stressed throughout the literature on supervision. In general, contracting can be defined as obtaining cooperation to work on a mutually agreed-on problem (Connell, 1984). It is important to remember that mutual cooperation does not assume equal power in the relationship. The supervisor has more influence over which expectations will be delineated in an agreement with the supervisee. Because of this greater power, ethics require that supervisors ensure that supervisees understand what the job entails and on what basis they will be evaluated (Levy, 1973). This clarification prevents the supervisor from misusing that power by catching the supervisee in a bind. Even without the ethical dimension, contracting is linked to evaluation because, to determine the criteria used for evaluation, the supervisee must be clear about the purposes, goals, and objectives of supervision (Bartlett, 1983).

The supervisory contract is sometimes formally or informally stated and, regretfully, often not addressed at all. The premise of this discussion is that both understanding and agreement are aspects of shared meaning. However, even when agreement is not possible, it is in the best interest of both parties to ensure understanding. For example, supervisees may well disagree about whether they should be evaluated on a particular aspect of their work. However, if it is a requirement of either the supervisor, the organization, or the profession that supervisees behave in a particular way, that requirement must be clearly stated.

Approach to treatment   The treatment approach relates to beliefs about what is helpful to clients. Many factors contribute to the development of one's beliefs about effective treatment. Practitioners' theoretical orientation, practical experience, and cultural and familial values and norms will lead them to emphasize and support certain types of client behavior in favor of others, offer particular kinds of help, and do so with a style that reflects their own personality and background. Finally, the organization within which the service is being provided defines the parameters for what can and should be done on clients' behalf. The following questions can serve as a guideline for the types of issues that may arise when considering the topic of approach to treatment.

1. What is therapy or counseling? Addressing this question requires focusing on such issues as whether the purpose of treatment is primarily to solve the presenting problems or whether practitioners should strive to help people restructure, on a deeper level, their relationship with themselves and others.

2. How do people change? Do people require insight in order to change their behavior? Do people change more when the worker educates them very specifically about the treatment process or when the process is more elusive?

3. What is the role of the practitioner? Should the treatment relationship be a major focus, or should the practitioner stand more outside the client system, offering interventions but assuming that the major work will take place outside the session? Should the practitioner be task-oriented and personally distant, or should there be sufficient time for more casual, personal interaction between client and worker in order to establish trust?

4. What constitutes "healthy" or "functional" behavior? This is an especially important question when working cross-culturally. Because counseling as a profession is primarily a Western endeavor, ideas about health are steeped in the values of this culture. Therefore, for example, individuality and autonomy are positive, and a family with extremely strong connections and deep involvement with one another is likely to be labeled "enmeshed."

Several links can be made between shared meaning and aspects of both accountability and competent service to clients. For example, the more education the supervisee receives from the supervisor, the more both will share an understanding of what constitutes effective treatment of clients. This is especially true if the supervisor is teaching a particular model of treatment. In addition, the more of the story the supervisee tells, presumably the greater will be the degree of understanding between supervisor and supervisee.

Trust

Many authors name respect and safety as important elements in the supervisory relationship (for example, Olson & Pegg, 1979; Heath, 1982; Liddle & Schwartz, 1983; Alonso & Rutan, 1988; Schwartz, 1988; Pirotta & Cecchin, 1988; Haas, Alexander, & Mas, 1988; Nichols, 1988; Liddle, Davidson, & Barrett, 1988; Wetchler, 1989; Kadushin, 1992;

Munson, 1993; Shulman, 1993). Respect, or a demonstration of the supervisor's esteem for the supervisee, can be experienced both by supervisors' expressing belief in supervisees' ability and in the value and relevance of their past professional and life experiences.

Safety is usually defined as the supervisee's freedom to make mistakes and to take risks without danger of an excessively judgmental response from the supervisor. To some extent, both supervisor and supervisee are vulnerable because both are asked to expose their personal, interpersonal, professional, and cognitive skills to each other, particularly in the context of live supervision. This sort of exposure most profitably takes place in an atmosphere of safety (Berger & Dammann, 1982; Liddle & Schwartz, 1983; Liddle, 1988). The supervisor also needs to be able to challenge the supervisee (Liddle, 1988). Challenge is most effective if the supervisee feels basically accepted and feels safe to risk new behaviors.

Two of the four functions of supervision named by Loganbill, Hardy, and Delworth (1982) relate to the promotion of the supervisee's growth. A common dilemma in supervision is the potential conflict between the growth-promoting and accountability-maintaining functions. The growth-promoting functions require a trusting relationship between supervisor and supervisee, a condition that may be threatened by the need to include a component of critical evaluation. As a result, some supervisors and supervisees make the mistake of sweeping the aspect of evaluation under the rug, rather than dealing with it directly.

Adding the ethical dimension helps address this dilemma. The ability to tell the truth about oneself, necessary for the process of accountability, is directly related to the degree of trust in the relationship. Boszormenyi-Nagy and Krasner (1986) stated that "personal accountability as a guideline for caring and relational integrity constitutes the foundation of trustworthiness and individual health" (p. 62). Doherty (1995) elaborated on this notion, stating that, in our human relationships we are obligated to be truthful with one another. If we are not, those relationships disintegrate.

Doherty (1995) also introduced the notion of practitioner's courage. His contention is that it takes courage to push oneself and one's clients past personal safety zones into areas that will promote growth and integrity in one's work and in that of one's clients. Peterson (1984) suggested that trust in the supervisory relationship is built, in part, by the confidence that the supervisor will go as far as necessary to understand completely the supervisee's work. When this is done without shame, supervisees experience that they have told the whole truth about themselves and their work, to the best of their ability; and, even when they are deeply challenged, they feel accepted by the supervisor. Also, if supervisors hold themselves accountable in the relationship, trust in the relationship will increase. Supervisors can increase trust by telling the truth about their impressions of the supervisee and about their own feelings, by treating the supervisee with integrity, and by taking responsibility for their own part in any tensions in the relationship. My story illustrates these points quite clearly. I trusted my second supervisor because she created an environment in which I could tell the whole truth without fear of being shamed or diminished. In addition, she acted with integrity in her ability to hold herself as well as me accountable. As commonly happens, both my supervisors' use of power also affected trust. If supervisees think their supervisors are treating them fairly, neither abusing nor abdicating their power, they are more likely to trust them.

The development of shared meaning, discussed above, promotes trust in the relationship by building the confidence of both parties in the mutual understanding between supervisor and supervisee. This becomes even more evident in cross-cultural relationships. Often both supervisors and supervisees are uncomfortable with raising problems or even addressing questions relating to racial or cultural differences. The silence itself can lead to increased mistrust, as issues such as differing expectations; supervisor insensitivity; and differences in personalities, opinions, backgrounds, and life experiences are left unaddressed and unresolved (McRoy, Freeman, Logagan, & Blackmon, 1986).

The Larger Context: The Setting

The context within which the supervision takes place has a significant impact on the supervisory relationship. With regard to shared meaning, the context influences both the contract and the beliefs about what treatment should consist of. The context may not promote a situation in which the expectations for supervisee performance are clear. In addition, the supervisor may not be in a position to attend to a particular supervisee's learning needs. In an agency, the relationship is not voluntary; even if the supervisor and supervisee cannot agree on the contract, they must continue to work together unless a transfer to another part of the agency can be easily arranged. If the relationship is voluntary, both can choose to end it without serious consequence.

An outpatient counseling service will provide very different treatment than will an inpatient psychiatric unit in a hospital, school setting, or crisis intervention agency. In addition, funding sources often dictate both the length of treatment as well as what types of services are necessary. All these variables affect the nature of treatment and therefore the content of the supervision. By virtue of their position, supervisors must find a way to endorse and promote the agency directives, while at the same time supporting the workers' commitment to competent service. Often there is real or perceived conflict between the two, and, to be effective, the supervisor must balance the needs of agency, supervisees, and clients (Shulman, 1993).

The context also affects the type and amount of power the supervisor exercises over the supervisee. For example, the prominence of the supervisor's evaluative role is directly connected to the degree of power vested in the supervisor by the context. When the degree of power is high, the level of trust between supervisor and supervisee may well be threatened, especially if either the evaluation is performed in a disrespectful manner or the shared meaning between supervisor and supervisee is not present.

SUMMARY

The supervisory relationship is the medium through which supervision occurs and, as such, deserves careful attention. Because the relationship is potentially a quite powerful one, which has a great impact on the quality of a practitioner's work with clients, its development should be set within guidelines derived from ethical principles.

In this chapter, I presented a model that describes supervision. The goal of supervision is to offer competent service to clients, and this goal is reached through the supervisee's use of perceptual/conceptual, executive, and personal skills. The process of accountability includes the telling of the story, evaluation, and didactic and experiential education. Accountability is defined as telling the truth to the best of one's ability and taking responsible actions. The supervisory relationship is the immediate context within which supervision takes place, and it is the primary focus of this text. Elements in the relationship include power and authority, shared meaning, and trust. The model assumes that power and authority constitutes the most important element because, by definition, a power differential exists in supervision. Finally, the supervision takes place in a larger context, which includes the agency setting and the community within which the agency exists and that it serves.

QUESTIONS TO PROMOTE CRITICAL THINKING

1. Discuss your own experiences as a supervisee. What were the salient characteristics of those that were most positive? most negative? What impact did they have on you?

2. Although many people define the goal of supervision as the development of the supervisee's skills, this model defines the goal as competent service to clients. Discuss the implications of the difference in emphasis of these two definitions.

3. One of the most difficult things for many people is to have compassion for others and simultaneously hold them accountable for their destructive behavior, either toward themselves or toward others. Compassion can appear to be "letting someone off the hook," whereas holding someone accountable can seem to be "blaming the victim." Discuss the implications of this dilemma in work with clients and in your own life.

4. The notion of reciprocity, or mutual give and take, is important in the theories of both Boszormenyi-Nagy and Noddings. Discuss the complications involved in creating reciprocity in hierarchical relationships. Give examples from your own experience.

Chapter Two

Power and Authority

Jose has been a supervisor for many years in a variety of settings. He directs a small group in private practice. In addition, he is well known in the professional community and is frequently asked to serve as a consultant to many individual practitioners as well as to other groups. No one would disagree that Jose is both a brilliant thinker and an excellent clinician. His knowledge of psychological testing is superior. In addition, he has a broad and deep understanding of several theoretical approaches to psychotherapy.

As is often the case, Jose's supervisees respond to him very differently, depending on their own perceptions of and feelings about both him and themselves. Both Howard and Sally work with Jose in the clinic. Although Jose is the director and leader of the group, all the clinicians are experienced and the group holds regular case consultation meetings. Jose defines himself as a colleague in these meetings, and presents cases of his own for feedback. Sally's perception, however, is that Jose presents his clinical work in a smooth, complicated, and abstract manner that makes it impossible to challenge him in any way regarding his work with clients. For example, when he talks about a child with behavior problems, he talks about developmental issues and possible therapeutic interventions using a number of technical terms. Rarely does he discuss any doubts he may have, nor does he share his emotional responses to the child. Sally resents what she sees as a lack of congruence between his self-description as colleague and his behavior, which puts him in a superior position relative to the others.

Howard takes his concern a step further, noting that Jose seems to promote a situation in which the others defer to him. No matter what the topic, Howard complains, all eyes turn to Jose for his opinion. Rather than challenge that practice, Jose accepts the invitation to act as expert. At one point, Howard asked him whether he noticed this dynamic, and Jose denied it.

Marsha describes herself as more of a feeler than a thinker. She states that she adores Jose because he is both extremely knowledgeable and a very warm man. Although she is a capable clinician, she describes herself as having difficulty comprehending and articulating complex ideas, and she feels ashamed when she doesn't understand someone. When Jose speaks, she attributes her difficulty following him to her own inadequacies, telling herself that she "should" know what he's talking about. Because she has never had the courage to tell him she can't understand him, she assumes that he just isn't aware he is leaving her in the dark. Therefore he shouldn't be held accountable for the impact of his highly theoretical and rapid style of presenting information.

Finally, Kim, who works in an agency for which Jose consults, simply views him as a capable teacher. Her feelings about him are relatively neutral.

This story contains some of the key power dynamics that can occur between supervisor and supervisee. As the example illustrates, the supervisory relationship is, of course, affected by the stance of both participants. Although all four supervisees are very aware of Jose's extraordinary knowledge and ability, they differ dramatically in their assessment of Jose's use of the power he derives from his expertise. Sally and Howard see Jose as working to maintain a superior position over the others, whereas Marsha sees Jose's greater power as purely a result of her own one-down stance. Kim views Jose as simply offering his knowledge and herself as learning from him, in a manner that seems unaffected by personal feelings of either superiority or inferiority.

The premise of this book is that, by definition, supervision occurs within the context of a power differential between supervisor and supervisee. In her discussion of professional/client relationships, Peterson (1992) listed several sources of the professional's greater power, all of which are applicable to the relationship between supervisor and supervisee. Peterson maintained that clients are dependent on professionals to help them meet their needs. Supervisees are dependent on supervisors for guidance and education. More significant, in many situations, supervisees are also dependent on supervisors for evaluations that will influence opportunities available to the supervisee vis-à-vis future jobs, salary increases, hiring and firing (Levy, 1973), accreditation, or licensure.

Society gives professionals power, with the attendant obligation and privilege to use it in the service of others. Supervisors are given the power to maintain their supervisees' accountability by their agencies and by licensure and accreditation boards. Professionals are given power because of their expert knowledge in the field, on which clients, who lack the training themselves, must have faith. Although supervisees often have similar training, new clinicians in particular must depend on a mentoring relationship to learn the job.

Professionals are also given power by their clients. The intensity of clients' needs and their willingness to ask for help in meeting those needs determines the amount of power they turn over to the professionals on whom they depend. This is also true in supervision. Supervisees who feel more unsure about their own abilities as practitioners are more likely to depend on their supervisors for guidance and to be more influenced by their responses. Finally, supervisors, like other professionals, have a sense of personal power. How they express that power is a reflection of their self-esteem, what they think they have to offer, and how they see themselves in the role of authority.

Kadushin (1992) applied to supervision a framework developed by French and Raven (1960), which delineates five types of power. The first three are formal, or vested in the supervisor by virtue of the title. They include *reward, coercive,* and *positional* power. By virtue of supervisors' position, they have the power to reward supervisees or to reprimand them if their behavior is not acceptable. The final two types of power are functional, or derived from the supervisor's personal characteristics. *Referent* power refers to those qualities in a supervisor that the supervisee admires. The more the supervisee respects the supervisor, the more impact that supervisor will have. *Expert* power comes from having knowledge about the field and about the nature of the job.

This framework suggests several questions related to the supervisor's use of power: How does the supervisor use the power to reward and coerce? Is competent behavior that effectively serves clients rewarded? Is only a particular style of treatment rewarded, leaving no room for supervisees who have other styles and strengths? Is coercive power used to set necessary limits in support of ethical behavior or to force particular actions by the supervisee that do not necessarily support either the client's or the supervisee's best interests?

As stated in the previous chapter, an important question regarding the power differential is whether the hierarchical nature of the relationship should be emphasized or minimized. Sometimes the decision is made on the basis of the need to have an isomorphic connection between the supervisory relationship and the approach to treatment being used. For example, strategic therapists view the practitioner as responsible for the outcome of treatment, and structural family therapists emphasize boundaries in the family. Both types of therapists stress the need for the supervisor to maintain a clear position of authority (McDaniel et al., 1983).

Wheeler and associates (1986) maintained that to promote feminist values and behaviors in treatment and in supervision, the hierarchical nature of those relationships should be minimized. The vehicles through which this can be accomplished in supervision include (1) giving shared responsibility to both supervisee and supervisor for contracting and for evaluation, and (2) the use of clear, understandable language as well as respectful encouragement of the supervisee's questions and ideas.

Others promote minimization for a different reason. They argue that the adoption of the learner/subordinate role can be quite stressful both for beginning graduate students, who are in that role in many ways already, and for established mental health practitioners, who have reputations as competent professionals. In an effort to reduce the stress, Haas and associates (1988) recommended avoiding behaviors that will emphasize hierarchy, such as being directive rather than suggesting possible actions.

A related concern is that of the degree of dependency versus autonomy the supervisor encourages. Clearly both elements are a necessary part of the process, as they are in any mentoring relationship. Like parents who are charged with the task of showing their children the way *and* letting them be themselves, supervisors find that knowing *which* aspect of the job to do *when* is a difficult and often murky challenge. An example of this concern is found in the literature on live supervision. The good news about live supervision is that it allows the supervisor to give on the spot feedback to the supervisee, rather than discussing things in retrospect; the bad news is that supervisees can begin to rely on those directives or suggestions and lose confidence in their ability to make decisions themselves. In addition, some supervisors literally take over the treatment instead of remaining in the role of supervisor (Montalvo, 1973; Lowenstein, Reder, & Clark, 1982; Liddle, 1988; Nichols, 1988).

As will be demonstrated in this chapter and the next, the manner in which both supervisor and supervisee approach power and authority result in a number of complex dynamics. In this chapter, we will look at relationship in light of the greater knowledge and expertise of the supervisor, the limit-setting function of supervision, the power of the supervisee in choosing supervision, and the attitude of both supervisor and supervisee toward power and authority.

THE KNOWLEDGE DIFFERENTIAL

As stated in the discussion of the conceptual model, the goal of supervision is to enable supervisees to provide competent service to clients through the development of supervisees' perceptual/conceptual, executive, and personal skills. A crucial issue is how supervisors manage the degree of difference between their level of expertise and that of the supervisee. Most supervisees state that they gain more from supervision when their supervisors have more information than they do about these skills. They are likely to add that the differential should become less significant as they develop, allowing them to become more autonomous. A typical example of this attitude is illustrated by the following comment by a supervisee:

In the internship situation, there should be a clearer distinction between you and the supervisor. The supervisor is clearly in charge. The supervisor is clearly the expert. Even toward the end of the internship, however, that relationship might change a little bit. The supervisee would become perhaps not completely equal to the supervisor, but the supervisor would become more of a person to bounce things off of, to get feedback from, rather than instruction or a lot of structure.

The supervisor's need for greater knowledge is clear when the supervisee is a beginning practitioner. In addition, a more experienced clinician might seek out a particular supervisor or consultant in order to learn that person's area of expertise. Clearly, the supervisee wants a supervisor who has something to teach.

I'm going to Clara every other week for supervision on working with eating disorders. She is clearly the teacher. She has a lot of knowledge. I enjoy what she does, and she does seem to be the authority.

When the knowledge differential does not appear to be present, the validity of the supervisor's feedback is questioned (Schwartz, 1988). One supervisee described her supervisor as not very bright or knowledgeable and stated that she didn't believe he had much to give her. Like many supervisees in this situation, she did not talk to him about what was really happening in her work. In the language of the model, she did not tell her supervisor a complete story. She met with him for the required hour a week and told him in a perfunctory manner what she was doing. She expressed no doubts, questions, or concerns and asked for little to no help in her work. He would compliment her on a job well done and she would leave, feeling unsatisfied.

Sometimes the issue of credibility relates to that of shared meaning. One aspect of shared meaning is that supervisor and supervisee need to arrive at, at least, a general agreement about what constitutes effective treatment. Within this parameter, most supervisors help supervisees develop their own approach. Conflict can occur if the supervisor uses an approach that the supervisee does not find useful and does not want to learn.

Gary supervised an agency unit that served gay and lesbian clients and that used a psychoeducational approach to the work. The unit's emphasis was on the impact of societal homophobia as well as on developmental issues related to being gay and lesbian. Gary, a heterosexual man, recognized the need to include the educational component, but he also believed that a sole emphasis on the societal and affectional preference issues neglected the intrapsychic and family-of-origin issues the client brings to bear on the situation.

Gary ran into resistance from a few of his supervisees, who discredited his position in part because he was not gay. They believed that his knowledge was inconsequential because he did not understand the unique needs of gay and lesbian clients. His solution was to invite the group as a whole to discuss this population's needs relative to those of other clients. ("Let's talk about why this client, because she is lesbian, needs only psychoeducational counseling, whereas a heterosexual client with many of the same issues would be encouraged to explore family-of-origin issues.") He chose the group setting because he knew there were members in the group who were themselves gay and whose approach to treatment were more similar to his. In doing so, he hoped both to strengthen his own credibility and to make the discussion more of a general treatment issue relevant to the work of the entire unit, rather than a power struggle between himself and individual supervisees.

The fact that Gary saw the need to avoid a power struggle suggests an overlap between a conflict in shared meaning and a power conflict. A question about who is right quickly can become a question of whose "way" will prevail. Thus, Gary attempted to define the issue solely as one of shared meaning and to expand each position to include that of the other. This effort might succeed if the supervisees, in discussions with their peers, develop what Gary would consider a more balanced approach to the work—not giving up their original approach, but adding intrapsychic and family-of-origin components to it. However, they may remain in deep disagreement with Gary, in which case they are likely to regard him as an ineffective supervisor with little to teach them.

This account illustrates another important dynamic, that of the influence of the larger context on the supervisor's credibility. In this case, the larger context is Gary's other supervisees. Often, supervisees' opinions of their supervisors are shaped at least in part by those of their peers. Gary hoped to use others in the group to influence individual supervisees who were in disagreement with him. This could backfire, however, with the group moving away from Gary, creating a situation where he and they maintain polarized stances and Gary's credibility is greatly diminished.

For a variety of reasons, supervisors frequently may not have as much knowledge as their supervisees or may not be able to teach what their supervisees need to learn (Kadushin, 1992). In agencies where the practitioners are quite experienced, supervisees are likely to develop areas of expertise greater than/or different from that of their supervisors. In some cases, people are asked to supervise others who have different training or experience than they do. School social workers, for example, are often supervised by school principals who have little idea about effective clinical practice, although they may be knowledgeable about education or educational systems (Garrett & Barretta-Herman, 1995). The challenge, then, is for supervisors to promote their supervisees' growth without stifling the supervisee in order to maintain a one-up position and without abdicating their position of power by providing no guidance or support for the supervisee.

To some extent, supervisors can compensate for the diminished knowledge differential by attempting to create an environment in which mutual learning occurs between them and their supervisees. I have supervised people for licensure who work in settings with which I have little or no experience. I tell them that they will need to educate me about the nature of their job; then I can educate them about general principles that can guide them in their work.

Although potentially effective, this solution has its limitations. Although a Caucasian supervisor, for example, may have a great deal of expertise regarding family counseling, he or she may have little regarding the culture of the supervisee and perhaps that of the clients with whom the supervisee is working. A Native American supervisee expressed a feeling of frustration about the fact that she frequently found herself in the position of educating supervisors about her culture. One source of this frustration was the supervisee's sense that a role reversal had occurred. She had come for help with her own skills and instead had to put energy into teaching the supervisor. Supervisors whose knowledge about their supervisees' culture is limited would benefit from gaining general knowledge about the culture from other sources, such as through reading or workshops, and then talking to their supervisees about their particular experiences.

It is ultimately unrealistic, however, to expect supervisors to completely meet their supervisees' learning needs. When supervisors cannot provide that education, their role shifts from that of doing the teaching to one of supporting the supervisee in making use of other resources for professional development. In-service training, conferences, workshops, courses, outside consultation, and peer consultation are all possible avenues (Weinbach, 1994; Garrett & Barretta-Herman, 1995).

Supervisors who feel threatened by the recognition of their own lack of knowledge may react to that feeling by sabotaging their supervisees' growth. Rebecca is a supervisee whose supervisor criticized new information she brought back from conferences, stating that the trainers were not sensitive to the realities of this agency and these clients and therefore were proposing naive and ineffective ideas. If Rebecca attempted to try some of the new approaches she learned in her work, she would find herself rated negatively in her yearly evaluations.

Misuse of the Knowledge Differential

Although there is little disagreement about the desire for a knowledge differential, Jose's story illustrates the potential for the differential's exploitation by the supervisor or unhelpful exaggeration by the supervisee. Given the powerful nature of both the therapeutic and the supervisory processes, it is not surprising that "gurus" have emerged in the mental health field. Jose was perceived by many as that sort of leader: brilliant and highly skilled in his art. The experience of having great impact on people's lives and being recognized for the positive effect of that impact can be quite exhilarating. Many of us have both a desire to help and a natural desire to be appreciated for our talents. It is easy to imagine Jose basking in the glory of the recognition and encouraging the admiration to continue to the detriment of his followers.

Marsha gave Jose so much power to know more than she that she failed to see her own strengths. This is not unusual for beginning practitioners, who are understandably overwhelmed by the complexity of the work. Clinical practice is far from an exact science, and even the most experienced workers have time periods when they are completely at a loss about how to proceed with a client. Those who are new often suffer both from a real lack of knowledge and from a lack of confidence in what they do know. Usually this very common lack of confidence naturally lessens as the practitioner gains experience. However, for some the lack of confidence is a deeper issue. Marsha actually had quite a bit of experience and expertise, but because of her embarrassment regarding her ability to comprehend and articulate, she was easily intimidated by Jose's brilliance. We can guess that she quickly deferred to Jose, and he willingly accepted the power she offered him. Jose could not have stopped her from idealizing him. Had he been concerned about the possible detrimental effect of this imbalance, however, he might have done more to encourage her. Perhaps he could work to point out her strengths or to ask her opinion. Perhaps he could challenge Marsha and others to look at what her behavior was communicating to herself and to him when she deferred to him.

Unlike Marsha, Sally and Howard described Jose's behavior as a misuse of the knowledge differential. They saw him as encouraging a situation in which his ideas could not be challenged. The extent to which supervisees receive permission to challenge the supervisor may affect whether supervisees experience the knowledge differential as promoting growth or as serving to keep them in a one-down position. This can be seen in the attitude illustrated in the following account by a supervisee.

Roberta stated very clearly that it was her belief, which had been reinforced by her supervisors, that the supervisor's job was to know and hers was to not know. She would hate to be a supervisor, she told me, because if she were, she would have to pretend to know all the answers. When asked how her supervisors communicated this idea, Roberta provided several examples. One supervisor would immediately ask whether Roberta had taken particular actions with a client before listening to what she had done. Roberta was left with the impression that she should have thought of those things and that her own actions were incorrect. Another supervisor was supportive in a way Roberta experienced as patronizing. A third would come into the session during live supervision and take over, giving the message that he knew how to do it and she did not. She did not experience permission to challenge them in any of these situations: "If you go in for supervision, you know that's how it's supposed to be. You've got to play that role." She attributed her acceptance of the inevitable one-down position as reflecting not only something about her own attitude but also something about that of her supervisors.

> I think supervisors like that role. Why would they want to be supervisors? To be the big shots. Isn't that true?

This dynamic may be affected by cultural dimensions as well. For example, a Hmong supervisee stated that she felt no permission to challenge the supervisor's ideas. She attributed that to her own beliefs about proper behavior with an authority figure, rather than to any message communicated by her supervisor. If her supervisor had expected her to challenge in that way, the pressure to break cultural norms and the underlying message that those norms were somehow wrong or unacceptable would have increased her discomfort and decreased her feeling of safety in the relationship. In response, her supervisor worked to create a balance between respecting her reluctance and encouraging her to be more assertive.

THE LIMIT-SETTING FUNCTION

Although the knowledge differential allows the supervisee an opportunity to learn, it is most effective when both supervisors and supervisees can balance the need to respect the supervisors' greater knowledge with the need to respect the supervisees' increasing ability to forge their own way. Forging their own way, however, has to be within the bounds of what the supervisor considers ethical and competent practice. The supervisor's requirement to establish and enforce this parameter forms the basis for the limit-setting function in supervision. Ultimately, limit setting occurs at the point at which the supervisor defines a bottom line by telling a supervisee whether certain behavior is acceptable. Any negative feedback a supervisor offers can be defined as limit setting.

Frequently, supervisors prefer to avoid this part of their job, focusing instead on the nurturing and affirming aspects. Quite naturally, supervisors often have a desire to be liked by their supervisees and therefore resist saying something that might be perceived as critical (Kadushin, 1992). This resistance potentially gets in the way of effective limit setting.

> In my early days, I saw myself more from the nurturing position, the younger parent. I was not clear enough about my evaluative role, partly

because I didn't know it well. I never dealt with a problem employee, dealt with kids not doing their chores. I just thought kids always did their chores and I'd just be there saying, "Good for you." Or, if they didn't do their chores, they would come to me and say, "It's really hard to do my chores." And I would say, "Well, how can I help you?"

This supervisor discovered, of course, that there were times when she had to take a stronger stance with her supervisees. Partly because she cultivated a reputation of being an unusually kind and understanding boss, her supervisees were often surprised and upset when she had to hold them accountable for not "doing their chores."

It is sometimes surprising to realize how very difficult setting a limit can be, even for those who consider themselves or who are seen by others as strong individuals. In a training seminar for supervisors that I teach with a colleague, we suggested that members role play a situation in which they had to set a limit with a particularly difficult supervisee. I was surprised to see several members of the group, many of whom are experienced practitioners and supervisors, attempt to hold the line with this supervisee, only to find themselves avoiding making clear statements about their concerns. Generally when people are defensive or aggressive, they are working hard to avoid seeing or admitting something about themselves. It follows then, that they will be skilled at deflecting others from pointing it out, through distortion of their feedback or through intimidation. It is easy for a supervisor to be thrown off base by the deflection, partly because it takes them by surprise and partly because it is threatening.

The notion of courage, discussed by Doherty (1995), is a useful one here. He contended that therapists are often taught to be caring, truthful, and wise, but one rarely talks about the need for them to have courage in their work. However, practitioners are in fact called on to commit acts of courage in major ways. Examples include dealing with suicidal clients; handling serious conflicts with professional colleagues; and confronting clients when to do so could cause the client to fire the professional, at best, and threaten the practitioner with a lawsuit, tarnished reputation, or physical harm, at worst. Doherty further suggested that courage is required in small ways on an everyday basis. Here he included addressing an uncomfortable issue that would be easier to avoid and being honest with oneself about internal issues and responses when they arise. His main message was that it takes courage to act with integrity, because to do so often requires pushing oneself past one's comfort zone. Supervisors must be prepared to push themselves past comfort to act on behalf of clients, the agency, and their supervisees' learning. In addition, they must be ready to push their supervisees past comfort to help them provide competent service to clients. Both acts may involve setting a limit with a supervisee who may react in a negative or aggressive fashion.

An equally important component of limit setting is that it be fair. At the core of Boszormenyi-Nagy's philosophy is a recognition of the fundamental human need for and right to fair treatment. Both he and Doherty (1995) addressed the need for clients to recognize and come to terms with the ways in which they have experienced injustice in their lives. They further stated that it is important to encourage clients to treat others justly as well, even those who, for whatever reason, might be considered "the enemy." Doherty gave a poignant example of challenging his client, a divorced man, not to treat his ex-wife unfairly, even though she might not recognize his behavior as such. Boszormenyi-Nagy contended that a person earns what he calls "merit" for treating another in an ethical manner, no matter how that person responds. He defined a just relationship as one in which there is a fair balance in the distribution of merit, and he described individuals who try to ensure that balance as trustworthy (Boszormenyi-Nagy & Krasner, 1986; Van Heusden & Van Den Eerenbeembt, 1987). As will be evident in the examples below, when supervisees are unhappy with the limits they face, it is generally because they perceive their supervisors as unfair in some way. Although supervisors are not always able to avoid that perception, they will enhance trust in the relationship to the extent that they operate out of a sense of justice.

A primary avenue through which the limit-setting function is exercised is formal and informal (ongoing) evaluation. In a study on the supervisory experiences of 83 licensed school social workers, Garrett and Barretta-Herman (1995) found that 40% of those surveyed had not received a formal evaluation regarding their client-centered work from their supervisor in three years or more. Although evaluation is essential to the process of supervision, many resist formal and even informal evaluation because of the risk of discomfort. Many supervisors are reluctant to give negative feedback, and many supervisees respond defensively on receiving it. The process of evaluation raises a number of complex questions, such as whether to evaluate someone in relationship to his or her own growth or capabilities, to the capabilities of the rest of the staff, or to an external standard of performance.

This delicate issue takes on even greater significance when we consider the variable of cultural diversity. Like many organizations, human services agencies and training institutions work hard to recruit and retain people from a variety of ethnic and cultural backgrounds to work with an increasingly diverse clientele. In addition, affirmative action and antidiscrimination laws have been implemented to protect those groups who historically have been oppressed by the dominant culture's members and institutions. The need to create a more equitable system, one open to the acceptance of differences, is of utmost importance, and efforts to move toward that goal need and deserve a great deal of support.

Because of a lack of opportunity, significantly fewer people from other backgrounds seek or have formal training to do the work than are needed, particularly in parts of the United States where populations are only recently becoming more diverse. However, even when extensive training is lacking, many agencies find that practitioners from diverse backgrounds bring an extremely important dimension to the work, thus making a crucial contribution toward the goal of competent service to clients. That contribution can be broadly stated in two ways. First, agencies that serve a diverse clientele need practitioners who understand the experiences and needs of the clients from the inside; and, when the clients' first language is not English, the agencies need practitioners who are fluent in the clients' language. Second, although the guiding principles of the traditional theories of counseling are grounded in European and Northern Caucasian American cultures, most if not all societies have ways to help people that serve a function similar to that of formal counseling (Sue et al., 1996). Those ways may be more than just helpful to those from whose society they are generated; knowledge of them also opens up more possibilities for helping people from all societies. Adding more diversity to the agency therefore potentially creates a more effective service for all clients. On the other hand, without formal training, many practitioners may lack important skills, which then need to be learned on the job. Consequently both schools and agencies are often in a position of having to weigh the importance of maintaining a particular standard of practice against that of increasing diversity.

Paula supervises in an agency that serves families with a multitude of problems. Many of the families who live in the area are Native American. Partly in response to pressure from the agency mandate to increase diversity and partly in response to her own belief that the clients would be best served by Native American counselors, Paula hired Susan and Mike, both Native Americans. Because her agency is a private nonprofit organization, it cannot offer salaries commensurate with others in the area, and highly qualified practitioners—particularly those of color—are able to find better opportunities elsewhere. Susan and Mike had some experience with families, but both their experience and their training were limited. The hiring committee determined that they would be effective on the job but only after several months of closely supervised work with diminished caseloads.

Clearly these two workers were not held to the same standard of practice or productivity as the other workers, who were asked both to take up the slack in the caseload and to help in the training process. This caused resentment among the staff, which created the danger of a backlash against the goal of accepting differences. A question was raised not only about the equity of workload among the staff but also about whether clients were ultimately being better served by practitioners who were less well trained.

A useful guideline for this and other, similar situations is to return to the goal of supervision—competent service to clients—and to the definition of clinical work offered in Chapter 1. Northern (1989) defined clinical work as "based on knowledge and theory of psychosocial development, behavior, psychopathology, unconscious motivation, interpersonal relationships, environmental stress, social systems and cultural diversity" with the "goal of enhancement and maintenance of psychosocial functioning of individuals, families and small groups" (p. 1). Certainly we can assume that Susan and Mike had a great deal of understanding of and sensitivity to what it means to be Native American, which brought an important dimension to their work. Paula acted on the assumption that with good on-the-job training, they would obtain the other knowledge and skills necessary to do the work.

This is a reasonable assumption. I frequently tell my students and supervisees that their training in school is tantamount to filling up a gas tank for a long journey. Most of their learning will occur in their jobs, through experience, good supervision, and continuing education and training opportunities. A significant difference in Paula's situation was that Susan and Mike began the job with less training than was required of other practitioners in the agency. However, as Susan and Mike are making an important contribution to the agency, it is in the agency's best interests to give them the support they need to succeed in the job. To ensure that the work with clients is not compromised, Paula should establish a mechanism for evaluation and a timeline by which Susan and Mike will be expected to obtain the skills necessary to perform at a level that does not require extra support. To minimize the staff's resentment, Paula must first create an environment in which all members of the staff are valued for their contribution. Susan and Mike are not the only ones who need to learn new skills. They also bring with them unique knowledge and skills, some of which they can teach the others. Then Paula should recognize and reward those who are doing extra work to support their colleagues.

Shared Meaning and Limit Setting

Some argue that the very notion of standards is a cross-cultural issue because standards themselves are culturally based and biased. Supervisors frequently need to decide whether a difference in treatment approaches is simply philosophical or whether it reflects poor work by the supervisee. Jerry told the story of an African American social worker who worked in a program with a strictly behavioral orientation. The expectation was that practitioners establish clear and measurable goals with the clients and gear treatment directly to the achievement of those goals. Alice was quite effective with clients, although she was unable to articulate either goals or a treatment plan. Her approach was more casual, more intuitive and less overtly task-oriented. Initially Jerry wondered whether her effectiveness would increase if she were able to develop better verbal skills and think more consciously about her work. He quickly recognized, however, that Alice worked with many families better than did those who used the program's usual linear, step-by-step behavioral approach. He speculated that culture was a large factor in the fit between Alice's approach and her clients. To try to force either Alice or her clients into a different mode was not only impossible but also not useful, at best, and destructive at worst.

Another example of this dilemma is in the area of written agency documentation. Many cultures do not value the written word as much as others do (Ryan & Hendricks, 1989). In addition, some workers either have English as a second language or have not had the educational opportunities to learn formal writing skills. Consequently, they have more difficulty than others do with the paperwork aspect of their jobs. The question raised is whether it is fair to hold those workers to the same performance standards used with workers whose cultural values and education support the development of those skills. On this question, Jerry takes a hard line. His position is that funding and accrediting bodies demand a certain amount and level of documentation. Therefore all his workers, no matter what their background, must achieve what he considers an acceptable level of skill in written work. Like Paula above, Jerry will offer extra help, through guidance or time and money for training in writing skills, for those whose written work does not meet the standard.

Although Jerry made clear decisions in the examples above, Tim, the supervisor in the following story, was more ambivalent. His supervisee, a Mormon whose clients were also Mormon, had different values than he about male and female roles in the family, as well as about domestic violence.

> Joleen was seeing a couple in which the wife was depressed. It came out over the course of some sessions that the husband shakes her. I expressed concern about this, but she kept saying, "It's just shaking. It's not pounding. It's not hitting. You're blowing this out of proportion. It only happens occasionally." She was not going to put a stop to that. She was going to teach them some alternative ways of conflict resolution. But she didn't think that she needed to really stop the physical abuse.
>
> We really did have some disagreements about that. I said that part of what she could do to support the wife, to give her a sense of empowerment, was to make hitting or shaking off limits. This is not something that should happen in this marriage. Make that a ground rule. While I'm working with you, this has to stop. As we would go from session to session, occasionally this would come up again. And Joleen wasn't asking them for information about it directly.

But it would come up. The wife would talk about him, and him "beating up on me," which turned out to be shaking, but she felt very intimidated by it. I asked Joleen to set the limit, but she told me she couldn't. She said that I was pathologizing him too much and that they were learning new methods. My response was, "She's still struggling with depression, and she's never heard anybody echo her by saying 'yeah, he is beating up on you.'" We never resolved that.

In this situation, Tim and Joleen agreed to disagree. The clients eventually left, with Joleen concluding that things had improved and Tim concluding that the deeper issues were not adequately addressed. Another supervisor might have taken a stronger stance, stating that Joleen's approach was jeopardizing the woman's safety and enabling both members of the couple to minimize the seriousness of the violence. The supervisor in this case might insist that Joleen change the nature of her intervention or risk receiving a negative evaluation, being taken off the case, or, at worst, losing her job. In my opinion, this situation calls for a strong stance. There was certainly a difference in values between Tim and Joleen, and, whether accurate or not, Tim determined that the difference was grounded in each of their cultural backgrounds. However, a core value of any human service profession is the enhancement of clients' personal safety. To accept physical abuse in the name of cultural differences is therefore to threaten a basic standard of good practice.

In a similar situation, Lon, a Caucasian supervisor, spoke of his work with Hmong supervisees on the issue of child abuse. According to Ly (1996), Hmong parents typically use corporal punishment to discipline children who do not obey. Physical punishment for serious misbehaviors, even if it leaves marks, is considered a tolerable practice, performed by loving and concerned parents. Ly also notes that Hmong families are traditionally very patriarchal and that conflict resolution is dealt with in a specific, orderly way. If there is a problem in the family that the father cannot resolve, the family will ask for help from the extended family.

This situation poses a dilemma for a practitioner in the United States. Most state laws dictate that child abuse be reported to the appropriate child protection agency. Although defining what constitutes "abuse" is sometimes difficult, the general guideline is that practitioners should report corporal punishment that leaves bruises (Kisch, personal communication, 1996).

Lon observed that the Hmong families served by his agency fit the description offered by Ly (1996). His supervisees, themselves Hmong, made the cogent argument that the family elders were in a much better position than the child protection agency to have an impact on a particular family's problems. They also argued that some of the corporal punishment, seen in the context of Hmong culture, was not really abusive.

Lon's response was a complex and sensitive one. He made it clear to his supervisees that corporal punishment extensive enough to leave bruises was considered child abuse according to the law and was therefore unacceptable. It was the job of his supervisees to help the family and the extended family elders understand this and to help them learn other effective methods for child rearing.

However, Lon also recognized that the ultimate question was how to best serve the client—in this situation, how to best protect the children. Although some cases were severe enough that an immediate report to child protection had to be made, many were not. Clearly, the family would be much more open to help from relatives than to help from a child protection worker: perhaps the family elders could be enlisted to help the family derive other strategies for disciplining their children. Lon and his supervisees worked together to determine whether a particular situation could be addressed first within the Hmong family, and only later, if necessary, through child protection.

Technically, Lon was breaking the law by not insisting that his supervisees immediately make a report to child protection. Nonetheless, he set a clear limit with his supervisees that upheld the professional value of enhancement of clients' personal safety and insisted that his supervisees do the same with their clients. He did so, however, with an understanding of and respect for the supervisees' and the clients' cultural values.

Supervisees' Responses to Limit Setting

As with the knowledge differential, the way in which supervisees experience the act of limit setting is a crucial component in the relationship. Usually supervisees want judgments from their supervisors and like Kyung, who tells the following story, are disappointed when the supervisor will not take a stand on an issue, or insist on a certain level of quality.

> I had a case where I was working with the mother and another therapist was working with the daughter. The mother was really worried about her daughter and wanted to try to resolve some things. I suggested a co-therapy session with the daughter and her therapist. The daughter's therapist said she would not do that because it would jeopardize her relationship with her client.
>
> I brought it up in our team supervision group, saying that I was concerned about it. I got no support from our supervisor. He just sat back and said, "Oh." He tried to analyze each of our issues about it but didn't really take a stand on what made some sense in terms of the clients. I talked to him about it later. I can't even remember what he gave me back. It was really a nonresponse.

Noah, another supervisee, compared several supervisory relationships, including one that was basically positive except that he and his supervisor seemed to have a "secret pact" to avoid certain issues that would be uncomfortable. The relationships he defined as "real supervision" were those in which he could count on his supervisors to take a stand and to push him when necessary.

Frequently supervisees will be upset with a supervisor but will not discuss it. Carla reported an instance in which she had criticized a supervisee for a stiffness in his style. Shortly after that, he moved to a new department. Two years later, his job changed and Carla again became his supervisor. His attitude was quite cooperative, but he seemed to have almost no clients to present in supervision.

> A few weeks went by and he still only had one client to talk about. I said, "Listen, every time I've worked with you, you have always had a lot to discuss. What's going on?" He said, "Nothing's going on." So we set a goal for him to present a couple more clients within the next month. A month came and the situation hadn't changed. I said, "Something's going on. Let's talk about it. What am I doing that's getting in the way?" He hemmed and hawed, and finally he told me that he was still stinging from the criticism he had received two years earlier. No one had ever called him stiff. He thought that I liked him, and then I told him he was stiff. Now he didn't know if I liked him.

Shulman (1993) recommended that supervisors "reach inside the silence" (p. 90) to get at underlying feelings or concerns. He assumed that when there is no response forthcoming, this is a clue to the supervisor that something is awry. Often supervisors will avoid the subject, to save themselves or their supervisees discomfort. In the preceding example, the supervisee was withholding the story as a way to protect himself from further criticism. Clearly what Carla intended as helpful feedback, the supervisee experienced as shaming. Carla saw the withholding as an indication that there was a problem. By addressing it, she was able to get to the cause of the supervisee's discomfort.

Sometimes a supervisor will use the limit-setting function in a way that feels punishing or threatening to the supervisee. Anne recounted the story of an evaluation process with the clinical director of the agency. Her clinical supervisor had done half of the evaluation, which the director then completed. This situation was problematic partly because Anne received different information from each of them about what was expected of her. The issue was productivity. Her understanding from her direct supervisor was that her current rate was within the acceptable range. When she met with the director, she was told not only that this rate was unacceptable but that if she was going to work at a rate of 83%, perhaps she should be paid 83% of her salary. The director then added that Anne's raise would have been better if her quota had been better.

> I went back to her and said the statement was really powerful, coming
> from a supervisor. I explained that if a colleague had said it, it would be
> an exploration; but from her, it sounded like a threat. She didn't get it.
> From her point of view she was just "pointing out an option."

As this example illustrates, the impact of the supervisor's feedback
might be a great deal stronger than the supervisor intends. Unfortunately, in this situation, even when the supervisor was told of her
impact she did not acknowledge it.

Supervisees often experience the supervisor as having a hidden
agenda, perhaps one of racial prejudice. Don, an African American
supervisee, recounted the following incident, which happened earlier in
his career.

> The first year I was at the agency, I figured I was new and had a lot to
> learn. I got a satisfactory rating on my evaluation. The next year it was
> better, but not outstanding. I asked my supervisor what I needed to do to
> get a rating of outstanding. He said, "You're doing a great job here, but
> to get an outstanding, you need to do more—like talk at a national con-
> ference or write a paper. He specified what I needed to do.
>
> During that year I did perhaps 15 presentations. I presented at a
> national conference. I also was on the agency's public relations commit-
> tee. It came to the evaluation process and I showed him what I did. I
> didn't get an outstanding rating. He got me on documentation. He said it
> was good but not excellent.

Don challenged the evaluation, but the administration supported
his supervisor's decision. Although it may be true that Don's documentation was not excellent, it appears that the supervisor did not mention
it when Don requested feedback and did not acknowledge Don's high
level of performance. Don concluded from this and other unexplainable
and subtle rejections that race may have played a part in the supervisor's action and perhaps in the administration's support of it.

It is not unusual for supervisees of color to believe that racism has
been a factor in a supervisor's decision making. Often, as in Don's
situation, the source of that sense is difficult to name. Rashon, for
example, spoke about the fact that, as an intern, she was given significantly fewer clients than the other students. She was an older student
who had relocated and was having understandable problems adjusting. However, her sense was that because she was a person of color,
those problems were seen as more significant, and her competence was
more closely questioned than that of her colleagues. Clearly those who
have a history of oppression and of being in a minority position are
more aware of and sensitive to subtle expressions of racism than are
those in the majority culture. The inability to explicitly pinpoint the
racism does not by any means negate its very real, although often neb-
ulous, presence.

On the other hand, some supervisors observe that supervisees who are unhappy with a particular limit may attribute the action to racism. From the supervisor's point of view, however, the real issue is performance or behavior on the job. Larry told the following story about his African American supervisee, Tom.

> Tom was assigned to work with me, and my agenda was different from his. At the same time, he got involved with some grant funding from the state and was focused on a program that was very near and dear to his heart. We got into a huge struggle because he wanted to work on this other program even though he was largely assigned to work on my programs. We would talk about what he needed to do and when it needed to be accomplished, but it wouldn't happen.
>
> When I would ask him, "Why haven't you done this?" he would talk about how racist his co-workers were and how difficult it was to work with them. He seemed to me to be unwilling to try to work out any differences he might have. I was losing sympathy with him. I was willing to listen and to learn only up to a certain point, and then I had to question whether he was simply calling everyone a racist.

In this sort of situation, it is often difficult to distinguish between the tensions that arise because of racial differences and what might be considered a more "objective" assessment of the practitioners' performance. Part of the difficulty comes from what Boszormenyi-Nagy calls "destructive entitlement" (Boszormenyi-Nagy & Krasner, 1986). This can occur when a person is not treated with the fairness and care that all human beings deserve. Some parents, because of injustices in their own lives, fail to give children the care they need, either on a psychological, spiritual, or physical level. In addition, children may not have the quality of life to which they are entitled for reasons outside the parents' control, such as poverty, serious illness, racism, or oppression.

Children who encounter injustice in their lives are entitled to be angry and even to want somebody to take the blame for their condition. However, the result is often that these children act destructively toward others in response to the injustices they have experienced. This sort of behavior is defined as a manifestation of "destructive entitlement." An example of destructive entitlement is when the relationship between parent and child becomes a vehicle through which the parent meets needs that should have been addressed earlier (Goldenthal, 1993).

It is clear that many who are in the minority have been and continue to be severely oppressed by the majority culture on many levels. The subtle and insidious effect of racism is one that permeates the culture and underlies much of the difficulty oppressed people encounter. It is difficult to measure the extent of the pain caused by a history of victimization of an entire people and the effect of that pain on any one individual. The term *blaming the victim* has been coined to describe situations in which those who are themselves oppressed are then blamed for causing the very abuse they suffer. It is of utmost importance that those in human services take care to curb any tendencies of their own to participate in this sort of blame. On the other hand, the notion of destructive entitlement alerts us to the reality that many who have been mistreated have a belief that the world "owes" them something in return. Often, as Boszormenyi-Nagy suggested, this belief translates into an expectation that people other than those who created the original problem are responsible for its cure. Although it is easy to see the unfairness to children who are expected to meet their parents' unmet needs, it is less clear in the arena of racism in the workplace. Indeed, affirmative action laws are in place precisely to make amends for past oppression and to ensure against continuation of oppression. In what situation, then, does the supervisor go the extra mile for a supervisee to make amends for oppression? And when does the supervisor simply refuse to accept certain behavior in spite of the pain that might have produced it? These questions must be addressed on a case-by-case basis, with the supervisor using as a guideline the notion of competent service to clients.

Influence of Context on Limit Setting

The positional power agencies ascribe to supervisors gives supervisors a great deal of responsibility for their supervisees' work. The worker represents the agency and is hired to carry out that agency's mission. In addition, the agency will ultimately be held accountable for the quality of that work. Supervisors connected to degree-granting programs derive their positional power from their influence over whether or not a student graduates and becomes a professional. A supervisor or consultant in private practice has little positional power unless the supervisee is seeking some type of certification. A reflection of this difference in the degree of the supervisor's positional power is that evaluations are often much more formal and structured, are taken more seriously by the supervisor, and have more impact on the supervisee when the supervisor has more positional power. In the private practice setting, evaluations are often extremely casual, if they occur at all.

In addition to ascribing varying degrees of positional power, the context can either support or interfere with the supervisor's ability to set firm limits because of other dynamics that are occurring. In one school setting, for example, a supervisee was sexually involved with several faculty members. Clearly this situation was fraught with problems, not the least of which was impairment of the faculty members' ability to support the supervisor's assessment that this person's work was unacceptable.

As mentioned earlier, another contextual influence is the reactions of others in the agency. Frequently, in the case of serious limit setting, other employees have strong feelings and opinions about what has occurred. Because of the need to respect the individual supervisee's confidentiality, often those reactions are based on limited information. Even if the supervisor has acted with integrity, other supervisees, hearing the story only from the point of view of their colleague, may believe that individual has been treated unfairly. They may also fear that they, too, will be similarly mistreated. Often supervisors who are concerned about this sort of negative response from others will lose the courage to set the necessary limit. It is important, therefore, that the supervisors' peers and superiors support the action.

Often there is more than one supervisor and one organization involved, as when the supervisee is a student and is therefore accountable to both the agency and the school. Most agree that schools should perform a gatekeeping function for the profession. However, the actual practice of effective gatekeeping requires careful and thorough cooperation between the academic and agency supervisors, as well as support from the larger institutions in which each are employed. If they do not support one another in setting limits for the supervisee, it is easier for the supervisee to play one against the other, just as a child may take advantage of inconsistent messages from his or her parents. The following story illustrates some of the possible complications.

Geri, a student in a counselor education program, had limited academic abilities and a history of drug abuse. She had maintained sobriety for 3 years. She was having some difficulty in her first year practicum, including arriving late on several occasions and coming to work apparently high one morning. Her supervisor confronted her and notified the faculty supervisor of the difficulty. Geri admitted that she had begun to use drugs again and agreed to return to treatment. After this incident, her performance improved to a satisfactory level. The agency supervisor, deciding that Geri had done what she needed to do, declined a request from the school to document the event on her final evaluation.

Geri continued in school, performing as a marginal student. She had difficulty understanding the concepts being presented and often turned in assignments that were barely satisfactory. She frequently complained about being overwhelmed by the demands on her. When she entered her second practicum, the school did not feel at liberty to share information about the first one, because Geri had in fact passed with a satisfactory grade and the supervisor did not document the problem. Geri's confidentiality and her right to be given a chance to improve needed to be protected.

A few months into the year, the practicum supervisor started noticing problems in Geri's performance similar to those Geri demonstrated in the classroom. She appeared to have difficulty retaining and processing information and thus was not doing an adequate job with her clients. After much discussion with the faculty liaison, the practicum supervisor was able to develop goals for Geri and strategies designed to monitor her progress. The strategies included having Geri give her supervisor both written documentation and tapes of sessions so that the supervisor could learn more fully what Geri was actually doing with clients.

In spite of very specific feedback from her supervisors, Geri did not acknowledge her own contribution to her difficulties. Rather, she attributed the problem to confusion and lack of direction in the agency and to an unrealistic amount of work she had for her classes. She refused to recognize that others in a similar situation were handling the work much more effectively than she was. Still, she was able to respond to the greater structure imposed by her agency and academic supervisors and finished the year with a satisfactory grade. Both supervisors, however, were left with the uneasy feeling that, although they were able to hold Geri to a minimum standard, she was not capable of the quality of work normally expected of someone at the masters degree level.

A significant larger contextual issue at play here is the mandate from the larger society to protect individual rights—in this case of the student, in other cases of an employee. Legal restrictions require that, before taking an extreme action such as expulsion or firing, one needs to carefully document that the supervisee has been apprised of the problems and given adequate support and opportunity to correct them. Many times, as in Geri's situation, the supervisee is unwilling to take even partial responsibility for the difficulty and may blame the supervisor or the agency. This makes the supervisor's job more difficult, as it becomes necessary to face not only the supervisee's anger and hurt at being mistreated but also the fear that the supervisee may seek retribution in the form of a complaint or suit against the supervisor. Therefore, this process is one that requires time, persistence, and a great deal of courage.

Although the importance of protecting the supervisee's rights is outweighed by that of protecting clients from harm, it is often quite difficult to determine whether harm to clients either has occurred or will occur. The supervisors cannot assume that because Geri is a below-average clinician who barely meets minimum standards, her clients are in danger. In this situation, even though both supervisors placed a high priority on cooperation and accountability, they were not completely confident that they had performed the gatekeeping task. Probably Geri would not hurt clients. She seemed, with close supervision, to be able to perform adequately. However, Geri clearly was not held to the kind of standards expected of other students.

The balance between the rights and needs of clients versus those of supervisees becomes even more complicated when we add the element of reporting laws imposed by boards who license mental health professionals. As stated earlier, the purpose of licensing is to ensure the public's protection against professionals' incompetent practice. To that end, licensing boards and some professional organizations have established codes of ethics and procedures for reporting and sanctioning those who break the codes.

The system of licensure is crucial in that it gives consumers of mental health services the confidence that those who are providing these services have specific training and are practicing at, at least, a minimum standard of competence. In addition, clients are hopefully protected from harm; if not, they at least have an avenue through which they can be compensated for the damages incurred. However, there are potential difficulties with the system that can lead it to work against its own goal of protection of the public. In Minnesota, for example, the reporting law developed in 1992 both for licensed social workers and for licensed marriage and family therapists reads as follows:

> A licensed health professional shall report to the appropriate board personal knowledge of any conduct that the licensed health professional reasonably believes constitutes grounds for disciplinary action under this chapter by any licensee, including conduct indicating that the licensee may be medically incompetent, or may be medically or physically unable to engage safely in the provision of services. If the information was obtained in the course of a client relationship, the client is another licensee, and the treating individual successfully counsels the other individual to limit or withdraw from practice to the extent required by the impairment, the board may deem this limitation of or withdrawal from practice to be sufficient disciplinary action. (Minnesota *Statutes*, 1992)

The implication of this law is that any information gathered in a supervisory or consultative relationship that meets the above requirements has to be reported. The law leaves no room for the supervisor or consultant to make a judgment about the degree of seriousness of the supervisee's action or whether the supervisee has made an error that can best be corrected through appropriate and therapeutically effective amends. In fact, the law explicitly states that even information disclosed by a licensee who is a client in therapy must be reported to the board.

Although this law is somewhat unusual among licensure boards in the broad nature of its scope, it is a reflection of what I like to describe as a climate of "ethical vigilance" that characterizes today's society. The exposure of serious ethical breaches in human services parallels a similar exposure in politics, business, sports, and so on. Because this discovery has created a feeling of betrayal by those in whom the public has placed its trust, there is a desire to control professionals' behavior through detailed legislation.

Such a global law potentially endangers the level of trust in the supervisory relationship. Many supervisees have commented to me that they would be afraid to tell their supervisor anything that might be reported. In the language of the conceptual model, they would limit the telling of their stories. By doing so, they run the risk of hiding problems in their work that are likely to worsen if not addressed, causing even greater harm to their clients.

THE SUPERVISEE'S POWER IN CHOOSING SUPERVISION

Although supervisors are in a more powerful position than are supervisees, supervisees also have power to enhance or sabotage the supervisory process. Supervisors need only the power of their position and the support from the larger context to exercise the limit-setting or evaluative function of their job. However, they need the cooperation of the supervisee to exercise the educational function. In the words of one supervisor, "Either they make me their teacher or they don't. That rests with them, not with me." In the act of making a supervisor a teacher, the supervisee in effect places the supervisor in a position of power. A supervisee described this process as one of putting himself in the care of his supervisor. To do so, supervisees must make themselves vulnerable on some level—that is, open to receiving what the supervisor has to give, as well as open to the notion that the supervisor is in charge. A supervisor who was a private consultant characterized this dynamic in the following manner.

> I've got the power. They hire me because of whatever they think I will bring to them professionally. I don't pretend to be equal. We're equal as human beings, but they're paying me to be in charge. They're saying, "Will you help me? I believe in you." That's wrought with power stuff.

The power to choose is most obvious to both parties when the supervisee is literally hiring the supervisor for private consultation. However, even in this situation, supervisees are not always in touch with the reality of their own power. There appear to be two sources of the ambiguity about where the power lies. The first is the one mentioned above: that by hiring a supervisor, one is assigning that person expert power and probably referent power as well. The second is that, particularly early in their professional development, supervisees may experience the power differential so acutely that it is difficult to recognize their own power.

Jasmine was a member of a group practice that hired various consultants. Over the years they had a number of different consultants, one of whom she experienced as both authoritarian and abusive.

> When we started, we were all really beginning practitioners. At that point, it felt very appropriate to have him be in the role that he was in.

He really had a teaching role. As we grew, the relationship didn't change. He saw himself as needing to be in control. Eventually that was not okay with us.

We had a few instances of him behaving abusively toward us. Once, early on, he made an outrageously sexist remark about a client. I objected to it. He jumped out of his chair and started yelling at me about how she deserved it. After a few of those encounters, we began to see that we were all acting like abused children. We were really afraid to confront him.

I think there was a culture in those early years that we turned ourselves over to anybody in authority. I don't think that's true anymore. I don't think a supervisor can come in here now and call the shots on any level. I think there really is a sense that we are grown-ups, that we know what we're doing, and that, as a group, we know what we need.

As indicated early in this chapter, the knowledge differential is expected to lessen as the supervisee develops professional skill. When more experienced practitioners seek supervision or consultation, they still need to become learners, but they do so with more sense of their own power to choose from whom they will learn and how that learning will occur. This is the phenomenon Jasmine is describing in her comments about becoming a group of grown-ups. She is referring not only to whether the supervisor has something to teach but also to whether the supervisor will treat group members with respect and whether they can agree on a mutually acceptable contract. The supervisor in the above account, although certainly knowledgeable, was not respectful to them or about their clients. At a later point in the group's history, the members fired a consultant when they discovered that he was unable to commit adequate time to meet their needs.

Supervisees frequently have no choice about who their supervisor will be because they are in an agency setting. However, the supervisee's need to become a learner to receive educational supervision still holds. As has been demonstrated in some of the earlier stories in this chapter, a common way for supervisees to avoid supervision in this situation is by withholding information. In the language of the conceptual model, they avoid telling a complete story. Generally they do so either because they don't think the supervisor has something to teach or because they are intimidated by their supervisors. In both types of situation, the supervisee is performing an act of personal power. Often, withholding may be a sound decision. However, a consequence of making this choice is that little to no learning can occur.

Variables named in the conceptual model influence whether or not supervisees choose supervision. Supervisees tend to base their choices on whether the supervisors have a knowledge base; whether they and their supervisors can achieve shared meaning, both in terms of what is effective treatment and how the supervisory contract will look; and whether they believe they can develop a trusting relationship with the supervisor. Jasmine, whose story is told earlier, offered the following comment.

> I believe that a supervisor ought to know more about something. Supervisors' power or authority comes from their knowledge base and from their own activities; not from their interaction with us, but rather from the fact that they are practicing clinicians who have expertise that we don't have. To the extent that their expertise is relevant to us, they will be credible. However, we will not get more personally vulnerable with a supervisor until we've worked together for a while so that we're clear that we trust his or her integrity as well as his or her competence and insight.

It is important to remember that, although the supervisee does have the power to choose, the supervisor has some avenues for handling a supervisee who is not willing to be a learner. In the consultation situation, the supervisor's primary option is to have an open discussion with the supervisee about the problem and try to determine what is blocking the learning. There may well be a way to correct the block. For example, as in the earlier case of Carla's supervisory relationship, the supervisee was hurt by Carla's assessment of him as stiff. Acknowledging the supervisee's pain and clarifying possible misunderstandings may alleviate the problem. On the other hand, either the supervisor, the supervisee, or both may be unwilling or unable to correct the situation. For example, the supervisor may simply lack the knowledge the supervisee is seeking, or one party may find the other too defensive to engage in honest discussion. In this situation, the consultant's only avenue is to end the relationship.

In the employment or training situation, the supervisor still has the option of open discussion and would be wise to begin with this approach. However, the supervisor also has the positional power to reward or punish. Again, no one can force another to be a learner. However, in this situation, the supervisor can use the avenues of formal evaluation, sanctions, and ultimately firing, depending on the seriousness of the problem.

ATTITUDES TOWARD POWER AND AUTHORITY

An important area to consider regards the attitude toward and level of comfort about power and authority that both participants bring to the relationship. A useful question to ask supervisors and their supervisees is how they experience themselves in their relationships with authority figures or as authority figures. Not surprisingly, their attitudes are influenced by cultural and gender factors, as well as by individual or family experiences.

Supervisors' Attitudes toward Power

On one end of a continuum are supervisors like Bev, whose comments reflect careful attention to the dynamics of power in the relationship:

> In the past few years, I have paid more attention to power. My role is not mutual. I believe in transference. And I recognize that I could be the mother, the aunt, the father, etc.—that somebody else's stuff could be projected onto anyone in an authority position. It's not that you ask for it. I think you have to be aware of it. It's not just who you are in the room; it's what people project on to you from their own past. That makes a big difference on how people act in supervision. It's huge. You can try to minimize it, but at the same time, you have to balance it. When I sit on a committee that hears cases of ethical violations by therapists, all of the violations are about the denial of power, the minimizing of power. They say, "I didn't know they were going to do that with what I said."

On the other side of this continuum are supervisors who are reluctant to focus on the subject of power. The following is Sonya's comment about her sense of her impact on her supervisees.

> I don't know how much I know about the impact of my power on my supervisees. I can say that my relationship with supervisees is positive, warm, responsive. I don't know what they see about my power because it's just not something you talk about. It feels to me almost as though to bring it up is to heighten that. That feels inappropriate. It just doesn't feel right. It feels as though you're on a bit of a fishing expedition for praise.
>
> I wouldn't want to do that. And I would feel very distressed if people felt the need to supplicate or in any way try to present themselves to me in a way that would mollify me if they saw me needing mollifying, or having to be on their best behavior with me, or any of that sort of thing.
>
> I just assume that what we will experience together will be primarily a positive interaction, and therefore there would be nothing from me that you would not expect. For example, once a supervisee was so grateful that I hadn't shamed him. It never occurred to me I wouldn't. Those kinds of comments tell me more about the individual than about me. I say, "That's true for anyone that this individual interacts with. They are the givers-away of power."
>
> So it's no more true for me than it is for anyone else. Therefore, it's really a nonissue. I'm not sure I agree with the notion that we have so

much power because of our position as supervisors. We pay lip service to that notion. But, for example, with clients, you know how little power we have in many ways. One can work one's toes off and not get anywhere.

But I also know that there's a piece of my own dislike of being in power. So one of the ways I deal with that is to pretend I don't have any. I work overtime to get out from under the burden of being in power. "I don't want your power. You keep it. Don't give it to me. I don't want it. I've got my own. You take it. You use it. It's a burden if you give it to me because then you have asked me to be responsible for it, in a not very subtle way. And thank you, but no thank you. That's your job, not mine."

I don't want to have special impact. I want to at least be heard. But, then I don't think one has to be in a supervisor/supervisee relationship to have impact. I think sometimes we get from our families, from our colleagues, from our friends, comments, ideas, challenges or support that is enormously impactful. I don't know that we'd describe that as power.

Many of Sonya's thoughts would be shared by people like Bev. Sonya observed that supervisees will react to her in ways that have to do with their own issues rather than with her directly. She recognized that supervisees have the power to choose supervision and that, in many ways, she may not be able to have much impact on that decision. She points out that it is dangerous to be in a position wherein the supervisee feels the need to take care of her (mollify her). Certainly most supervisors would agree that the hope is that supervisees will increase their sense of their own power and that this is the important focus in supervision.

However, there are some fundamental differences between Sonya and Bev. Sonya appears to join together the notions of closely attending to the significance of her place in the power differential with that of taking away power from the supervisee. The way to enable the supervisee's growth toward greater personal power, therefore, is to minimize, as much as possible, her own. In addition, she assumes that, if supervisees respond to her out of their own issues rather than because of something she is doing, there is nothing she can or ought to do about it.

By contrast, Bev was quite clear about her power and thought the best way to handle it was to acknowledge it, both with herself and her supervisee, and to use it in her work. She feared that if she tried to pretend it doesn't exist, she might unintentionally hurt a supervisee, because the act of pretending hides her awareness of her impact. Perhaps the difference is related to comfort. Sonya acknowledged that part of the issue is her own dislike of the notion of being in power. She further stated that her own first experience with authority figures was with her authoritarian, dogmatic father, with whom it was no doubt true that her own power was in jeopardy because of his.

Supervisees' Attitudes toward Power

Supervisees have a range of experiences with supervisory power. Sometimes they are uncomfortable with the supervisor's use of power, and other times they experience the supervisor's use of power as appropriate and positive. It bears noting that supervisees are rarely if ever comfortable with supervisors whom they experience as abdicating their power to provide expert knowledge and to set appropriate limits.

Although supervisees' perceptions of their experiences reflect their supervisors' actions, these perceptions also reflect their own approach to authority figures. As demonstrated by the story of Jose that began this chapter, several supervisees can have very different responses to the same supervisor, in part because of what each brings to the relationship. Those whose past experiences have been comfortable and positive are likely to accept the supervisor's position and use of authority more easily than are those whose experiences have been negative. Supervisees who are more aware of their own personal power may ascribe far less to their supervisors than will those who lack this awareness. The supervisees in this chapter's first story serve as an illustration. Although both Marsha and Kim were comfortable with Jose as an authority figure, Marsha deferred to him, discounting her own competency in comparison to his. By contrast, Kim seemed to be quite aware of her own strength, while at the same time eager to learn from Jose. We do not know what Sally and Howard bring regarding their own attitudes toward authority, but it is possible that their reactions were colored by their own mistrust of those in greater power.

A stunning example of this sort of mistrust was expressed earlier by Roberta, who stated that supervisors believed they had to know everything and that she was to know nothing. She added that she presumed supervisors were in the job because of their desire "to be big shots." Naturally, if they are in it for the power, they are in no way interested in acknowledging her power, and in many ways she does not acknowledge her own. If her job is to not know, and she believes she knows—especially if she knows more than her supervisor—she must keep it a secret from her supervisor (which in fact she did in several situations). Although Roberta's supervisors may indeed have influenced her perception, it is quite possible that she came to the relationships with a background of having those in authority over her feel threatened by any show of her power, strength, or knowledge. She is clearly cynical about the integrity of anyone who would want to be in a position of power, and makes many perhaps unfounded assumptions about their intentions.

Sam's statement is an example of a supervisee who is aware of the effect his previous experience with authority figures has on the way he relates to his supervisors:

I make him very much the expert. I see him as just a real confident person, with a lot of knowledge and skill, and I think I see him as kind of a father figure. Maybe it's difficult to let go of the image and see the real father, because that's not what you're looking for. What you're looking for is a mentor. So some of this male stuff could play into it. Maybe he does represent more of a father, and my female supervisor represents a mother and is therefore more approachable in my eyes.

As a kid, I had authority problems. I really went against the grain in terms of what people were telling me to do. For example, my teachers appeared to project detachment or lack of understanding. Power. One up, one down. I start out relationships with people in authority carefully. I monitor my own antiauthority responses.

Sam's comments reveal a man who has historically been distrustful of male authority figures, whom he experienced as misusing their power, and more trusting of females, whom he experienced as more nurturing. Also implicit in his account is his desire for a male figure whom he could admire and emulate. It is apparently important for him to hold his male supervisor in high esteem, as someone with enormous skill and expertise. It is unclear whether Sam will move beyond the stage of idealizing his supervisor to one in which he claims his own power.

Sam's story is, among other things, an illustration of the impact of gender on power dynamics in supervision. Clearly one's assumptions about appropriate behavior for men and women will influence the relationship. For example, women in authority who present themselves as primarily nurturing are often labeled unclear thinkers, whereas those who present themselves as more in charge are seen as dangerous. Furthermore, if a female supervisee is working with a male supervisor, it is possible that she will be doubly constrained by the greater power of her supervisor as both a male and an authority figure (Caust, Libow, & Raskin, 1981; Aulte-Riche, 1987). In a discussion on the issue of dependency versus autonomy, Reid, McDaniel, Donaldson, and Tollers (1987) suggest that women's greater tendency to depend on their supervisors may put them in a better position than men to adopt the role of learner rather than engage in power struggles. The danger, of course, is that they may not give as much credence as they deserve to their own authority.

Men with male supervisors may assume and respect their supervisors' theoretical expertise but not their relational expertise, typically thought to be more highly developed in women (Nelson, 1991). This phenomenon is illustrated by Sam's comments that he saw his male supervisor as the one who is the expert, with knowledge and skill, and his female supervisor as more nurturing and approachable.

The Influence of Culture

Those who have a history of being oppressed because of race, class, sexual orientation, and other nonmainstream conditions may well come to supervision with a mistrust of those in greater power. This mistrust would likely be exacerbated if the supervisor is Caucasian, middle class, or heterosexual (Cook & Helms, 1988; Kadushin, 1992). In addition, one's ethnic background may well affect how one views the notion of power in general. Miguel, a male Hispanic supervisor, remembered a story from his own days as a supervisee. He had a Caucasian supervisor, a woman, who insisted that he call her by her first name: "I can't call her Barbara, because to do so would be to pretend that we are on the same level." It is worthy of note that Barbara interpreted Miguel's reluctance to treat her more informally as a sign that he did not respect her. From his point of view, the opposite would be true.

Miguel's observation is that in the dominant Caucasian culture, there is a sense that everyone is equal. People in the majority culture are often uncomfortable with the notion of power and tend to minimize or negate power differentials. By contrast, notions of hierarchy are clear in Miguel's culture. The Spanish language includes formal forms of address for those who have greater power and informal forms for those who are equal or who have less power. Because of these differences, Miguel uses a more authoritarian style with his Hispanic supervisees, whom he imagines would be uncomfortable with an egalitarian approach. On the other hand, he gives his Caucasian supervisees a lot of room to challenge his directives, assuming that to be authoritarian would create resentment and resistance.

In contrast to Miguel's approach, Maria, also an Hispanic supervisor, uses a consensus approach. Miguel believes gender is the variable that explains their different styles.

> The top of the pyramid in my culture is the man, whether it is a priest, father of a family, or whatever. Right next to that is the mother. It is the mother who runs the whole show. The father makes the decision, but whenever anyone wants anything done, they work with the mother. Mother controls all the information. She is the mediator. She has to be skillful, because she can't directly challenge the authority figure, so she has to find out other ways to do that.
>
> I think women are more consensual because of traditional tasks in our culture. The man's task is to be in charge of the outside world, bringing resources to the family. The woman's task is to be in charge of the inside world, which is the family. This is a big task because in Mexican society families are large and there are many people to care for. You can't do the work by yourself, so you get together with others and

talk while you do your work. Men just do the work and are into tasks, power, and status. Women are into doing things together.

So, when you have a female vision of the world within the Hispanic family, I think what happens is that the woman thinks, "I can't do this all by myself, nor would I want to, so I'll see who else is available to help me with these tasks." This sort of cooperation leads to more consensus rather than the male way, which is to work more independently.

One could argue that Miguel's explanation not only applies to traditional Mexican culture but also describes traditions in many cultures. Certainly his ideas are commonly expressed by many other observers of gender dynamics. For example, Tannen (1990) observed that men often relate to one another through competition, whereas women are more likely to relate through emotional connection. Miguel's distinction between a culture that is comfortable with the notion of hierarchy versus one which is not, however, is worth noting. Given the political ideology of the United States, which above all else values the notion if not the fact of democracy, it is reasonable to assume that many in this culture resist acceptance of a power differential. One could surmise that some of the difficulties supervisors and supervisees encounter in their relationships derive in part from a societal confusion about the very notion of power.

This observation is of course a generalization, as is always the case when one attempts to describe an entire group's attitude toward something. However, sensitivity to the implications of cultural differences is useful in understanding power dynamics in supervision. Rick, for example, is aware that, as a white male supervisor, he is both resented and in some cases feared by some whose cultural groups have been traditionally oppressed by white males. He must factor in this possible reaction in any analysis he makes of his own behavior or of his supervisees' responses to him. Darlene, a white female supervisor, observes that her agency, which is run entirely by white women, may not see their own biases. She thinks they have at times been hard on others, particularly on men from other cultures, and missed the extent to which their approach has been unfair or insensitive.

Beth, a Native American supervisee, talked about the contrast between what she sees as the cooperative approach of her culture and the more individualistic approach of white society:

In our culture everything is a shared kind of thing. It's not who has power over whom, it is who works best with whom; and in our tribal system they are set up as a tool for action. When we put an American Indian in a supervisory role, he or she would use a model of consensus. We collaborate. The attitude is that you do your part. If you don't, you get left behind. You simply are no longer a part of the collective project.

I think this is why a lot of American Indians have not been a part of so many things in white society. White society operates in a totally different way, coming at things in an egotistical, individualistic manner, in which we are doing things for our own personal satisfaction or gain, rather than for the good of the group.

Beth stated further that if a supervisor approached her from a power stance, she would not be able to cooperate. She would not be consciously resistant, but she would simply be unable to give her soul to the task at hand. She in fact had never thought of supervisors as having power over her; to do so was repugnant to her. In Beth's opinion, the very concept of power is connected to a focus on individualism rather than on collectivism.

This notion was supported by Norma, an Hispanic supervisor who noticed a difference between Caucasian supervisees and supervisees of color, primarily those who were Hispanic and African American.

With the white folks, there is an underlying feeling that my authority was not acknowledged to begin with. I had to prove myself in a way that I did not with people of color. For example, with white supervisees, I would be talking about a theory and would apply it to a particular case. They would engage me in a debate about it. I felt like I was not believed. It felt disrespectful.

It's a subtle difference, but I think it has to do with seeing the world through a lens of individualism rather than collectivism. The questioning from the white supervisees feels like a challenge about whose argument will win, and questioning from the supervisees of color feels more like an attempt to understand something, to connect it to a context that is familiar to them.

A different side of this picture was offered by a Laotian supervisee, who described her culture as one in which those in authority are rarely challenged. She had a positive experience with her Caucasian supervisor, who encouraged her to be more assertive and more of an equal in the relationship.

As will become even clearer in the chapter on shared meaning, a significant challenge in cross-cultural supervision is the fact that wide differences in interpretation are often made about the same behavior. What someone from one cultural background interprets as a disrespectful challenge to authority, another may perceive as a demonstration of competence, confidence, and appropriate assertiveness. An extremely important dimension of cross-cultural supervision, therefore, is a consistent and thorough conversation about the differences between supervisor and supervisee and the implications of those differences for their relationship.

SUMMARY

A theme that ran throughout this chapter, and that will be apparent in subsequent chapters as well, is that both supervisor and supervisee contribute to the content and quality of the dynamics between them. Whereas a knowledge differential between supervisor and supervisee does not always exist in the relationship, if the supervision is to be effective, either the differential has to be in place or the supervisor at least needs to take the role of enabling and encouraging the supervisee to continue the learning process. The knowledge differential was discussed in terms of its importance in the relationship, the ways in which the differential could be misused by both supervisors and supervisees, and the relationship between the knowledge differential and both shared meaning and trust.

The limit-setting function was defined as the act of the supervisor's establishing parameters for acceptable practice. It was discussed in terms of attitudes of supervisors and responses of supervisees toward limit setting, the influence of both the agency and larger societal contexts on limit setting, and the relationship between shared meaning and limit setting.

Although the supervisor clearly holds the greater power in the relationship, both parties recognize the supervisee's power, which is manifested in the ability to choose to be supervised. The act of choosing, the basis on which the choice was made, the connection between the supervisee's professional development, and the manner in which supervisees exercise their power to choose were all addressed.

A key factor underlying the dynamics of power and authority in the supervisory relationship is the attitudes toward power and authority that both supervisor and supervisee bring to supervision. Supervisors and supervisees express varying degrees of comfort with their own power and comfort in relating to others who have greater power, as well as varying interpretations of what constitutes positive and negative use of power. Both culture and gender are significant variables contributing to the development of these attitudes.

QUESTIONS TO PROMOTE CRITICAL THINKING

1. Trace your own development as a supervisee with regard to your learning needs. To what extent were your supervisors able to meet those needs? How did this affect your relationship with them? What changes have you noticed over time about those needs, and how did these changes affect your supervisory relationships?

2. Imagine a situation in which all of Jose's supervisees (pp. 25–26) discuss with him their feelings about his supervision. What are some ways that Jose could respond to the feedback? What effects might those responses have on the individual supervisees and on the group as a whole?

3. Assume that Gary (pp. 29–30) is unsuccessful in his initial attempt to gain credibility with his gay and lesbian supervisees. Speculate as to how the supervisees might be experiencing Gary's attempts, and suggest several possible courses of action he might take to improve the situation. Create a role play in which Gary approaches his supervisees, and evaluate the outcome of Gary's attempts. What helped you decide the appropriate actions, and what were the implications of your decision?

4. Using the story of Paula, Susan and Mike (pp. 36–37) as a basis for discussion, discuss the question of how to establish standards in the context of cross-cultural supervision. What is your opinion of the issues that must be taken into consideration?

5. Using the same story as in question 4, speculate as to what reactions Susan and Mike might have to the requirement that they initially receive additional supervision and diminished caseloads, as well as their reactions to the staff resentment that developed. How do you think these factors might influence Susan and Mike's ability to perform on the job?

6. Analyze the positive and negative implications of Tim's approach to his conflict with Joleen (pp. 38–39). If you found yourself in a similar situation, how would the fact that your culture differed from that of your supervisee and the clients affect the way you would approach it? Would the supervisee's particular culture make a difference? For example, would you respond differently if the supervisee were a fundamentalist Christian than if he or she were Vietnamese? If so, why?

7. Consider the stories of Don (p. 42) and Larry (p. 43) from the points of view of Don's supervisor and Larry's supervisee. What factors might be operating that either Don or Larry may not be aware of? Create a role play in which Don talks to his supervisor and one in which Larry talks to his supervisee about their concerns.

8. Talk about a time when you were challenged to state your own limits of acceptable behavior with a client or with a supervisee. What did you think and feel about the situation, what did you do, and what were the results of your action?

9. Using the story of Geri (pp. 45–46) as a basis for discussion, explore the implications of the notion that schools should act as gatekeepers to the profession. How does this role affect the permission for the student to be able to make small and large mistakes in the process of learning?

10. What do you associate with the words *power* and *authority*?

What is your perception of yourself as an authority figure? How do familial, cultural, and gender variables contribute to the development of this perception? Compare your attitude to those of Sonya and Bev (pp. 51–52) and to those of Beth and Norma (pp. 56–57). How does your attitude affect your behavior with supervisors, supervisees, colleagues, and clients?

Chapter Three

Power: Dual Roles in Supervision

For the past several years, I have been serving as a faculty member in a social work program as well as maintaining a private practice on the side. In my job at the university, I act as advisor and mentor to several students, teach practice courses, and act as a faculty liaison for student interns in the field. Some years ago, I developed an important mentoring relationship with Jeffrey, who took several courses from me. Jeffrey came to the program from a rather unorthodox professional background. He had engaged in a number of dual relationships—as a student, a client, and a supervisee with teachers, therapists, and supervisors. These experiences were characterized by confusion and pain mixed with enormous enrichment and satisfaction. As a professional, Jeffrey was drawn to treatment modes that encouraged deep involvement between practitioner and client and a challenging of more traditional boundaries.

My initial contact with Jeffrey occurred when, in the role of his academic advisor, I was alerted to some actions he had taken indicating a lack of knowledge of appropriate boundaries. In our discussion, Jeffrey freely told me about his background and his struggles with the value versus the problems inherent in more conventional professional boundaries. He was a willing learner, although he also expressed some concern that his openness to me would jeopardize his standing in the school.

At some point during my work with Jeffrey, some former students with whom I had a very positive relationship asked me to serve as a private consultant in the agency where they now worked. This was a wonderful opportunity for me, as I was interested in building the consultation aspect of my private practice and had a desire to maintain professional connections with students once they left the program. I was pleased to accept the offer and began negotiations with this agency.

Shortly after receiving the initial request, I learned that Jeffrey was interested in an internship at that same agency the following year. Because of my excitement about the consultation opportunity, I ignored my internal warning signals that told me this association could be problematic. I established the condition that interns would not be in the consultation group and concluded that this would protect Jeffrey from any confusion because of my involvement at the agency.

As the time drew near for both the internship and the consultation to begin, I began to question the wisdom of my decision. I sought advice from other colleagues to see whether there was a way that I could safely proceed with the plan. It soon became clear that the plan was fraught with potential problems.

What if Jeffrey became unhappy with the agency? Would he feel free to discuss this with me, his academic advisor and teacher, considering my involvement in the agency? Would I be able to fully support Jeffrey if I were worried that by so doing I was jeopardizing my own standing with the agency? What if the agency was unhappy with Jeffrey? Would Jeffrey feel betrayed by me if I supported the agency over him? If I had to confront Jeffrey with negative feedback about his behavior in any way, would Jeffrey trust its authenticity or suspect that I was protecting my own interests in the agency? What if Jeffrey or the others decided they were dissatisfied with my work with them? Would Jeffrey experience a loyalty bind? What sort of impact would it have on Jeffrey to realize that, because of my involvement, he would be unable to participate in a consultation group that otherwise would be available to him? In any of the above scenarios, would Jeffrey's concern about my power to evaluate him negatively at school keep him from being able to freely express concerns about the agency? Finally, given Jeffrey's history with boundaries, what kind of message would I be giving him if I engaged in a dual role, which both intricately involved Jeffrey and in which I stood to gain both professionally and financially?

I came to the conclusion that accepting the job as consultant would diminish Jeffrey's learning, and I withdrew from the position. Jeffrey felt let down. He respected me a great deal and wanted as much exposure to me as possible. In addition, he was observing problems with the work of others at the agency, whom he thought could benefit from my supervision. He saw none of the possible complications I envisioned and was unhappy with me for making the decision without giving him an equal say. The agency also was disappointed, and my former students expressed regret about not being able to work with me. I struggled with my own natural pleasure in being admired and respected, my temptation to accept the notion that I was "the one" to do the job, and my disappointment at losing the opportunity.

The past several years have seen an increased sensitivity to the concept and impact of boundary violations both in direct practice and in supervision (Jacobs, 1991; Peterson, 1992, 1993a, 1993b; Goldberg, 1993; Tomm, 1993; Gartrell, 1994). Peterson (1992) suggested that because of the power differential between professionals and clients, professionals must protect the trust that has been granted them by their clients. Boundaries keep both professional and client clear about the purpose of the relationship. They contain the professional's power so that it is used only for the agreed-on purpose of attending to the needs of the client in a respectful and competent manner. A boundary violation occurs when professionals use the relationship to meet their own needs rather than those of the client. When this occurs, the purpose of the relationship becomes unclear, and the lack of clarity is often painful for the client. However, the pain often does not emerge until the client experiences a detrimental consequence.

Because of the increased awareness of the potential of boundary violations, a rising concern has developed about the impact of dual relationships in supervision. With that concern comes a certain amount of confusion about what exactly constitutes a dual relationship. For a variety of reasons, dual roles in supervision are frequent, often both inevitable and desirable. In an agency, particularly a small one, supervisors and supervisees commonly engage with each other in social and informal ways as well as in the formal supervisory setting. Even when they do not socialize, supervisors and supervisees are colleagues because they are both employees in the same organization. In addition, most supervisors perform both administrative and clinical supervisory tasks. Finally, as will become clear in the following discussion, a significant focus of much clinical supervision is on the practitioner's use of self. The ambiguity of the line between supervision and therapy often raises the question of whether the supervisor is acting as a therapist by exploring the supervisee's personal issues, thus creating a dual relationship.

There are other examples of situations in which dual roles exist. In rural settings or small communities within a larger city, people often have more than one role in their relationships with one another. Sometimes private practitioners obtain paid consultation, either from another otherwise equal member of the practice or from another colleague with whom they might have an otherwise peer relationship. Academic institutions often provide supervision for students in clinical internships. My story, recounted above, illustrates multiple roles; I was already Jeffrey's advisor, mentor, and professor, and I considered the possibility of adding the role of consultant. It is quite common for members of an academic institution to serve as consultants to agencies in the community. This situation raises a question about the implications of doing so when students from the institution are involved with the agency.

Peterson (personal communication, 1995) helped clarify the confusion in the following manner. She maintained that there are inherent dualities in the supervisory relationship, all of which are congruent with or support the purpose of supervision. She contrasted this relationship to a situation in which supervisor and supervisee are engaged in a relationship whose purpose is separate or different from that of supervision. In this framework, administrative and clinical supervision are dualities in that they both support different aspects of the goal of service to clients. A supervisor's multiple roles with a student in an academic environment all are geared toward enhancing the student's learning. The collegial relationship between supervisor and supervisee in an agency is also congruent, because both are employees of an agency whose purpose is to work with a specified client population. Finally, because the supervisee's use of self is integral to the work, addressing personal issues enhances that work and is therefore consistent with the purpose of supervision.

By contrast, a social relationship meets the participants' mutual needs for friendship and is not congruent with supervision. In the preceding story, because I would be acting not in my role as faculty member but as private practitioner, my own purpose and needs would be different from and potentially in conflict with my obligation to my student. By this definition, Jeffrey and I would be engaged in a dual relationship. In addition, when a colleague hires another colleague for consultation, they are forming a dual relationship. The discussion in this chapter will focus on dual relationships in supervision, types of information shared by supervisors, and exploration of supervisees' personal issues.

DUAL RELATIONSHIPS IN SUPERVISION

An important discussion about the topic of dual relationships is taking place in the field of marriage and family therapy supervision. Although there is little disagreement that the power differential between the participants needs to be taken into careful consideration, there is some disagreement about what it means to do so. The American Association for Marriage and Family Therapy Code of Ethics (1991) warns against dual relationships in supervision. Many supervisors are concerned that this standard interferes with their ability to supervise effectively, because it so narrowly restricts the possible ways in which supervisors and supervisees can interact, curtailing interactions that can potentially enrich the relationship. Others raise the issue that dual relationships are a natural evolution because, in contrast to the practitioner/client relationship, supervisors and supervisees are professional colleagues (Storm, 1993).

Peterson (1992, 1993a, 1993b; Storm et al., 1997) contended that the structure of dual relationships—that is, the fact of their existence—is not the problem. Rather, a problem arises when there is a covert dual *agenda* in the relationship, whether or not a literal dual relationship exists. The overt or official agenda is the attention to the supervisee's needs, and the covert agenda is the attention to the supervisor's needs. For example, a supervisor may give a supervisee information about a colleague with the expressed goal of helping the supervisee deal with that person more effectively. The covert agenda may be that the supervisor is hoping to form an allegiance with the supervisee in a conflict with the colleague. The supervisee then becomes, to use the language of Nell Noddings (1984), the cared-for and the one-caring. This situation creates confusion for the supervisee, who feels powerful and special because of being asked to meet the supervisor's needs, and who at the same time feels diminished because those needs are in competition with his or her own. The confusion caused by the dual agenda leaves the supervisee unclear about which reality is operating and how to proceed in a way that feels safe. As the one in charge in the relationship, the supervisor is responsible for being aware of the potential binds in which a dual relationship places the supervisee and for protecting the supervisee from experiencing those binds (Storm et al., 1997). If the supervisor fails to do so, one of two things might occur: Either (1) the supervisor may abuse the power differential inherent in the relationship by using it for personal gain, or (2) the supervisor may abdicate the power by denying its existence and ignoring its impact.

Karl Tomm (1993; Storm et al., 1997) argued that dual relationships are part of the reality of life and that, in fact, dual relationships have the potential to enrich the supervisory relationship because they allow for a more authentic understanding of the supervisee as a complex human being. Setting up artificial protection for supervisees unnecessarily increases the power differential in the relationship and denies the supervisee opportunity to develop skills for dealing with the normal complexities that occur in relationships. Rather, Tomm stated, it is more effective to monitor possible problems by engaging in dialogue with the supervisee about the potential for difficulty, and, if necessary, asking for feedback from an uninvolved third party.

Both Peterson and Tomm agreed that there is an increasingly dangerous trend in the profession toward trying to regulate behavior through rule making instead of living with the discomfort of the ambiguity derived from attempting to make difficult decisions in the context of specific relationships. Such rule making, as discussed earlier in this book, has the potential for creating its own difficulties. Both Peterson and Tomm also would argue that one must assess dual relationships in context, rather than simply applying a blanket standard. Their disagreement is over whether, in doing so, the supervisor takes greater responsibility or whether the supervisee is considered an equal partner in the process. This is an important distinction, as it raises the issue of how to work most effectively with the overt as well as the more subtle dynamics inherent in the power differential between supervisor and supervisee.

The story about Jeffrey and me illustrates many of the concerns raised by Peterson and by Tomm (Storm et al., 1997). This is certainly a scenario in which both supervisor and supervisee had needs that could eventually create a conflict. One might conclude that I acted in an overprotective and thus disempowering manner toward Jeffrey. Jeffrey was sure that my involvement in the agency not only was not problematic but would in fact enrich his learning there. I concluded, however, that as the one in charge, I needed to take responsibility for drawing a boundary that, because of his past experience as well as his investment in the current situation, Jeffrey was unable to recognize the need for, much less to draw for himself.

In the following account, Jeanette discusses a situation in which she had multiple relationships with a supervisor. Because they worked in a small agency, they related to each other as supervisor/supervisee, as colleagues, and as friends. In the course of their 5 years together, she reported, they learned about identifying the boundaries and about clarifying the issues involved in their different relationships with one another. She characterized this supervisory relationship as somewhat unsatisfying, although she had great respect for her supervisor and thought the experience was a valuable one for both of them.

> We liked and respected each other a great deal. But, we had some difficulties in confronting each other about things. I think maybe we had a secret pact to not talk about some things. There were times when we did talk about uncomfortable issues. I believe that we only went so far, though. I think our social relationship got in the way.
>
> In terms of professional development, there was no power differential between us. In terms of the structure and hierarchy of the organization, there was. But the growth that happens in supervision, like learning new therapeutic theory or approaches, happened mutually. We didn't really know what supervision should look like. We went through the motions, but it wasn't really supervision as I would define it now.
>
> If there had been form or structure, such as guidance about how to present a case, do intake, etc., it would have made the supervision more effective. I'm not saying it would have been great, but it would have been better.

Jeanette attributed the pact not to address certain issues to a desire to avoid discomfort that could threaten their friendship. This was a reasonable assumption, although it is possible to form such a pact without the existence of a friendship as well. The problem, whether due to a social relationship or not, was that the comfortable connection between them became more important than Jeanette's learning. When supervisors are invested more in being nice, in being liked, or in keeping things comfortable than in enhancing the supervisees' learning, the supervision is compromised. This is an example of the dual agendas discussed above (Peterson, 1986, 1992, 1993a, 1993b; Storm et al., 1997). Jeanette contrasted this relationship to another relationship that she described as an excellent supervision experience. In this case, the supervisor, who also became a friend, was clearly more knowledgeable than she. In addition, the supervisor had a powerful impact on her personal and professional growth. She identified her feelings toward her supervisor, particularly in its early stages, as being influenced by strong transference reactions to her. One could assume, therefore, that a friendship would be difficult to form.

Jeanette attributed her ability to establish a friendship with this supervisor to the fact that they were close in age and that she could balance the knowledge differential with her own greater knowledge about life issues, such as parenting. In addition, the friendship did not develop until later in the 6-year supervisory relationship, at a point when Jeanette was more developed professionally and the power differential was not as great.

Even in the later stages of the relationship, however, Jeanette felt somewhat inferior because of her supervisor's greater intelligence, and she acknowledged that this feeling made it more difficult to address problems in the relationship. There was a point at which the friendship interfered with supervision, but some clarity in terms of the contract alleviated the problem.

> There was a time when I hadn't been able to see her for a couple of months. I have negotiated a fee with her, per hour. We spent more than a good share of the time we negotiated just catching up on our personal lives and how our practice is going and that sort of thing, not in supervision issues. She wanted to catch up, and I wanted to catch up. I paid for the whole time anyway, which was her expectation. I knew that I had to say to her, "If we want to catch up we have to schedule extra time, because I need to be efficient about my supervision dollar." It was really scary for me to address the money issue with her, but I did. We talked about it and she understood.

The money issue is significant because it is the symbol of the power differential that exists in the supervisory aspect of the relationship. Jeanette experienced this interaction as successful. She was clear that her needs for supervision had been superseded by the friendship and that she had the power and right to ask for clarity about the agendas operating in the relationship. If the agenda is supervision, she said, this is what we must do. If it is friendship, then we schedule extra time, for which I don't pay you, so that my supervision is not compromised. In addition, the supervisor was receptive to Jeanette's feedback and willing to redraw the boundary to protect the supervisory relationship. One can imagine the potential difficulties if Jeanette had not felt her own power strongly enough to overcome her fears about addressing the issue or if her supervisor had been less receptive to the feedback. In such cases, Jeanette would have struggled with the conflict between her sense of gratitude for the friendship of this very powerful and helpful supervisor and her experience of being exploited by the same supervisor, who took her money for supervision that did not occur. Her fear of losing both the friendship and the supervision would have rendered her powerless to advocate for herself. She very likely would have been confused about the legitimacy of her feelings because, as she stated, she also wanted to catch up. It is noteworthy that Jeanette continued to experience a sense of being "inferior to" her supervisor, even with the success noted here. Thus, even though the friendship appeared to Jeanette to be basically unproblematic, it was certainly not free of complications. Her admiration of the supervisor continued to negatively influence her sense of herself and, therefore, potentially her sense of personal power in the relationship as both friend and supervisee.

Another example of this type of relationship is offered by a supervisee who saw no problem with the fact that she not only received supervision from her supervisor but was also her peer in a different work setting and was being paid to decorate her supervisor's house.

> When I was in supervision, I knew I was there to learn. I knew my place, but it didn't feel like a generational boundary. I was voluntarily putting myself in her care, so to speak, for my development. As an example, when she decorated her house, she turned to me to do it for her and put herself in my care to do that, because that's what I do. And she trusted me to deliver that to her. So, we changed roles entirely. Then we went to supervision and we flipped the role around; I was in her care.

This supervisee credited her life experience for her ability to make this shift. A latecomer to the profession of social work, she was already established in her career as an interior designer; therefore, she felt that she was meeting her supervisor on an equal professional level. So although she recognized and respected the need for the knowledge differential, she also clearly recognized and exercised her power to choose.

These examples suggest that the success of dual relationships rests partly on the supervisee's sense of power, both personally and professionally. They suggest, as well, that the success rests on the supervisor's ability to use the power inherent in the relationship in an appropriate manner. It is clear both from these examples and from others discussed in this book that, although dual relationships can be quite positive, they have the potential to complicate the supervisory relationship or harm the supervisee. As illustrated in previous sections, for example, supervisees often experience their supervisors' actions as more powerful than the supervisor intended. Therefore, as Peterson (Storm et al., 1997) pointed out, although the supervisor might attempt to minimize the impact of the power differential by engaging in dialogue with a supervisee regarding implications of a dual relationship, the supervisee might not feel capable of equal partnership and participation in that dialogue. The supervisee's sense of this capability is directly related to the power to choose supervision. As mentioned in the last chapter, this power is affected in part by the nature of the formal relationship between the parties—that is, how much positional power the supervisor can exercise over the supervisee. This power is affected as well by the degree to which the supervisee experiences the power differential. No matter what the degree of positional power the supervisor holds, supervisees who attribute a great deal of expert or referent power to their supervisors are less likely to feel the power to choose, and they are therefore less likely to be able to participate equally in a discussion about dual relationships.

In contrast to what occurs in the relationship between clinician and client, the understanding shared by both supervisors and supervisees is that supervisees are colleagues who often become their supervisors' peers. With this in mind, supervisors tend more to treat supervisees as peers than they would their clients and so are more open to dual relationships. Recognizing the possibility that treating them as equals can cause difficulties for the supervisee, many supervisors monitor the nature of their dual relationships.

> I have friendships with some of the people I supervise. Two of the people I supervise have gotten married in the last year. I've gone to their weddings. I've been to people's houses for parties. I don't date them, but I have relationships with people outside of work. But I don't have a strongly intimate friendship with any of the people I supervise. I very likely would say I just had a fight with my children, but I would not reveal to them what the fight was about. That's where my limit is, because then I feel that it unduly burdens them. That would be a role reversal in which they would feel the need to take care of me.

INFORMATION SUPERVISORS SHARE WITH SUPERVISEES

The preceding example shows that the selective sharing of information is a major method by which supervisors both create a sense of collegiality and monitor the extent of that collegiality. The supervisee can experience the effect of that sharing in both positive and negative ways, depending on both the intention of the supervisor and the supervisee's personal reactions. In the preceding excerpt, the supervisor expressed a concern about placing a burden on the supervisee, thus creating a role reversal in the relationship. This is probably the key factor influencing whether the supervisee experiences the supervisor's information sharing as something that creates trust in the relationship or as something that creates a feeling of discomfort. Three major types of information (other than educational) are frequently shared by supervisors: organizational policy and politics, supervisors' relationships with other supervisees or colleagues, and supervisors' vulnerability.

Agency Policy and Politics

It is commonly accepted that the supervisor's position as middle manager is perhaps one of the most challenging ones in an agency. Shulman (1993) described the supervisor's main function in an agency as one of mediator between line staff and administration. An essential aspect of the job, therefore, is to communicate relevant information from staff to administration, and vice versa. Many variables contribute to the supervisor's choices about what constitutes relevant information, including whether the information is confidential, whether it will help or only burden the staff, and whether the supervisor is in agreement with the person or group he or she is representing.

It takes a great deal of skill to advocate for two groups of people whose points of view, by virtue of the nature of their jobs and often their training, are frequently in conflict with each other. Supervisors are pulled by the tension of being responsible for ensuring that the mission and mandates of the agency are carried out and being responsible for ensuring that the needs of their staff are adequately met. They may also be pulled by a personal tension. On the one hand, they may want the approval of administration personnel who have power over them to evaluate, compensate, hire, and fire. They may also want the respect and regard of their staff, who have the power either to cooperate and perform their jobs well or to sabotage the efforts of the supervisor and the agency. Their supervisory style may be predominantly authoritarian or predominantly egalitarian, and this style may or may not reflect that of the agency administration. It is not surprising that supervisors are often confused about how much, what type, and to what end information should be shared with supervisees.

John worked in a residential treatment setting and had several different supervisors, all of whom varied in the amount of information they shared regarding policy and politics. On one end of the continuum were those who shared very little of the process. Decisions were presented in final form with a message that John could have little impact and that his feedback was not particularly valued. In addition, if a political situation influenced a decision, these supervisors would be likely to deal with it without including him in any way. On the other end were those who regularly solicited feedback and conveyed the message that it was always possible to have impact. These supervisors also shared quite a bit about the political factors surrounding particular issues.

John's reactions to all these approaches were complex. His response to the more directive and withholding supervisors was to experience them as "they"—closer to administration and higher up in the hierarchy. His relationships with them were somewhat distant, and he did not feel particularly supported by them. Part of this problem, he acknowledged, had to do with his own relative youth at the time he was in those relationships. He made the following comment about his relationship with his first supervisor:

> I don't think I ever would have talked to her about a policy I didn't like. I wouldn't have dared say, "This is too hard." I was just so grateful to have a job.

The positive side of this experience for John was that he felt protected from the extra stress that becoming involved in organizational politics puts on an already difficult job. In addition, he felt comfortable knowing that there was a structure in place on which he could depend.

> Her style created a structure from within which I worked. If I'm told to do something, I can do it. There was never any question about whether the task was required, and I didn't have to get all bent out of shape about it. Then I could concentrate on my clinical work. In a way, she really protected me.

One of John's supervisors shared quite a bit of information with him. He learned a great deal from her and, although a part of him would rather have been protected from the political dynamics of the organization, he came to see the value of his greater awareness. The information helped him make sense of tensions and previously confusing responses from others in the agency. It gave him some tools with which to advocate more effectively both for himself and for his clients. Finally, he learned the lesson that you never know whether it is possible to have an impact unless you speak out. A further effect of this style of supervision was that John experienced this supervisor as one of "us" rather than as one of "them" in the system. He saw her as being willing to listen to him and to advocate for him with the administration when necessary. In this respect, she was quite different from his previous supervisors, who appeared to come to him with nonnegotiable directives. Clearly this second situation, although it left John less protected from the complexities of the politics, also gave him a sense of empowerment and greater knowledge.

John rated this supervisory relationship as excellent but he did feel uncomfortable at times with the degree to which this supervisor was "fluid" about her hierarchical position. His discomfort came from his sense that sometimes her own agenda influenced the way she shared the information.

> Sometimes I think the fact that she solicits feedback is based on her own disagreement with the directive that's been sent down. As a unit, we would probably be angry with this thing that we were told to do anyway, and would give that feedback to her. It's not like she puts words in our mouths, but maybe she opens it up sometimes, and she's ready to stir it up a little bit. Sometimes I think she has her own issues with authority

figures and so is kind of provocative with that stuff, and possibly she uses our reaction as ammunition to back up her own feelings.

I think she really does believe that we can have some impact if enough of us talk about what's going on and it gets relayed back. In fact, I think that is only true one out of five times. I can deal with things not changing, but I don't want to be misled and think that I can have an impact when I can't.

Although John's first supervisors were distant and seemed less supportive and approachable, they did provide a clear definition of their role and their supervisees' role. The second supervisor was obviously more supportive and approachable and drew less distinct boundaries between her role and that of her supervisees. She let her supervisees know about agency politics and invited them to participate. In communicating the message that "we" are on the same "side," she ran the risk of covertly implying that they needed to be as loyal to her as she was to them. To the extent that John experienced her as sharing information to push her own agenda rather than to advocate for him and his colleagues, he felt manipulated and betrayed.

Conflicts with Other Colleagues

The supervisor's talking about conflicts with other colleagues is almost always experienced by supervisees as a burden. Quite often, supervisees find themselves in a position of attempting to fight the supervisor's battle.

There was a very strong, nasty conflict between myself and another trainer that erupted into a political battle. It affected the trainees. His trainees hated my trainees, and my trainees hated his trainees. People weren't talking to each other: "My trainer is better than your trainer."

I called the group together one day after I realized what was going on and told them, "Look, I can fight my own battles. There's a problem here, but you guys keep out of it. This is my problem. I don't need you. Stay away." Their reaction to this was relief, I think. I think they felt better. It worked.

In this situation, the supervisor alleviated the problem created by inappropriately shared information by redrawing the generational boundary. In the following account, the supervisor, Doris, appeared to want to use her supervisee, Kasha, to fuel her competition with her colleague. This was complicated by the fact that Kasha trusted neither Doris nor the colleague in question, who was also above her in the hierarchical structure.

Doris was so against Ted. She had her own ax to grind. When this job he's in now opened up, they both went for it and she didn't get it. I know her attitude toward him affected me. Sometimes I would use it. I would say little things indicating that I was suffering on the other end of the hall so that I could get her to make some comment against Ted. Then, she would make the comment; I wouldn't be making it. Doing that sometimes would kind of help. It was a little release of some kind. I'd always feel ashamed about it later inside myself. And I didn't let her know that part. So in some ways I didn't respect that, but I used it at the same time.

It is not unusual for supervisees to have some good feelings from this type of information. They might feel special because their supervisors choose to confide in them. Like John, they might feel that they and their supervisors are on the same "side" against a common enemy. By her own account, Kasha covertly encouraged her supervisor to speak negatively of Ted in order to get some support for her own difficulties. However, she soon learned the information came at a cost, both to her own integrity and to her respect for Doris.

Supervisors' Personal Vulnerability

A useful tool for creating trust in the relationship is for supervisors to share their clinical work, particularly their mistakes or feelings of vulnerability as they relate to their work. When the knowledge differential is large, supervisees can easily assume that if they were only more experienced they would not be having the same doubts about their work and would know how to "do it right." Supervisors can help mitigate against this myth by being open about their own imperfections. In addition, supervisees are more likely to trust the supervisor's integrity when they have some information regarding the type of struggles a supervisor experiences.

The effect of sharing vulnerability becomes more ambiguous when the supervisor is sharing something personal, rather than work related. This type of sharing can lead to a feeling of role reversal.

A couple of times my supervisor has come to me to ask for my feedback about how she came across. On the one hand, it's nice 'cause I think she trusts my opinion. I try to be honest with her about my perceptions. I've ended up feeling sort of awkward and confused. I don't always know what to do with that. If somebody's my supervisor, then that's really clear. But I don't know how to be friends with the supervisor, too. That sort of request feels more like something you would ask of a co-worker or a peer.

That just troubles me a little bit. It's nice because it feels that she trusts me, but it feels almost too personal. Then I have to talk to her about the fact that I don't know how to negotiate the other stuff in the relationship. I think she's really okay being more peer outside of supervision, but I don't know how to do that.

The common thread running through most of the problem stories in this section is that the supervisees experienced the supervisors as offering information with a dual agenda (Peterson, 1992, 1993a, 1993b; Storm et al., 1997). In those situations, supervisees became confused about how to respond and how to interpret their own feelings. In this last example, the supervisee felt trusted but was unclear how to manage what she experienced as a dual relationship. She concluded that the problem was hers. Her supervisor was apparently comfortable with being "peer outside of supervision," but the supervisee was not, and she assumed that her uneasiness reflected her lack of ability to act as a peer.

EXPLORATION OF SUPERVISEES' PERSONAL ISSUES

Early in my career, I had a supervisor who warned me, "You'll see yourself coming and going in this job." Never has a statement been more accurate. Many are the days a client comes into my office asking for help on the very question I am grappling with in my own life. Perhaps this happens because when I am working on something, I tend to be more attuned to a similar aspect of a client's problem. Perhaps it happens because of an unconscious coming together of two people who are drawn to one another because of what they have to teach and learn from the other. Perhaps it is just coincidence. My internal reaction to this occurrence has ranged from "Why are you asking *me* this, when I obviously have no idea how to handle it?" to "I'm the perfect person to help you, because I have thought about and worked through so much about this issue." Because I am in the role of practitioner to client, it is of paramount importance that I not use my relationship with my clients to further my own needs for personal growth. However, the fact that we are both human beings with lifelong lessons to learn influences the way we respond to and interact with one another.

This relationship is complicated by the fact that the very nature of clinical work is such that a practitioner's primary tool is him- or herself. My own belief is that the phenomena of transference and countertransference exist and they affect the way an individual experiences current relationships. Both Boszormenyi-Nagy and Noddings offered some concepts about these phenomena that add an ethical dimension to the need to attend to them in our work. In Boszormenyi-Nagy's first book, *Invisible Loyalties* (Boszormenyi-Nagy & Spark, 1984), he described loyalty as an obligation based on the reality that all children are indebted to their parents, not only for life itself but also for the inheritance of the strengths, weaknesses, legacies, and laws of the family. This indebtedness creates a permanent bond that shapes an individual's relationship to self, family, and the outside world. The concept of *invisible* loyalties relates to the fact that people are often not conscious of the act or of the effect of remaining loyal to their origins (Van Heusden & Van Den Eerenbeembt, 1987). An example of the impact of invisible loyalties is the child of an alcoholic who does not drink but becomes a workaholic, thus remaining loyal to the addictive pattern (Goldenthal, 1993).

Being bound through an invisible loyalty to a past relationship will restrict one's ability to respond in an unencumbered way to a current relationship. Furthermore, the concept of destructive entitlement, discussed earlier, suggests that those who have not come to terms with injustices in their own lives may unconsciously strive to meet unmet needs from an old relationship by making unfair demands of a current one. In a discussion of therapists' training, Boszormenyi-Nagy and Krasner stressed that therapists need to create and maintain fairness in their own relationships (Boszormenyi-Nagy & Spark, 1984; Boszormenyi-Nagy & Krasner, 1986; Boszormenyi-Nagy, 1988). Supervisees who are unaware of either their invisible loyalties or their unmet entitlements are less able to relate to clients in a "clean" manner, unencumbered by their own unresolved issues. For example, a supervisee, angry and unresolved about her own experience of sexual abuse, may push a client to confront her perpetrators without carefully assessing either the client's readiness to take such action or whether doing so would be appropriate or useful.

Noddings (1984) distinguished between natural and ethical caring, and she suggested that the latter derives from the former. *Natural caring* refers to situations in which we act on behalf of someone else because we want to. *Ethical caring* is called for when we need to act in a caring way but don't feel a natural inclination to do so. This derivation of ethical caring is an important concept for both practitioners and supervisors, who are bound by the obligation to treat both clients and supervisees with integrity. Our ethical ideal, or our sense of how best to treat another, is developed from our best memories of natural caring and being cared for. It derives from a feeling of caring not only about the other but about our best self as well.

An important characteristic of this ideal is that it is constrained by what we already have done and by our particular capabilities and vulnerabilities. Therefore we must remain accountable to who we are and to the potential impact we have on others. Practitioners, acting in the role of the one-caring, must not only strive to be their best possible caring selves but must also be aware of their particular vulnerabilities, their propensities for faulty judgment or hurtful behavior vis-à-vis clients, and their particular strengths.

Another aspect of the ethical ideal is that it will be diminished when one experiences a lack of alternatives. Noddings (1984) contended that a person who is highly committed to the ideal will be less likely to compromise it. However, given the right circumstance, anyone can feel forced to react or behave in a manner that compromises the ideal. Because of the highly charged atmosphere of clinical practice, it is easy to imagine the possibility of such a compromise. The right circumstance for a practitioner could result from a combination of that worker's personal feelings, unresolved issues (invisible loyalties or destructive entitlement), and reactions to a particular client's presentation. To work effectively with clients, the practitioner must be aware of those situations in which the ethical ideal would be compromised. An important aspect of supervision therefore involves attention to the clinician's feelings about and responses to clients and the clinician's ability to create and maintain therapeutically beneficial relationships.

The Line between
Supervision and Therapy

As stated in previous chapters, the relationship between client and practitioner is the medium through which the work occurs, and the dynamics of parallel process and isomorphism are integral to both treatment and supervision. Springman (1989) introduced the terms *therapist-induced* and *client-induced* countertransference. He contended that distinguishing between the types of information the supervisee is presenting can help determine the direction of supervision.

In the case of therapist-induced material, further exploration into the supervisees' personal issues may be necessary to keep those issues from clouding therapists' responses to clients. A sign that this intrusion may be occurring is when a supervisee has a pattern of a similar kind of difficulty with several clients. For example, Jenny found herself frequently becoming anxious and feeling inadequate in response to what she experienced as demands from clients to "fix" their situation. In turn, she would demand that her supervisor give her solutions, evoking the same feelings of anxiety and inadequacy in him. The supervisor responded in three ways: First, he commented on the parallel process; second, he declined the request to "fix" the problem and "take away" the supervisee's anxiety; third, he explored the origins of Jenny's discomfort. Jenny revealed that, in her own family, she was often in the position of having to "fix" unfixable dilemmas for her parents, who appeared unable to tolerate their own anxiety or to trust in their own ability to find solutions to their problems. As a result of the supervisory process, she was able to see more clearly that her job was not to "fix" problems but to enable her clients to tolerate their fear and to find answers to their own dilemmas.

In the case of client-induced material, the supervisee's behavior is generally uncharacteristic. Often a simple change in the supervisor's behavior to alter the dynamics will quickly enable the supervisee to make an effective change in the treatment. A supervisee who is usually quite focused may have a client who presents information in a scattered and disorganized way, and the supervisee may in turn have difficulty focusing in the supervisory session. The supervisor can both comment on the difficulty and help the supervisee gain clarity and direction regarding the current situation, modeling skills that the supervisee can use with the client. Peterson (1986) stressed that parallel process is not a phenomenon that occurs simply in times of conflict or when the worker is stuck. Rather, it happens continuously and can be used as a tool for accessing sometimes illusive information about the interaction between therapist and client.

An area of considerable controversy and confusion for both supervisees and supervisors is defining and drawing the line between the activities of supervision and therapy. Supervisors generally agree that some degree of self-awareness is important for practitioners to be effective in their work. In addition, most would probably agree with Bernard and Goodyear (1992) who state that personal issues should be addressed in supervision only to the degree that they enter into or interfere with the work. It is generally considered inappropriate to spend supervisory sessions talking about supervisees' personal concerns when those issues are not in some way connected to practice. Finally, most supervisors would say that those personal issues, when identified, should not be "fixed" or "worked through" in supervision. Rather, if the issue keeps reappearing, the supervisee should be encouraged to seek further personal help elsewhere.

However, despite a certain amount of theoretical agreement, how this question is actually handled varies from supervisor to supervisor. Among the factors that influence a supervisor's decision is whether he or she believes that primarily supervisee-focused or primarily case-focused supervision is more likely to lead to competent service to clients. The following statements by three different supervisors illustrate points along that continuum.

> In supervision, my philosophy is that an issue can be highlighted and that many issues that have to do with unresolved family of origin pieces or whatever would require therapy. So in supervision, it would be acknowledged. It would be addressed. I'm not there to be their therapist, but there's a therapeutic element in so much of the feedback, especially when there's something that someone isn't getting. How much I intrude depends on my belief system and standards for what is ethical practice. I will be as intrusive as I need to be to have someone get something important. I feel that's my professional responsibility.

Genna, the supervisor who made this statement, offered the following story as an illustration of her point. Her supervisee was a young woman who had a tendency to "over-mother" her clients. She did several things with one client, including going to her poetry reading, accompanying her to the stairway after a session, and giving her a ride home. At first, Genna attempted to help her supervisee see the problem by using a gentle manner. Genna made the decision to become more intrusive after the supervisee gave her client a ride.

I said, "We've got to talk," and I asked her, "Why do you have to give her a ride home? How far in do you have to go with her?" She was overly invested in this client. I asked her what she was feeling in reaction to the client, and where she had experienced that feeling before. I asked her what her understanding was of her belief as a person, not as a professional, about how one treats someone who is in pain. I told her that my expectation was that she address this issue, preferably in therapy.

Although I started very gently, I finally had to just come on really strongly and say, "That isn't your place," and that she was ripping off the client by doing that. I had to get to her. She did hear me, finally, but if I hadn't said it that strongly, she wasn't going to get it. It really had to be a loud knock on the door.

Before that, she would acknowledge and seem to understand what I was saying, but then I saw she really didn't. That's when I will intrude more, because I feel that it's my responsibility to make sure she does ethical work. I can't collude with her by not calling this to her attention in a dramatic way, if necessary. I think what I did with her was therapeutic, giving her the feedback, but it was certainly in the work. So, while it was therapeutic, I couldn't ignore it. Nor could I say, "Go work on that in your own therapy" and only focus on her work with the client here. That wasn't okay. It was too integral to her work.

In the following account, the supervisor attempts to work around the supervisee's personal issues rather than address them directly. Although he wouldn't discourage the supervisee from exploring his own issues, he also did not see a reason to insist on it.

I had a fellow who was really afraid of anger. He had an angry, angry father, who would go along and do his thing and be pushing the family to the appropriate degree until somebody got angry. Then he would instantly back off. There would go his whole plan for the family, crashing around him. He wouldn't know what to do to get out of that.

Initially, I worked on trying to get him to deal with anger more comfortably. I tried to help him realize this wasn't the end of the world and that he wasn't a little kid any more. It didn't work. He really wasn't willing to deal with his family issues. We finally agreed that when he got stuck that way and realized it was happening again, he'd say, "It's time for us to take a break so we can go discuss the case." And we'd go off and sit in a different office and decide where he was going to go from there. Then he would go back in the other room and continue the session. My approach is to try to find a different way, if you're not going to deal with the issues, a way to get around them.

Unlike the supervisors in the first two examples, the one who made the next statement would actively discourage exploration of personal issues in the context of supervision.

I tell people I don't care about their development. What's important is their work with clients. I suppose this is not really what I mean. I suppose this message is a method for trying to get people to pay attention to what I think is important for their craft. I think they should attend to their interaction with people, and not with themselves and their own development. Their development is of course important, because you're building skills in your abilities to influence others. But you don't want to spend time with your own processes. If you pay attention to the craft aspect, your own development will come out of that. You'll get better if you pay attention to your interactions with clients and not so much to interactions with the questions about yourself, of whether you're competent or not competent, proving something to yourself for your own journey.

The Use of Power in Drawing the Line

Although establishing the line may be seen as purely a question of philosophy or approach, it carries a strong dimension of power. Particularly in the first and last examples, we can see the supervisor's use of power; the supervisor is unquestionably in charge of the direction the supervision will take, either toward or away from the supervisee's self-exploration. Furthermore, in the first situation, the supervisor clearly connects her more intrusive stance with the limit-setting function. Her obligation is to insist that the supervisee look at a personal issue that is negatively affecting her work. The middle example illustrates more of a posture of giving the supervisee a choice. If he wants to look more at his family issues, the supervisor will help him; if not, the supervisor will help him find a way to circumvent the problem.

The dimension of power is significant not only because of the influence the supervisor has over the direction of the supervisory session but also because it is intricately connected to the evaluative function of supervision. The most common duality in supervision is one in which the supervisor performs the roles of clinical and administrative supervision. Although both are functions of the job, each has different elements, which can create complications. It can feel quite dangerous, for example, for supervisees to share their personal sense of vulnerability in their work with the same individual who decides their salaries. If the supervisee is given the message that addressing personal issues is of value, any reluctance to do so has the potential to be seen as resistance to supervision and as a weakness in the supervisee's ability as a practitioner. If, on the other hand, attention to personal issues is strongly discouraged, any vulnerability on the part of the supervisee has the potential to be interpreted as a lack of competence. These interpretations might be made by the supervisor, the supervisee, or both; and although these interpretations may at times be valid and useful, they may at other times have a damaging effect on the supervisee, and potentially on the client. Because of this potential complication, supervisees often find themselves going outside the agency for private consultation, where they feel safer to be more vulnerable. A model for supervision exists in Holland (Van Kessel & Haan, 1993), in which the administrative and educative functions of supervision are performed by two people in order to allow freedom for both supervisors and supervisees in both arenas.

George, who had many years of experience as a supervisor, traced his own metamorphosis regarding this question throughout the years. He began supervising in the 1970s, at a time when the field was in a stage of revolution against the rigidity and impersonal nature of the Freudian, psychoanalytic approach to treatment (Burton, 1970). There was a push toward greater authenticity in the therapeutic relationship, characterized, for example, by the humanistic approaches to treatment (Turner, 1986; Corsini & Wedding, 1995). These approaches gave credibility to the notion that the full person of the practitioner and that of the client needed to be brought in to both treatment and supervision. George was a powerful leader and teacher in his own community, and many practitioners, both beginners and those with a great deal of expertise, sought him out for supervision. They found that this experience often led them to significant personal growth.

Since that time, George has gradually moved more to the position that there needs to be a clear distinction between therapy and supervision, with supervision being much more heavily case focused. He sees his own earlier belief that we are in the field ultimately for our own personal growth as encouraging supervisees to meet their needs through their clients. By the same token, George now believes that supervisors may pursue exploring a supervisee's personal weakness to meet their own needs in some way.

> To me, the line between therapy and supervision means being careful not to intrusively explore something that's personal and vulnerable for the supervisee. It's there, and we can identify it, but to go further than just identification is problematic. I like to help. I like to rescue. It's so tempting. And supervisees often have few defenses against me if I decide to pursue personal issues. But it would be a violation. I've done it. I know how to do that, and people can be very impressed by it, and awestruck, and all that. However, I think it's a rip-off in that I get a wonderful adrenaline rush about my power and my wisdom and my miracle-worker abilities. But to me, it's a violation.

The Impact of Exploration
on Supervisees

From the supervisee's point of view, a supervisor's insistence on exploration of a personal issue well may seem to be a violation and, as such, an abuse of the supervisor's power. Although any boundary violation damages the relationship, the extent of the damage cannot be measured by simply looking at the outside behavior. It is necessary to look as well at the amount of pain the client or the supervisee feels, because each individual may experience the situation differently (Peterson, 1992). Sergio offered an example of this situation, in which he connected the issue of hierarchy with that of feeling personally exposed to his supervisor, without having a choice about how open he wanted to be.

> There have been a couple of times where I've been intrigued with the line between personal issues and supervision versus professional issues. In my way of thinking, there is no line. There's a gray area that could change from week to week.
>
> On one occasion, my supervisor and I were talking about shame. I recounted a shameful experience in my life. Then I started wondering if this was supervision. So I asked him directly, "Is supervision where I'm talking about my life, or what?" He said if he felt I needed therapy, he would refer me out. So we left it at that.
>
> That statement never settled properly with me. I didn't quite understand what that meant. I started thinking about the hierarchy in our relationship when the same sort of thing came up again. He made a statement about me talking about my behavior in a couple of sessions and that I said twice that when I got angry in a session, I withdrew.
>
> And of course, I immediately applied that to myself in a general way; "Well, yeah, sometimes when I get angry I withdraw." Then I found myself feeling that I needed to clarify that for him, as if his next statement was going to be, "Well, that's it. You need therapy." I got uncomfortable because we somehow jumped out of the arena of supervision to speaking about my personal life, and I wasn't ready for it.
>
> That's when I felt the hierarchy. I think that there was a level there where I felt exposed. I don't know, maybe it's out of control. Or, I've said too much. Or is this really what we're here to deal with? That was the discomfort. I felt that we shifted suddenly from case consultation to me. I felt that I had to respond. I guess I felt that I was defending something.

The supervisor does not appear to have violated Sergio in the sense of meeting his own needs instead of those of his supervisee. However, Sergio clearly felt unable to make a choice about how far to go with his supervisor because of the supervisor's greater power in the relationship. If the supervisor told him he needed to look at his response to anger either in the context of supervision or by going to therapy, Sergio would need to follow the direction. Implied in his account is Sergio's belief that the suggestion to go to therapy would indicate some sort of failure or weakness on his part. This sort of attitude, certainly not unique to Sergio, placed him in a double bind. He felt compelled to pursue the topic of his reaction to anger but, at the same time, feared that such self-exposure placed him in danger of being seen as someone with problems severe enough to need therapy. A noteworthy feature of this account is that the supervisor appears to have done a minimal amount of exploration. It is possible that a different supervisee would not have felt so exposed by the supervisor's observation that he appeared to withdraw when angry. We are reminded again that supervisors may have an impact far greater than they either intend or realize.

On the other end of the continuum are those supervisees whose very nonintrusive supervisors are experienced as missing or glossing over important information or feelings. Duncan elaborated on his ambivalence about the question of intrusiveness. He described himself as someone who is scared of really knowing himself on a deep level. His supervisors were people who were quite careful about erring on the side of nonintrusiveness rather than overintrusiveness. At first, Duncan expected and liked this treatment, comfortable with the fact that the supervision contract meant he could count on his supervisors' respecting his limit regarding personal exploration. Duncan speculated that had he encountered a supervisor who pushed him further, he probably would have closed himself up more. Even if he might have learned something from the process, it was more important to him to have permission to make the choice. However, he made the following observation.

> I think I'm limited as a therapist because of my own fear of exposure. I think that causes me sometimes to not push clients far enough. Sometimes I think that the fact that I struggle with getting stuck in the mid-phases of treatment may have to do with my own stuckness and fear of exposing myself. If I had to look back I would have to say that I probably wasn't confronted enough by my supervisors. My perception, at this point, is that the focus on my personal awareness could have been stronger in general. Otherwise, it's almost as if the work becomes something that you do rather than what you are. And I think what we do brings in what we are.

One wonders, then, what the most effective supervisory intervention for Duncan would be. He believes that, because he has never been pushed past his comfort level, he has not reached his potential as a practitioner. However, he is also clear that had he been pushed, he would have become resistant. Perhaps it was his supervisors' awareness of his discomfort that influenced them to avoid behavior Duncan would consider intrusive. Perhaps they saw him as a limited practitioner but one whose work was satisfactory; therefore there was no need to push him into areas he was reluctant to enter. Another possibility, however, is that they were scared to go there themselves. If this was the case, they did not push him because of a desire to protect both themselves and Duncan from discomfort.

Michelle compared two supervisors, one of whom tended to pursue more aspects of her own vulnerability, the other of whom would tell her to "get back in her head" and talk only about the case. She believed that each approach had both merit and difficulties for her. As she is a very emotional person who is easily vulnerable, it has been important for her to have a place to talk about her personal reactions to clients. In addition, Michelle sees supervision as a place to explore the ways in which her personal issues block her ability to work effectively with some clients. However, there were times when she experienced the degree of intrusiveness of the first supervisor as an abuse of power.

> I had a client with whom I needed some help. I was not bent out of shape by this to start with. But, as I talked to my supervisor, it suddenly became huge because of how she was reacting. She reacted really strongly, making interpretations about what was happening that didn't fit for me. She started telling me what she saw as my blind spots about this. I thought, "This is something I don't know anything about. She must be right, and I must be wrong." And I got really upset.
>
> Another time, she asked me to look at something I was doing with a client, and then somehow it got switched into my relationship with my father. My father does not have good boundaries, and he can be very intrusive and difficult. I got a little emotional about it while I was talking.
>
> She strongly suggested that I confront my father about this. That seemed to be a therapy issue. When I thought about it, I decided that because my father's 80 years old, I didn't really think it was appropriate or productive to deal with him about this. This was one of those things that just is, as far as I'm concerned. I don't have to take it on. But she was so convincing in her position that I thought, "I really should do this."

The supervisor's feedback carried particular weight both because of the forceful nature of her style and because of her position of power over the supervisee. Michelle clearly did more self-exploration in the supervision setting than was comfortable for her. In addition, although she later realized that she could choose not to follow her supervisor's advice, initially she experienced it as a requirement. Again, it is important to remember that Michelle herself is part of the equation. Another supervisee might not have so quickly discounted her own opinion in favor of the supervisor's.

In her experience with the other supervisor, Michelle valued an approach that gave her the opportunity to learn more about "staying in her head" and being more cognitive. This was helpful for her because she had the tendency to be vulnerable in situations that were not safe for her. In addition, she found that by not focusing so heavily on her own responses, she was able to think more clearly about her work with the client and to react less personally to difficult situations. However, she was aware of limitations in this supervision in that personal issues, about which she might feel more vulnerable, appeared to be off limits for discussion. This left Michelle with the sense that to share that aspect of herself would incur a negative judgment from her supervisor regarding her abilities as a clinician.

Michelle concluded that her ideal supervisor would have both capacities—"head" and "heart"—and that she would have the power to choose whether or not to "bleed" and how far to go. This conclusion matches that of other supervisees, who appreciate supervisors who recognize supervisees' need to address stuck areas and, at the same time, not only respect supervisees' limits but impose some of their own.

The stories presented here demonstrate the dilemma of how to balance the value of supervision that focuses on the practitioner versus supervision that focuses primarily on the case. Clearly, there is no one right answer to this question. As Michelle's accounts illustrate, a single supervisee might have a variety of learning needs and could both benefit from and have difficulty with varying degrees of attention to her personal issues. The stories demonstrate, as well, the need to balance the supervisor's authority with the supervisee's autonomy. Should the supervisor, as the one in charge, insist on a level of personal exploration by the supervisee as part of a commitment to competent service? In doing so, is the supervisor violating the supervisee's right to choose how much to self-disclose? Is it a form of abandonment if the supervisee is discouraged from or allowed to avoid discussing personal vulnerabilities in the supervisory context?

As I stated earlier, my own belief is that transference and countertransference issues exist and need to be addressed in supervision. The most important tool that practitioners bring into the room with a client is themselves. Their understanding about their own responses gives them valuable information both about their clients and about themselves as clinicians. To ignore transference and countertransference would be to ignore one of the most important sources of data available to them in their work. However, the focus on the supervisee's use of self should not supersede the need to focus on the client and on developing the perceptual, conceptual, and executive skills of the supervisee. The decision about where the major attention should be focused depends on the particular supervisee's needs. As mentioned previously, some supervisees, having done a significant amount of personal work, may quite easily identify their own responses and be able to use themselves effectively. Others may have a great deal of difficulty with this process or be uncomfortable exploring themselves in much depth.

The deciding factor must be how the work with clients is affected. Even practitioners with a great deal of personal insight can become so entangled with a client that they need enormous support and personal exploration to see clearly what needs to be done and muster the courage to act on the client's behalf. Those who are less willing to talk much about themselves in supervision may still be doing competent work with their clients. Furthermore, some supervisees might be much more comfortable talking about their own issues than about the work with clients. They may use a focus on personal insight to avoid what for them is more difficult—understanding in a more dispassionate or detached way what is occurring for the client. For them, a supervisor's strong focus on personal issues may enable supervisees to use the work to meet their own needs rather than those of their clients.

SUMMARY

Dualities and even dual relationships in supervision are common and sometimes inevitable and desirable. The discussion centered therefore not on whether they should occur but on the impact of the power differential in those relationships. The concept of dual agendas was also introduced. A related topic is the types of information shared by supervisors and supervisees. Supervisees experience information sharing sometimes as positive and sometimes as burdensome, depending on how the supervisee perceives the supervisor's intention in the sharing. In addition to information meant to educate, types of information generally shared include agency policy and politics, conflicts with colleagues, and the supervisor's feelings of personal vulnerability.

There is often confusion and controversy in the field regarding exploration of supervisees' personal issues in supervision. Supervisors and practitioners alike struggle with the notion that although one must understand oneself well to do effective clinical work, too much or inappropriate exploration of personal issues in supervision is a potential violation of the supervisee's privacy. The topic was discussed with regard to the ethical dimension of the practitioner's use of self and the dynamics of parallel process, establishing the line between supervision and therapy, the use of power in drawing the line, and the impact of various levels of supervisor intrusiveness on supervisees.

QUESTIONS TO PROMOTE
CRITICAL THINKING

1. How would you have approached the dilemma I faced with Jeffrey that opened this chapter? Make an argument that agrees and an argument that disagrees with the position I took. In your discussion, speculate about how Jeffrey may have experienced this incident.

2. A supervisee who has a great deal of admiration for her supervisor leaves the agency. Later she decides she would like to receive therapy from this supervisor. Discuss the possible complications and benefits of such an arrangement. What if the situation were reversed— that is, a former client seeks supervision? Would your response be the same? Why or why not?

3. A supervisor, as part of training for students and new employees, offers a family-of-origin group, in which each participant describes his or her family to the group. The purpose of the group is to help the participants understand the ways in which their family experiences affect their work with clients. The hope is that the experience will provide both the supervisor and supervisee data that can be applied in future sessions to issues presented in supervision. Analyze this idea in light of the concepts of dual roles, dual relationships, and dual agendas.

4. Compare your own experiences as a supervisee with those of Sergio, Duncan, and Michelle (pp. 81–84). What is your belief about how to draw the line between supervision and therapy? How have your supervisory experiences affected this belief?

5. At a party that both supervisee and supervisor attended, the supervisee became quite intoxicated. The next day she called in sick to work. How should the supervisor handle this situation?

6. A supervisor learns from a colleague that his supervisee has recently had some serious family problems. In addition to being concerned about the supervisee's work, he is hurt that the supervisee has not trusted him enough to share this with him. What should he do with the information? What variables and principles should guide his decision? Assuming he decides to address this in some way, create a role play in which he approaches the supervisee after learning this information.

7. The supervisor in question 6 begins to notice that the supervisee is losing more clients than usual and appears to be labeling many more clients as resistant or difficult. However, the supervisee has not offered any personal information that could affect his attitude toward clients, and he seems to dodge the supervisor's more indirect attempts to give him room to bring it up. What should the supervisor do now?

8. The agency is going through some major policy changes that will affect the quality of service to clients. Length and type of treatment will be severely restricted. As a supervisor, you are quite angry about this policy, as are several of your staff. What do you need to take into consideration as you make your decision for how to proceed with the changes and how to discuss them with staff?

Chapter Four

Shared Meaning

Liz is a Caucasian supervisor in a large state agency with an ethnically diverse staff and clientele. Her staff includes African American, Hispanic, and Southeast Asian practitioners. She sees herself as having the least amount of experience and knowledge about those from a Southeast Asian background, as compared to the other cultures. One of her supervisees is Neng, a Hmong worker. Neng had a client who was a 14-year-old Hmong girl who, along with her aunt and several cousins, was living with the Caucasian family who had sponsored their arrival in the United States. The young girl was in individual therapy for depression and suicidal tendencies with a psychologist named Sam, a Caucasian with a great deal of experience working with the Hmong people.

Mai, a very powerful member of the Hmong community, is a child protection worker who became involved in the case when the sponsoring family reported the girl's aunt for hitting her. The girl expressed a strong desire to live elsewhere and threatened suicide if she could not move. Mai agreed that the girl was being mistreated and took the girl into her own home, a licensed foster home. Not only was this action somewhat questionable with regard to the need to establish boundaries between the child protection services and the foster home, Mai also did not follow correct procedures in making this placement.

Neng was called by the girl's aunt, who wanted her niece returned home. She expressed a common Hmong view that suicidal threats are only an attempt to manipulate. In addition, she was concerned that, because her niece was removed from the home, she would be blamed and would lose face in her community. Neng thought Mai had acted inappropriately. Neng also believed that the Caucasian culture gives children too much power, to the detriment of the family and community.

By the time Neng became involved, however, the girl had been in the foster home for a month and had not been suicidal the entire time. In addition, she was now threatening suicide if she were forced to move back home. Her therapist, Sam, therefore supported her staying in the foster home for the time being.

Neng asked for a meeting among Liz, Sam, and Mai to decide what to do. The ultimate decision rested with Liz, who had a sense that in addition to the conflict about what was best for the child, there was a larger and deeper conflict in the community, the nature of which she could only guess. This sense stemmed in part from Mai's comment to her during the meeting that "when there are two tigers on a mountain, one of them leaves alive." Liz was in a quandary. If she did not support Neng, she would be abandoning her supervisee as well as supporting an action that went against agency guidelines. Although Liz sought consultation from the others involved in the case as well as from colleagues, she did not have access to other Hmongs who could help her make the decision.

Liz concluded that she had to make the decision based on what she could determine was in the child's best interests. Liz had a great deal of respect for Sam's abilities and insights. On the basis of his report and her own observation that the girl was certainly safe where she was and not suicidal at this point, Liz recommended that the girl stay in the foster home while a reunification plan was developed and implemented. Liz thought this was not only in the girl's immediate best interests but also best for the family members, who were facing other stressors that would increase if they had to deal with the girl's ongoing instability.

Liz never felt completely comfortable with her decision. Even though she attempted to make the decision based on the child's best interests, she felt very unclear about what those actually were. In addition, she suspected that by deciding against Neng, she caused Neng to lose face in her community and may have therefore impaired Neng's ability to be as effective with other clients. Neng felt unsupported by her supervisor and was left with a feeling that Liz was not sensitive to the values of Hmong families and had therefore harmed her, this particular family, and potentially the larger community.

We could describe shared meaning as the grease that allows the smooth running of the supervisory relationship. Broome (1991) used the term *shared meaning* (p. 235) to describe an ongoing process of discussing, adjusting, and correcting perceptions to arrive at a "third culture" (p. 242) of understanding. Shared meaning is created in the context of the relationship between speaker and listener. Certainly, supervision will be more effective if supervisor and supervisee come to a mutual understanding that takes each of their viewpoints into account.

I have defined *shared meaning* as both mutual understanding and, ideally, mutual agreement between supervisor and supervisee. As the story above begins to illustrate, arriving at a shared meaning can become quite complex. For example, there clearly is no *one* Hmong way, given that the two Hmong workers in the story strongly disagreed with each other about how to proceed. In addition, it is common for a conflict between professionals to arise when several are involved in a case. Each has a unique role and a unique position from which to understand and approach the client. The fact that in this situation the practitioners and clients represented two different cultures added even more room for misunderstanding, clashes in values, and confusion about what should guide the decision-making process. Finally, this story illustrates the impact the larger context has on the treatment approach. Here the context included a myriad of human service agencies, each of which had rules and expectations regarding the clients. In addition, Neng, Mai, and the clients were all a part of the same community. The Caucasian workers involved in the case were unaware of how the interactions among all the participants in this story affected and were affected by that community.

The supervisor's ability to communicate clearly and directly is often cited as a necessary component of the supervisory relationship (Farmer, 1987; Liddle, Davidson, & Barrett, 1988; Wetchler, 1989; Kadushin, 1992; Munson, 1993; Shulman, 1982, 1993). This communication includes such actions as offering clear feedback about the supervisee's performance and establishing clarity about the supervisory contract and expectations regarding job duties. It includes, as well, understanding what is meant by both verbal and nonverbal behavior, such as the use of particular words, tone of voice, and direct versus indirect styles of communication. Although this may sound unidirectional, a process by which both participants work together is necessary if mutual understanding is to be achieved.

Challenges of cross-cultural supervision are most evident in the area of shared meaning. The potential for complexity exists in any relationship, given that both supervisor and supervisee bring to the table a variety of assumptions, values, and experiences that all influence the individuals' attitudes toward each other and toward the job. The greater the differences between supervisor and supervisee, the greater is the possibility for blocks in the achievement of shared meaning. I begin this chapter with a general discussion about shared meaning and then discuss in more depth some of the issues that pertain especially to cross-cultural supervision. Two major areas that require both mutual understanding and mutual agreement for the supervisory relationship to operate effectively are the supervisory contract and approaches to treatment.

THE SUPERVISORY CONTRACT

Contracting in supervision is the means by which both supervisor and supervisee achieve a mutual understanding about what will happen in the supervisory process. Although contracts vary in formality and level of explicitness, any discussion that addresses the question, "What will happen here?" can be seen as a form of contract development. For the duration of the supervisory relationship, it is useful to clarify the contract on a periodic basis (Schwartz, 1988). This clarification could include both an overall review of the expectations of supervision and job performance as well as what Shulman calls "sessional contracting" (Shulman, 1982, p. 89). For example, the supervisee might want the supervisor to help identify particular patterns of interaction in a family or possible reasons why the supervisee keeps getting stuck with a client at a certain point. Perhaps the supervisee is practicing a particular technique and is looking for feedback from the supervisor. More often, the request might be for general feedback. Setting the agenda at the beginning of each session keeps the supervisor from simply moving ahead without attention to the supervisee's immediate needs.

A discussion about the contract invites the supervisee to become more engaged in the process. In addition, because contracting between practitioner and client is an important part of treatment, contracting in supervision can provide the supervisee an experiential lesson (Shulman, 1982). The following questions can serve as a framework for contract development.

1. Is the structure clearly delineated? Structure includes the times and place of the supervisory sessions and the processes for case presentation.
2. Are the standards and process for evaluation understood by both parties?
3. What does the supervisee need from supervision at this point, and is the supervisor prepared to provide it? If so, how? If not, how can the supervisor help the supervisee find and utilize appropriate resources?
4. What sort of information will the supervisee be expected to share in supervision? For example, should the supervisee expect that the supervisor will encourage an exploration of personal issues?
5. How will sensitive information provided by the supervisee be handled? For example, on what basis and with whom will it be shared, and how will it affect evaluation?

For sessional contracting, the following questions might be asked.

6. What are the priority topics for this session?
7. What type of feedback would be most helpful?

Power and Contracting

A power dimension permeates all aspects of the contracting process between supervisor and supervisee. By asking the question, "What do you want?" the supervisor is acknowledging the supervisee's need to take part in setting the agenda. As supervisees grow, they often become clearer about what they want in supervision. Concurrently, they may become more aware of their power to ask for what they want, to choose supervision that is useful to them, and to terminate or more subtly avoid supervision that is not useful. An example of this change in awareness is illustrated by Heather's following comment.

> I was getting clearer and clearer about what I wanted and I knew exactly what I didn't want. And I wasn't afraid anymore, so I wouldn't just with-hold from my supervisor when he was focusing on things that weren't helpful to me and tell myself "Well, I'll just let it go on." I knew I wasn't going to benefit as much from the supervision experience if I was hold-ing back resentment. So, I let him know more clearly how I wanted our supervision time to change.

To some extent, however, the word *contracting* is misleading because it connotes a situation in which each participant has equal say. This interpretation, of course, is not accurate. Although both supervisor and supervisee have some power to state their needs, desires, and require-ments about how the supervision will proceed, the supervisor has the power to make a final determination in the case of an unresolved con-flict. Again, the definition of shared meaning is mutual understanding and, *ideally*, mutual agreement. This definition acknowledges that even if the latter is not achievable, the former can help alleviate some ten-sion. If supervisees are clear about what is expected of them, then, even if they don't agree with it they are in a better position to make decisions about how to respond to those expectations.

Structure of the Supervisory Process

Although few contracts are put in writing, many supervisors and supervisees make rather explicit agreements about the structure of the supervision. Issues typically addressed include frequency, length and time of sessions, and method of case presentation. Difficulty arises if there is either a lack of understanding or a lack of genuine agreement about these basic issues.

When Carlotta went to work in a psychiatric unit of a hospital right after receiving her graduate degree, she was enthusiastic about the learning opportunities and was frankly relieved to have found work. Her supervisor, Paul, was a warm man who had quite a bit of experi-ence, and Carlotta anticipated that he would teach her a great deal.

In the job interview, Paul emphasized the independent nature of the work at the hospital. He also said that because of his own respon-sibilities, he would often be quite busy, although he would certainly make every effort to be available for guidance and support, especially at first. Carlotta, who had always enjoyed a great deal of autonomy, readily accepted these conditions.

However, when she began the job, Carlotta realized that her defi-nition of independence and Paul's were actually quite different. She had counted on regular, hourly, uninterrupted supervisory sessions like those she had experienced in her graduate school internships. She was quite surprised to discover that her sessions with Paul were sporadically scheduled and subject to interruptions and changes in response to emergencies that arose on the floor. Although she found Paul's feedback quite helpful, her resentment and frustration at his lack of availability grew as time went on. Paul thought that he had been quite clear from the beginning that he could not guarantee Carlotta a regular structured supervisory session and was surprised by her resentment. Unfortunately, he felt unable to meet her request for more regular sessions.

To some extent, this story reflects a communication problem: Paul and Carlotta had different meanings behind the words they used with each other. Because initially the words were left vague, there was no opportunity for Paul and Carlotta to discover the lack of common understanding. In addition, Carlotta may have agreed to things she later regretted, possibly convincing herself that she was satisfied with those agreements because of her desire to obtain the position. Supervisors and supervisees should periodically revisit the initial agreements to make sure they are still working for both parties and, when possible, to make necessary revisions. Even when revisions are not possible, clarity about the reality helps alleviate some of the potential strain on the relationship.

Supervisees' Expectations

An additional part of the contract often involves a discussion about what the supervisee wants to learn in supervision. A tool such as Munson's Educational Assessment Scale (Munson, 1993) can help both supervisor and supervisee determine appropriate learning goals. On occasion, such a discussion can reveal fundamental differences, such as those that emerged in Laura's discussion with a new employee.

> Shari had just graduated from a family program and begun working at the agency. One of the first things that I try to find out is what a person's beliefs are. I want to know what theoretical model they operate from. In doing that with her, she seemed to take my questions as somewhat insulting and challenging. We began to talk about the definition of supervision. "Well," she says, "I see supervision as honing my craft. You should give me pointers and teach me specific technique."
>
> I responded with, "Techniques are meaningful to the extent that they relate to your beliefs. So, what are your beliefs about change?" Using the things she told me, I tried to map out my understanding of her belief about change. It looked sort of like a hodgepodge of things to me. There was an educational piece, and an insight one, and a building of awareness, and it was surrounded by a kind of systemic notion.

As we talked about her graduate program, it became clear that eclecticism was promoted. I said, "I don't agree with that. I think your best bet is to train in a particular form and know that well, and then to develop some others. Then, if you come up against things that you're not sure how to explain given your understanding, redraft your theory of change, but there should be some centrality to it."

Well, that didn't go anywhere. She continued to consider my feedback insulting and contrary to her definition of supervision. She said to me, "I've gone through training. What I want from you is technique, not a challenge about my epistemology."

In this story, there is significant overlap between contracting and agreement regarding approaches to treatment, which is discussed next. However, the conflict here is about the supervisee's learning needs. Laura was not necessarily advocating a particular model. She was insisting that Shari adopt one of her own, rather than randomly using techniques from a variety of theories. In addition, whereas Shari saw herself as having already developed an adequate grounding in theory, Laura saw this area as something in which Shari needed further work. Unless they are able to resolve this fundamental difference, the supervision is likely to suffer.

Standards for Evaluation

Evaluation determines whether the supervisee has met the goals and expectations that were established either through mutual agreement or by the supervisor alone. In Chapter 2, Don gave an account of a situation in which he asked what he needed to do to receive an outstanding rating. After following all the supervisor's recommendations, Don still did not receive that rating. At that point, the supervisor said Don's written work was not good enough. The most benign interpretation of this incident is that the supervisor simply forgot to mention that this was a significant area in which Don would be evaluated. It is also possible that the supervisor did not anticipate that Don's paperwork would be problematic, but noticed it only when the time came to do the evaluation. Don's interpretation, which may well be correct, was that the supervisor was racist and that he added the paperwork as an afterthought to keep Don from receiving the high rating.

Whatever the explanation, the story reminds us that formal evaluations should not contain surprises. Rather, supervisees should know all along what is expected of them and whether they are meeting those expectations. Sometimes it is necessary to reestablish goals when new problems emerge between formal evaluation periods. Emily's student intern wrote a set of learning goals early in the year that followed the standard format provided by the school. Emily had some concerns about whether the goals were complete enough. However, she assumed that the student was adequately meeting a rather general requirement set by the school, and she approved the goals. Some months into the internship, Emily and the student added to the original goals to address problems that emerged that were not covered in the initial learning contract. Emily's action in this situation had two positive outcomes. First, by rewriting the goals, she called attention to the student's problems and redirected the focus of the supervision to deal explicitly with those areas of the student's work. Second, the student was made aware, within a reasonable time period, of what would be expected of her in order to receive a satisfactory evaluation at the end of the school year. Too often, supervisors fail to give this kind of timely feedback, probably because they are either too busy to notice or because they are uncomfortable with a potential negative response from a supervisee. When issues are addressed for the first time in an evaluation, supervisees are likely to feel angry and betrayed at having been led to believe that their work was satisfactory. Furthermore, they may often have grounds to file a grievance of some sort against the supervisor.

It is worth noting, however, that it may be difficult to reach a shared understanding regarding evaluations because the supervisee is unable to hear or accept the feedback. Ramon had many discussions with Cheryl, who was not performing her job adequately. However, Cheryl consistently responded defensively and seemed on each occasion not to have understood or retained feedback Ramon had offered in previous conversations. She was angry when she received her evaluation and told many colleagues that she had not received any of this feedback previously, nor did she understand why she was being negatively evaluated. Her response not only reflected a lack of trust and understanding between herself and Ramon but also created a group dynamic in which Ramon's other supervisees became worried that they too would be caught by surprise during an evaluation.

Shared Information and How It Will Be Used

As was discussed in Chapter 3, defining the line between supervision and therapy is confusing for both supervisors and supervisees. Many supervisors seek to alleviate the confusion by clarifying how the line will be maintained. The supervisor in the following excerpt described how he would talk to a supervisee about establishing the line if a personal issue arose during the course of supervision.

> I would say, "This is an issue. What are you going to do about that? We won't process that here. We'll identify it in a way that is respectful, open, and direct. We're not going to mess around with it."

This example illustrates some of the potential difficulties in achieving shared meaning. The supervisor's statement raises as many questions as it attempts to answer. What constitutes a respectful manner in this situation? How will we know when we have crossed the line from "identification" to "messing around"? Clearly, different supervisees will interpret this statement differently. In addition, as mentioned before, although many supervisors say similar things about where the line will be drawn, they may actually behave quite differently from one another.

This is an issue that requires an initial discussion in which both supervisor and supervisee talk about their philosophy regarding the sharing of personal issues in supervision. The topic may well be revisited later, as specific issues arise and as each learns more about the other's style and needs. Ji came to supervision from a previous supervisor whom she experienced as violating her and others in the way in which he conducted exploration of personal issues. Because of that experience, Ji was quite clear with Ed, her new supervisor, that she considered such discussion off limits. After some time, she began to realize that Ed would use the information in what she considered a respectful and useful manner, and she was willing to renegotiate the contract.

An accompanying concern for many supervisees is whether and with whom the supervisor intends to share the personal information the supervisee reveals. This is a particularly important question when the supervisor performs the dual functions of administrative and clinical supervision. The following is an account from a supervisor in an agency setting, describing how she attempted to clarify the way this would be handled.

> I said that I like to learn about where people come from—their family of origin, etc. I told my supervisee, "I think that this will help me as your clinical supervisor, because it will help me understand how you relate to your clients and what sort of feedback and guidance you will need from me. This is not related to administrative supervision. As your administrative supervisor, I will pay attention to things like your productivity and your caseload."
>
> I think that by setting those ground rules ahead of time, he felt free to ask me if I would ever reveal anything that he told me in our unit. I said, "No. As far as I'm concerned, that's private information that you would need to give me permission to reveal." I think he felt reassured.

There may be times when the supervisee reveals information the supervisor does feel the need to share in order to protect clients. As was discussed before in the section on limit setting, it is not always easy to sort out whose rights must be protected—the supervisee's or the client's. In an effort to clarify the procedure for the handling of sensitive information, the agency or school can create a policy that is shared with all practitioners. The following statement was developed by Yepez, Reeser, and Wertkin (1994) and is in the process of adaptation by Director of Field Susan Cochrane for the College of St. Catherine/ University of St. Thomas MSW Program in St. Paul, Minnesota.*

Gatekeeping is one of the responsibilities of social work educators. Sharing relevant student information is essential in field education. This information needs to protect the confidentiality of students and field instructors. The following policy deals with sharing sensitive information.

Policy Statement: Because social workers serve vulnerable people, affect the welfare of the country, and reflect the credibility of the profession, it is critical to graduate students who are competent to begin practice. The field component is one of the most important avenues in social work programs to evaluate student's ability to practice. Students, fieldwork instructors, field faculty, and the directors of field are a team collaborating to assure continuity and accountability in goal-oriented field instruction. To this end, relevant student information, written and oral, will be shared with involved parties—fieldwork instructor, faculty supervisor, associate director, or director of field as appropriate. This information will be shared to protect clients, protect students, and facilitate the learning process as well as to facilitate appropriate field placements and encourage informed choices by field instructors and students. Faculty supervisors may share relevant student information from communication in field seminars with field instructors. It is expected that field instructors will share relevant information from field placement with faculty supervisors. Student, faculty, and fieldwork instructors will have knowledge of the policy before the placement process begins.

Definition: Relevance is defined as having direct impact on field placement. Information is relevant when it affects students' work with clients, field instructors, agency staff, or the learning process.

Procedures for the execution of this policy include the following:

1. The policy will be located in the field education manuals. It will be discussed in field seminars and field instructor orientations.
2. Appropriate self-disclosure and possible outcomes of sharing will be discussed with students in seminars.
3. Field instructors are encouraged to include in their descriptions for the "Opportunities Listing" topical areas they consider necessary for students to consider as potential conflicts. Students can then make informed choices whether or not to apply to particular agencies.
4. Field instructors will be encouraged to ask students well-directed questions at the placement interview. The social work department is available to consult with agencies.
5. Relevant information will be shared with the next placement's faculty supervisor and fieldwork instructor. First-year students'

*This material is adapted with permission from "A Model Policy on Sharing Sensitive Information with Field Instructors" by L. E. Yepez, C. Reeser, and R. Wertkin. Unpublished paper, presented at the Council on Social Work Education Annual Program Meeting, Atlanta, Georgia, 1994.

evaluations will have a line to indicate students' consent to sharing their junior/first year graduate field evaluation with their prospective senior/clinical field instructor. In the event a student does not choose to sign the consent, the student will meet with the Associate or Director of Field to discuss reasons and a plan of action.

6. If concerns arise about a student, either during the interview process or while in the placement, the faculty supervisor will discuss the concerns with the student, including implications for future placements and social work as a profession.

7. When a student leaves a placement before the scheduled ending time, the student and faculty will sign an agreement stating what information will be shared with any future placements about the student as well as about the field work instructor/agency. Another placement will not be made official without this agreement.

8. Students will be informed of the limits of confidentiality if they are unwilling to share information that affects performance in the field with a field instructor when the field faculty supervisor believes the information is important for the field work instructor to have. Students will know what information is shared.

9. Students will use the grievance procedure outlined in the field manual when they believe the information may be or has been misused or not shared appropriately.

This policy makes overt the reality that supervision is indeed a process of accountability. Therefore, although supervisees need to feel free to share with their supervisors without inappropriate recrimination, the overriding concern is that supervisees serve their clients well. The positive effect of such a policy is twofold. First, it helps guard against the possibility that a student will feel betrayed by a supervisor's sharing of information without prior agreement. Second, it provides all involved with clarity about exactly what can be expected in this very delicate arena.

TREATMENT APPROACHES

In the past few decades, there has been an explosion in the field of mental health of new theories, techniques, and approaches to treatment. Often ideas that are strongly promoted by some clinicians and theorists are equally strongly challenged by others. Recently two societal forces have significantly influenced the way practitioners think about and approach their work. One is the advent of the managed care system, bringing an increased demand from third-party providers and others that clinicians work more effectively and efficiently with clients. This development has contributed to a significant movement toward more solution-oriented, behaviorally specific, brief treatment methods.

Tension has emerged between those who value the brief treatment mode and those who view long-term, more insight-oriented treatment as more effective. Another societal force is a rise in skepticism about practices that, only a few years ago, were considered by many to be an acceptable standard of care. The most obvious and probably most controversial target of the skepticism is the practice of retrieving repressed memories from people believed to be victims of abuse. A very short time ago, it was considered important to give victims of abuse the room and permission to acknowledge what had been a dark and ugly secret kept from others and even from themselves. Practitioners and clients alike were encouraged to identify signs of possible abuse. Practitioners who ignored those signs were seen as continuing the victim's denial of the experience and not validating his or her reality. Now, the serious challenging of the accuracy of repressed memories that emerge later in life has led many practitioners to carefully avoid "leading" the client toward or even supporting a belief that cannot be substantiated by some external source.

The good news about the undercurrent of change is that it reflects a field that is constantly growing and seeking creative approaches to dealing with increasingly complex problems. In addition, practitioners are challenged more than ever to examine the efficacy of their approaches. A negative consequence of this trend, in my opinion, is that the constant push to find something "new" and "better" can result in rejection of perfectly good and useful ideas simply because they have been around for a while and are therefore considered dated. An even more dangerous result of the trend is that many practitioners are continually second-guessing their own intuitive responses and becoming frozen with fear of the possible consequences, either to the client or to themselves.

The simple explanation for all the confusion is that clinical practice is at best an inexact science that has as a general goal some sort of positive effect on very complex organisms—human beings and human systems. It is not surprising that beliefs about what constitutes a positive effect—not to mention what will help achieve it—are steeped in one's personal experiences with family, culture, training, and life events, as well as in one's professional experiences with clients and other practitioners.

Teaching a Particular Approach

When I began doctoral work in marriage and family therapy, I had already been a social worker for 16 years. Although familiar with many family systems theories, I was steeped in an individual-focused approach. During my first year in graduate school, everything I had learned and cherished was turned on its head, its very validity challenged. The result was a combination of confusion and insecurity. While questioning everything I had previously done, I was not convinced that this new way was right. But I did try a systems approach and, over the next few years, began to integrate those aspects of the approach that worked for me. Many specific family therapy theories were more directly compatible with what I had previously known. Some were less so, but they added an important dimension to my work. Some I ultimately discarded as, although probably worthwhile, not useful to me because of my particular strengths, weaknesses, and style as a clinician. I have come to understand this experience as a reflection of a fundamental aspect of learning; that is, most students have a certain degree of resistance to new learning that at least appears to, if not in fact does, deeply challenge what they have known before. It is naturally threatening to shake the ground under one's feet. However, students who are closed to any possibility of such a threat may miss the opportunity to expand their knowledge and understanding of the world. Sometimes, as in the following example, supervisees are not overtly resistant but simply have a difficult time incorporating a fundamental conceptual change in their thinking. Ed, a private consultant, described some of the pros and cons he encountered when teaching his family systems approach to clinicians who had a great deal of experience in a different method.

> I think I usually have quite a bit of respect for what they bring from their contexts. Often they've brought something from their context that I don't know about. However, they also bring rigidity. This isn't always obvious. I present some new ideas, some alternate ideas, and they agree and think they've got it.
>
> It later becomes clear that they don't have it at all. They've got their way of thinking about things, and these new ideas don't change that. They just fit into their old framework. They might use some of the words, but they haven't changed their overall approach to one that has a systems perspective. I find that frustrating.

This observation raises an interesting question: Is it more beneficial for the supervisor's model to be one that contradicts or challenges the supervisee's previous learning or one that supports it? The answer to this question depends on the supervisee's particular learning needs and developmental level. Does the supervisee want or need to move in some new directions, or does the supervisee need more in-depth understanding and development of an already familiar area? In either case, it does appear that when the supervisor is teaching a particular model of treatment, both supervisors and supervisees consider it important that the supervisee find it a useful one. Marie, a supervisor whose approach is mostly psychodynamic in orientation, observed that some of her supervisees discovered that a solution-based approach made more sense to them. Marie encouraged them to seek training in that approach with either someone in the agency or someone outside the agency who had that particular expertise.

Basic Compatibility in Approach

When the goal is not to learn a particular model, it is more effective for the supervisor to give supervisees as much room as possible to develop their own approach. It is helpful, however, if they share at least in a general way a sense of what constitutes good treatment. Sandy, a supervisee, told the following story.

> I certainly think it's better if a supervisor has an orientation similar to mine. One time I was really stuck with a couple and I had done everything I knew to do. I brought it into supervision. Early on, I had talked to the woman about the possibility of sexual abuse and she had said "No." I took her word for it.
>
> When I presented the case to my supervisor, he said, "I just don't believe she hasn't been sexually abused." I went back into the next session and said, "I want to talk about it again." She burst into tears and said that since the first time I asked her, she had been thinking about it but never would have brought it up had I not asked again.
>
> I don't know what my previous supervisor would have said about that. She didn't believe in pursuing the issue of sexual abuse if the client didn't volunteer it. She might well have suggested that my client was ready to terminate. I think if my supervisor has a similar framework, she or he is likely to push me to another level that is useful, rather than sending me in another direction.

As mentioned previously, questions about how to deal with the issue of past sexual abuse abound in the mental health community. This is a good example of how one's philosophy about a topic influences the way in which both the treatment and the supervision will be experienced. Sandy clearly thinks that if her supervisor had not insisted she pursue the question, the clients would have been poorly served. They may have ended their work without dealing with a crucial issue that could potentially improve their relationship as well as the woman's well-being. The information we have about this case so far supports the hypothesis that pursuing the question of sexual abuse was a positive move. However, we are unable to predict what the ultimate outcome would be. As in many situations, it is nearly impossible to determine whether the supervisor's advice was right or wrong by some objective standard. To some extent, this issue is simply a practical one. Supervisors' feedback will naturally be grounded in their own framework; the question is whether this framework will be helpful to the supervisee. A supervisor made the following comment.

What comes out of my mouth is going to reflect my model. That's the way I think of the universe. I try to ask whether it will be useful to them to be supervised by me given that that's going to be my major approach. I try to help them fit it into their approach. So far, I think that's worked. But if it didn't, there's no way I can really change the way I think.

Probably the most important factor from Sandy's point of view was that she felt supported and challenged to pursue something she found difficult but valuable and that seemed to lead to a positive result. A supervisee with a different orientation might have the opposite reaction to Sandy's supervisor's advice. This supervisee might see the supervisor as advocating an intrusive and possibly destructive approach, one that might ultimately create more problems than it would solve. In this scenario, the supervisee might overtly or covertly resist the supervisor, a dynamic that could itself affect the outcome of the intervention with the clients.

Dealing with Differences

Frequently, supervisors and supervisees do not agree about which direction to pursue with a client. As discussed in Chapter 2, the supervisor is then in a position of deciding whether the difference in the supervisee's approach is one of philosophy or one that is beyond the parameters of acceptable practice. One might assume that it makes sense to support the supervisee's decision, assuming the difference is merely philosophical. However, it is not always easy to make this distinction. In addition, even when the supervisor is reasonably sure the issue is not one about acceptable practice, it again raises the question of whether the supervisor should be supporting the supervisee or challenging the supervisee to move beyond the familiar and comfortable. Both are legitimate directions for a supervisor to take. In the words of one supervisor:

People have a right to practice in what I consider to be a narrow way. On the other hand, I have the right, and probably the obligation, as a supervisor to try to make other options available and accessible.

In the following account, Sam, a supervisor, described the way he offers another option.

Betty, who was a student intern, thought that people having insight into their problems and really understanding themselves was important. I don't agree with that, so I told her, "What we do here is a certain kind of treatment, with a certain kind of philosophy behind it. I understand you see things differently. If you want to give my way a trial for three months and see what you can get out of it, we'll talk about maybe changing the focus at that time."

She agreed to try it. At the end of that period of time, we discussed it and agreed to continue because that's what she decided she wanted to learn. At the end of the year, we discussed it again. She had not changed her opinion, but she thought she really learned a lot over the year, and this would add to her abilities.

Sam encouraged Betty to put aside former beliefs in order to take in what he was trying to teach. He went on to say, however, that if she had continued to feel uncomfortable with his approach, he would change the focus, provided she achieved competency in basic skills. Thus his style was one of negotiation, with a goal of helping Betty expand her repertoire.

Another way to deal with a difference in approach is for the supervisor and supervisee to arrive at a common understanding of their differences. Jana spoke about one of her employees, whose approach was much more psychodynamic than hers. In an effort to avoid a power struggle, she encouraged her supervisee to teach her about his approach while she concurrently taught him about hers. As a result, they were able to avoid the power struggle, achieve a feeling of mutual respect, and achieve shared meaning by arriving at a common language that included both approaches.

If the difference is too great, however, most supervisors and supervisees would probably agree that supervision will not be very effective. The connection between shared meaning and the knowledge differential is quite clear here. Recall that it is clearly more desirable if the supervisee thinks the supervisor has something valuable to teach. Although it may be ideal for a supervisee to transfer to another supervisor whose approach is more compatible, this is frequently not possible. Both supervisor and supervisee are left with the need to continue to try to achieve some kind of constructive shared meaning or, as is unfortunately too often the case, remain at a standstill.

Shared Meaning and Telling the Story

Supervisees are aware of their supervisor's particular approach. With this in mind, they may well choose which cases they share based on whether they think the supervisor's approach will be useful. This decision can be seen in a positive light, if the supervisee has more than one person with whom to consult. As one supervisee stated, "I go to different people with cases and questions about which they have expertise. I present my work, knowing the kind of help I can expect." Through this method, supervisees can match their needs with the gifts of supervisors or consultants.

Supervisees who find themselves in conflict with their supervisor regarding shared meaning often deal with the problem by withholding the story. The following account by Alan, a supervisee, illustrates a potential pitfall of this action. The conflict in this case was a relatively minor one. The supervisor made it a practice, as part of his initial assessment of a client, to take a sex history. Although Alan did not object to obtaining this information when it seemed necessary, he did not see the need to ask for it if it did not seem relevant to the case. Although he discussed this difference of opinion with his supervisor, it was not something they discussed at length, and Alan did not think they reached a satisfactory resolution. As a result, Alan would attempt to avoid the issue by not mentioning it, experiencing private relief whenever he presented a case and his supervisor did not ask about the sex history. Because of the lack of clear resolution about the conflict, Alan was left with some self-doubt.

> Sometimes I did get a sex history, but there were other times when I thought, "Whew, he didn't ask me about the sex history and I didn't take it this time, and we just don't have to talk about it. I don't think it was defiance. I just didn't believe I had to have that information for every client. On the other hand, I was also aware of my shame about my own sexuality and I was never clear how much that influenced my decision to avoid the issue with clients.

As this example illustrates, often the avoidance of one issue can lead to avoidance of others. Alan was left questioning whether his attitude toward his own sexuality was interfering with his work. It is not clear why he was reluctant to pursue the discussion with his supervisor to a more satisfactory resolution. Perhaps he thought such a discussion would lead to a stalemate, or perhaps he was afraid to expose his feelings about his own sexuality and thought a discussion about doing sexual histories would inevitably lead to that disclosure. In any case, it is clear that by avoiding the issue, Alan suppressed some of his concerns and questions, and one could surmise that he did not learn all he might have if he had felt free to discuss the topic more fully.

SHARED MEANING AND CONTEXT

The context can have an impact on shared meaning with regard to both treatment approach and contract making. There is an important connection between the philosophy of treatment being promoted by a particular organization, or by a particular group within that organization, and the same issue in the supervisory relationship. The organization's philosophy of treatment is often, but not always, connected to the population that organization serves and by the agency's mission. The following comment offered by Ryan, a supervisor in an inner-city agency, illustrates this point.

> The streets are mad. People are mean. If you work with a family and you've got a gang kid in the family, they're not going to come into a meeting looking like clients described in a lot of the family therapy literature. They're not going to want to get in touch with their feelings or analyze their motivations. You're going to be hit with some very inner-city street behavior. So in supervision, I have some interest in making sure my supervisees know, understand, and can function in that dynamic.

A potential source of conflict can occur if the agency asks the supervisor to promote a particular approach, and those on the staff are more familiar with a different one. The supervisor is in the delicate position of influencing the staff's ideas while attempting to circumvent a power struggle. Often the push to change treatment approach occurs when the organization, in response to other needs, requires actions that are at odds with what supervisees (and perhaps supervisors as well) consider productive for clients. These needs often relate to financial concerns. Molly, a supervisee, described the dilemma in the following account.

> I work in an inpatient unit for adolescents. Sometimes, when you're working with a kid, you are actually working with a symptom of some of the family dynamics. I think in a lot of cases you just change the formation of the symptoms, rather than resolving the actual problem itself. This is especially true with insurance companies that set time limits on the coverage. You don't have time to deal with underlying issues, so you just focus on the immediate symptom.
>
> Frequently my supervisors make recommendations for treatment based on financial pressure. Everything has to be behaviorally specific. There's no support to look at the years of unresolved hurt and anger. I don't think this is helpful, but they're the bosses, and it doesn't pay to disagree, especially when I don't think they have much choice about it.

We see here the influence of the larger context on the approach to treatment and on the power dynamics. Not only did Molly feel powerless to challenge her supervisors; she also experienced her supervisors as powerless to challenge the organization, which in turn may have felt powerless to challenge the insurance companies. This example is reminiscent of the discussion in Chapter 3 about what type of information supervisors should share with their supervisees. Although Molly may well be correct that her supervisors have little choice, they apparently have not invited discussion about this dilemma. I would suggest that they do so, because a frank discussion could have several benefits.

First, Molly might simply receive some support and affirmation for her frustration. Second, it is possible that both she and the supervisors have more power to change or modify the treatment plans than Molly assumes to be true. Third, through discussion in supervision, Molly perhaps can develop some treatment strategies, within the current restrictions, that seem more effective than those she is currently using.

The primary impact the context can have on the contracting process is in relation to the clarity of job expectations. Zoe, a supervisor, provided the following example.

> My supervisee and I were hired at the same time. She was given promises about being able to do some creative program development work. I was given similar promises. When I began work, it became clear that the expectations for both of us were somewhat different than we thought they would be. So at the same time that I was taking that fight to my supervisor, who had hired both me and her, she was fighting with me about it.

Because both were hired at the same time, Zoe was not in a position to offer a clear job description to her supervisee. In fact, she was misled during her own hiring process about what would be expected of each of them. This created both confusion and tension as she attempted to advocate for both herself and the supervisee as well as to represent the agency to the supervisee.

CROSS-CULTURAL SUPERVISION AND SHARED MEANING

As stated at the beginning of this chapter, it is in the area of shared meaning that many issues pertaining to cross-cultural supervision emerge. Pederson (1991) suggested that the term *culture* be broadly defined to include variables such as age; gender; place of residence; social, economic or educational status; formal and informal affiliations; nationality; ethnicity; language; and religion. Using this definition, Pederson concluded that all counseling is in fact cross-cultural. We could surmise that this description applies to all supervision as well. As has already been demonstrated, both supervisor and supervisee bring a wealth of experiences to the relationship that affect their responses to each other. Certainly, supervisors and supervisees whose life experiences are dramatically different are more likely to encounter barriers to understanding and agreement than are those whose experiences are similar.

Differences in interpretation of such things as tone of voice, eye contact, assertive behavior, use of language, and direct expression of feelings and ideas (Ryan & Hendricks, 1989; Sue & Sue, 1990), can lead to deep, often unintentional misunderstandings. For instance, because Western culture generally values the open expression of ideas and feelings, Caucasian supervisors are likely to encourage their supervisees to bring their problems to supervision. Someone from an Asian culture may see admission of problems as a lack of self-control and may view talkative behavior as self-centered and rude. A supervisee with these beliefs may respond with silence to a supervisor's expectation of openness, and the supervisor could interpret this behavior as passive or uncooperative (Ryan & Hendricks, 1989).

Arriving at a shared meaning with someone whose meanings may be quite different from one's own is exciting and also enormously challenging. The stories that follow are about specific supervisors and supervisees who come from a variety of cultural and ethnic backgrounds. I recognize that the issue of how to refer to another's ethnic identity is a personal and sensitive one. For example, many Native American people prefer to be identified by tribe; and many people prefer to be called Hispanic, whereas others prefer Latino (or, for women, Latina) or to be identified by their specific country of origin. For sake of simplicity, I have identified people's backgrounds primarily by large categories, for example Hispanic or Latino(a), Native American, Caucasian, or African American, although at times my references are more specific—for example, Laotian. In-depth information about specific cultures is beyond the scope of this book. However, the reader is encouraged to become familiar with the growing body of literature on multicultural counseling and multicultural awareness. (Examples of recent contributions include Kiev, 1964; Sue & Kirk, 1972, 1973; Cromwell et al., 1979; Toupin, 1980; Marsella & Pederson, 1981; Sue & Morishima, 1982; LaFramboise, 1983, 1989; Pederson, Sartorius, & Marsella, 1984; Trafzer, 1985; Asante, 1987; Denton & Massey, 1989; Kinzie, 1989; Sue & Sue, 1990; Bernal et al., 1991; Cross, 1991; Swinomish Tribal Community, 1991; Jones, 1992; Leong & Whitfield, 1992; Boyd-Franklin, 1993; Leong, 1993; Pederson & Ivy, 1993; Cheung, 1994; Felix-Ortiz et al., 1994; Martinez, 1994; Pederson, 1994a, 1994b; Uba, 1994; Sue et al., 1996.) The examples in this book are not meant to provide general "facts" about specific cultures, nor do I mean to ignore the enormous variety that exists among any group of people. Rather, the following discussion is an attempt to elaborate on some of the dynamics pertaining to shared meaning that can occur in the cross-cultural supervisory relationship.

Biculturalism

Because the Euro-American culture is dominant in most places in the United States, people from a different culture who live in the dominant culture confront on some level the reality of their own biculturalism.

This is particularly true of those who work in organizations that are a part of that culture. Chau (1990) offered the concepts of *dual perspective* and *sociocultural dissonance*, which refer to the complexities of trying to manage often-conflicting values and norms from two or more cultures in which a person is operating.

The issue is further complicated by the fact that many variables contribute to any individual's process in dealing with biculturalism. For example, people who have recently immigrated to the United States may be quite unfamiliar with the new culture and fully identified with the one they just left. Teenagers immigrating to this country may be more willing, anxious, and able than their parents to assimilate into the larger U.S. system, and this difference may cause many conflicts within the family system. Others may have been raised far away from their traditional roots and may be out of touch with those cultural values; perhaps they are in a process of discovering and affirming the influence of those values in their lives for the first time. Others may have a lifetime of experience grappling with the influences and pulls of two, often conflicting, cultures. This is only a small list of the possibilities.

Generally speaking, practitioners who have been professionally trained in the United States have learned the rules of the dominant culture through the educational process. Many, however, are aware of an internal struggle to maintain the integrity of their heritage and personal identity, while at the same time operating within the parameters defined as professionalism. Understanding an individual's relationship to biculturalism is important for effective cross-cultural supervision. In many cases, for example, practitioners with cultural backgrounds similar to those of their clients may have a different opinion than their clients about what constitutes desirable treatment. This situation was evident in the story of the Hmong workers with which this chapter began. Recall that Neng and Mai had differing opinions and that Mai's opinion about what constituted appropriate treatment of the child was at odds with that of the Hmong family.

Doreen, a Caucasian supervisor, spoke about the dilemmas facing some of her Laotian supervisees.

Our philosophy has been to work on solutions within the culture first. In the Hmong population, we work with family members and with the clan members, trying everything we can within the system of that culture the way it's set up. If that doesn't work, then the social worker discusses with the family the fact that another option is to go with the American system. For example, usually if a woman is experiencing domestic abuse, she goes to her relatives, who then go to the relatives of the spouse to discuss the conflict that is happening and the way she has been treated. They figure out what they are going to do. Sometimes the husband's family has to pay some money to the wife's family to make amends. This can be quite difficult for the social worker, who is torn because he or she believes an order of protection could be helpful but is concerned that this would be unacceptable in terms of the community.

Song, a Hmong supervisee, described a similar dilemma from her point of view.

> I have to be extra careful in my community, because I don't want them to know me as a social worker who helps battered women. In the community a few years ago, an agency in town helped battered women and it created a conflict. I try to be careful to not take sides and to avoid the community seeing me as just helping the woman. If the woman is in my office and she is being beaten by her husband, I may not call the police for her, but will give her the number. I don't call because if the couple gets together again later on, I don't want the husband to have negative feelings. Those are some of the cultural things I have to be careful about.

In this situation, Song struggled with her need to be both effective and loyal to her community versus her sense that there is something useful for the women in the U.S. system. She negotiated a fine line between the two cultures. She made a further comment that she was pleased to be half American and half Hmong in her orientation and values. From her point of view, she had the best of both worlds.

Debra, an Hispanic supervisee, experienced more of a struggle with both cultures.

> Even in the Hispanic community I sit at some meetings and I'm so identified as both a social worker and a woman that I think that first I'm a social worker, then a woman, and then Hispanic. When the meeting has mainly men I get a headache because they are very patriarchal and they try to tell us what to do. I dislike that very much, even though that's part of my own culture.

Many people of color perceive that the burden is on them to adapt to the dominant culture. This feeling was documented by Matts (1995), who interviewed supervisees of color who had Caucasian supervisors. Nearly all the participants reported that they worked quite hard, without the active participation of their supervisors, to learn and adapt to their supervisor's culture. This difficulty may be partly a result of sheer numbers. Usually those in the majority in any group have more impact on the group's norms and values. In addition, they often are unaware or fail to acknowledge the experience of those in the minority. Debra, who made the last comment, went on to say the following:

> It is even more of a challenge, though, to work in a mainstream agency. I worked in my hospital job for several years before I began to feel a part of it. The people that I work with are very professional with me, and yet working with people in the majority culture is very painful. I get so tired trying to learn how to relate. Most people don't make the effort to try to move into someone else's reality. I feel that I don't really have a choice if

I'm going to survive here. I think that is also true of African Americans and American Indians. They have no choice either.

Her observation about the lack of choice was supported by Jaime, now a supervisor himself, who made the following statement.

I think that being a supervisee in a white system is basically easy. All you have do is learn what the rules are and the procedures. And you know already because you live in the white culture your whole life. Anyone who is bicultural in this society has to know the white rules. There is no way around them. None whatsoever. Anyone who chooses to be viable in the culture has to know that stuff and be competent in it. But the price of being competent is going against your own values.

Although, from Jaime's point of view, working in the white system is easy, for many that price is too big to pay. In fact, many find that if they deny important parts of themselves, they are less competent. Sara, an Hispanic supervisor, realized that her training in the dominant culture led her to behave in an unnatural and therefore ineffective manner. Only when she began to behave in a fashion that was more congruent with her heritage and cultural identity did she feel truly comfortable and empowered as a supervisor. Ron, an African American supervisor, made a similar observation.

For me to be effective, I've learned I need to bring who I am as a black man into the room. The reason I wear an earring now is that on my 35th birthday I said, "I'm not going to try to fit in any more." Over the past 10 years, I have been trying to fit into the system and it's not working. For me to be powerful and effective, I need to be myself. I will value your difference, and you need to value mine.

One way I do this is to tell stories, so that people can see my values and see how I see things and how I was raised. People asked me about my energy because I kept staying late to work on a project. I told them my story about my Uncle Billy. I always wanted to be like him. He raised seventeen kids, worked in the post office, and also was a minister. There would always be a lot of energy at his house. When I married my wife, I told her I wanted seventeen kids. She told me I had to have the first seven.

Sometimes I talk black English. My English is not great because I'm black and my parents come from the rural south. I let the people at work see this part of me.

Both Sara and Ron found ways to bring themselves into their work in a way that allowed them to be more effective. It is indeed important for bicultural practitioners and supervisors to learn to operate in a manner that integrates both their own and the dominant culture. Jaime was accurate in his statement that one must become competent with "the white rules." However, in my opinion, supervisors can and should do a great deal more than Matts (1995) reported they currently do. The supervisor needs to encourage and facilitate an ongoing discussion about cultural differences and the impact of those differences both on the supervisory relationship and on the understanding of treatment. By keeping the discussion on the table, supervisors are able to help supervisees honor those differences within the context of the core values and goals of the profession.

Style

As Ron's story suggests, an important way he brings his identity as a black man into his work is through his style of dress (his earring) and his style of speech ("black English"). Adriana, an Hispanic supervisee, described a meeting with her colleagues in which they talked about their cultural styles. She saw a number of similarities between herself and her other colleagues of color, who were African American and Native American.

> We are not as formal as many Caucasians. And we have an understanding of family and extended family as well as other important people in one's life. If we are doing family therapy, we don't tell the next-door neighbor to go home now, or tell them to turn off the TV. That's because the next-door neighbor is watching it with you and because if they want them there, they are part of the family. The culture of verbalization, how we talk to each other, is similar. We sat one day with each other and talked about what happens when we are with our own people. The African Americans said, "Well, when we are all together, it is loud and people would describe it as emotional and crazy because we get loud and we interrupt each other and everyone is talking at the same time." Latinos have been known as emotional people also. This is somewhat different in the Native American people, as I understood it from that meeting. They are more quiet and listen to the person who is talking.

This quality of informality, according to Adriana, also extended to the manner in which written work is done and the way in which meetings are conducted. She noted that she had learned in graduate school to write in a more formal manner than was comfortable for her. She appreciated the fact that her supervisor, an African American woman, did not demand that of the staff, as long as the content was accurate and useful. In addition, she compared meetings in agencies that had primarily Caucasian staff with her more diverse agency. In the former, meetings tended to be task-oriented, quickly getting down to business. By contrast, the meetings in her current agency were characterized by an initial period of informal "chitchat" about driving their children to school, what they did for lunch, "getting to know each other and getting comfortable" before attending to the task at hand.

Key differences exist between cultural and ethnic groups regarding such behaviors as use of language, intensity of tone of voice, expression of emotions, and eye contact. One person's very natural behavior may be interpreted as offensive by another. Nancy, a Native American supervisee, interpreted her African American supervisor's more forceful style as critical and controlling. However, she acknowledged that this may well be her own interpretation and not what Nancy meant to communicate. Jon, a Caucasian supervisor, described his awareness of both his own style and that of his supervisees.

> I have worked with people from a variety of backgrounds. My Cambodian supervisee acts in a much less assertive way than some of the others. In response to that when I want to listen to him, I make a point of stopping and focusing on him during a meeting. I think some other people see that as favoritism on my part. I don't do that for people who are more vocal.
>
> I am a New York Jew, so by nature I'm more argumentative, and a lot of animated discussion with strongly stated points of view seems normal to me. I think my Cambodian supervisee would see that as pushy and not know that it's OK to push back. On the other hand, I have a few African American women who are verbal, say whatever is on their minds, and say it forcefully. I engage in more banter with them, and sometimes give them a hard time about things they are doing as a way of connecting.

It is difficult to determine Jon's success without speaking to his supervisees; but Jon was attempting to modify his own style and to meet those of his supervisees in a way that he believed would benefit his relationships with them. With less awareness, Jon could easily intimidate a supervisee whose approach was more hesitant than his own. It is interesting to note the group dynamics here. Jon was also concerned that his effort to be sensitive may be creating other problems, such as the perception that he was showing favoritism.

The use of direct versus indirect styles of communication appears to be a significant issue in many cross-cultural supervisory situations. Doris, a Caucasian, supervises Southeast Asian supervisees from Cambodia, Laos, and Vietnam. She notes definite differences between the characteristic styles in each of these cultures, such as her impression that the Vietnamese tended to be more assertive than the Hmong. However, she also observes that many of her workers from all three cultures communicate in what she describes as an indirect manner. Often she is not exactly sure what their concerns are or whether they experience her as helpful. She second-guesses her own reactions: "Am I being too bossy? Is my definition of bossy the same as theirs? Is my style too linear and Western?" Like Jon, Doris attempts to blend her understanding of herself and of her supervisees. In part because of the very difference she is attempting to bridge, she feels unsure of her ability to assess whether she is succeeding.

An interesting comment was made by Brenda, a Native American supervisee who had two supervisors, one Indian and one European (English). She observed that they all chose to speak to each other on the job in a direct manner, although that style was not particularly characteristic of any of their cultural groups. The direct style seemed more effective and efficient for that situation. This observation was echoed by Youa, a Hmong supervisee who defined professional behavior in part as the ability to communicate in a direct fashion. This may be an indication of those from minority cultures adapting to the dominant culture's definition of acceptable style. However, it is also quite possible that the nature of the work in an agency is such that direct communication simply works better. This may be particularly true in a cross-cultural situation, where the chance of misunderstanding is increased. Directness is an effective way to check out each other's interpretations and assumptions.

Although it is crucial to recognize and honor differences in style, it is equally necessary to distinguish between those behaviors that are simply stylistic and those that are inappropriate or ineffective. Jim, a Caucasian supervisor, offered the following account of his interaction with Wes, an African American supervisee, as an illustration of the difficulty of weighing style differences against issues of acceptable performance.

> He did a lot of good stuff. He did a parenting class really well and was excellent about paperwork. He talked openly about a previous negative relationship with a supervisor. I believed his story, and put all of the blame on the supervisor.
>
> When he got here, he would be angry at times and blow up at me. We all take turns working in the resource center, and sometimes he would blow up about doing this in front of other staff. I would deal directly with it: "I have a problem with your anger. It scares clients and staff." There was a woman on staff who really loved to do the resource program, and had put it into good working condition. I asked her to explain to him how the system works, as she had done for all of us.
>
> I let him know that I asked her to do this, and he said he wouldn't be supervised by a woman. In a staff meeting, she brought it up and he was rude to her. I took him aside and said she was acting under my orders and that I didn't care if he didn't like it, he was going to do it. He responded with "Absolutely not." There was a real issue of insubordination.
>
> I told him specifically what I liked about his work but that I couldn't pass him off probation until I saw improvement both in the way he handled his anger with colleagues, clients, and outside organizations and his attitude toward work required of him that he was not enthusiastic about doing. He stated that the problem was my lack of experience with dealing with a strong African American male who is comfortable with his aggressiveness and his anger.

It may be true that Jim was uncomfortable with Wes's aggressive style of expression and that he therefore interpreted as hostile or intimidating behavior Wes did not intend that way. However, whereas Wes saw Jim's discomfort as the central issue, Jim saw Wes's anger as causing major difficulties in his work. Because he evaluated the behavior as impeding his ability both to serve clients competently and to be a cooperative member of the staff, Jim set a very clear limit with Wes.

Use of Language

In addition to differences in communication styles, there are differences in the use of language. A supervisor who identified himself as Chicano stated that the Spanish language has both a formal and an informal use of the word *you;* therefore one's choice of formal or informal style has a significant impact on the tone of the interaction. It may either minimize or maximize the power differential between supervisor and supervisee. A supervisor who invites a Spanish-speaking supervisee to address him or her in the informal manner is giving the message that "You can treat me more as an equal." Addressing that same supervisee formally may also afford the supervisee more power in the relationship. By contrast, insisting that the supervisee use formal language may reinforce the hierarchical relationship between them.

An obvious but sometimes neglected issue related to use of language is the extent to which someone from another culture has command of the English language. Matts (1995) noted that many supervisees struggled to understand what was being asked of them. This struggle was exacerbated by the fact that they felt "dumb" and often believed that their supervisors either viewed them in a negative light or did not take the time to make sure they understood. On the other side of this coin is the mistaken assumption that someone who looks different will not understand English. This assumption can be insulting as well. Lien, a Vietnamese supervisee, told the following story.

> Our agency went to the use of computers, and I didn't know anything about them. I had to learn, so I took a class, but I was slow in understanding. I kept asking the teacher to repeat what he was saying. The teacher became very irritated and asked me whether I knew English. At this point in my life, I was a social worker—a senior social worker—and somebody asked me if I knew English. I felt really ridiculous, but instead of walking out and protesting, I just stayed and finished the class. It bothered me for a long time, though.

Fortunately, in this situation, Lien's supervisor was quite supportive of her and helped her go to the teacher and give him some feedback on the impact of his question. Left to her own devices, she said, she would not have pursued the matter. This incident raises the issue of whether supervisees and supervisors feel free to talk to one another about questions pertaining to cultural or racial differences. Unfortunately, often either one or both participants are reluctant to address these questions, perhaps out of fear or perhaps out of ignorance (Matts, 1995).

Approaches to Treatment

As previously discussed, we arrive at our sense of what is helpful through our particular personal and professional experiences. Clearly, the cultural backgrounds of both supervisor and supervisee have an enormous impact on each of their views about treatment. It is equally clear that the cultural background of the clients being served influences what they experience as helpful.

This cultural influence is particularly important to recognize in light of the fact that many theoretical approaches to therapy and counseling are grounded in Euro-American culture, and each of those approaches is grounded in a particular historical and cultural context. The worldviews behind these theories carry certain core assumptions, such as the importance of individualism; the value of rational empiricism and linear, cause-and-effect thinking; the requirement of openness and self-disclosure as a prerequisite for effective treatment; and the notion that the process of counseling is most useful for those who are articulate, assertive, and able to identify and express their feelings (Sue et al., 1996). Therefore, especially when working with clients and supervisees whose cultural backgrounds are not Euro-American, it is important to challenge these core assumptions with questions about their applicability.

In the story that opened this chapter, Liz made her best attempt to decide what was in the child's best interests. At the base of the decision was her own value that the child's interests must be served above all else and that the child's safety must be ensured. Although it is often difficult, even when all parties are of the same culture, to make a clear assessment about a child's safety, Liz made her decision based on her best guess about what would protect the girl from harm.

Apart from the bottom-line question of the child's safety, one's definition of what constitutes best interests is culturally determined. Primary attention to the child's best interests may not be shared by someone from a cultural group that considers the well-being of the family or community to be more important than that of any individual. Furthermore, it is highly possible that someone could view Liz's action as one that gave the child too much power and was therefore actually detrimental to the child. Liz was not able to assure herself that the child was being helped appropriately, particularly in the context of the Hmong culture in which the child lived.

Treatment approaches is an arena in which one often has to juxtapose the values and norms of the dominant culture with those of the client's culture. Within the framework of the core values of the profession, there are many culturally sensitive options available to the practitioner. It is the supervisor's job to help the supervisee arrive at and exercise those options. Doris, who struggled with the indirect communication styles of her Southeast Asian supervisees, also observed that they were unlikely to express feelings of any kind to one another in the manner that was familiar to her. These stylistic tendencies had an impact on their approach to and definition of family therapy.

> If a Hmong father is referred to us, he is visited. If the workers find out there are marital problems, another worker will talk to the mother, and perhaps a third person will talk to the children. It is rare that they would all get together and talk. That is more the Western way.

Doris described her struggle with her own Western values; not only do people have to talk to one another, but it is also important to verbally express caring. She worked to blend this value with her growing understanding of what is valued and effective in these families.

> I'm walking a very fine line all of the time. I can't stop trying to get people to tell each other they mean something to each other. It's the basis of everything I believe in. I find myself couching my words, like, "I know you don't like to talk about this, but I have to tell you that right now I can see that you love him more than anything in the world." I try to throw in a little Western culture. I'm changing my own style as well. I've noticed that my supervisees are much more directive with their clients than I would normally be. They say things like, "You have to be nicer to your husband. It's the wife's job to smile." I find myself telling the kids, "You have to have respect for your parents, you know."

Doris is an example of a supervisor who is learning, from both her supervisees and the agency clientele, what constitutes effective treatment in their eyes. Her statement demonstrates her effort to blend her values with theirs. It also demonstrates her understanding that, although family therapy might look different from what she is used to, it is just as powerful when practiced in a manner that is more fitting for the clients.

In another example, Sara, a Latina supervisor, viewed spending "unproductive" time with clients as an integral part of the work. In her culture, the development of relationship is paramount, and the way to accomplish this is to simply be with clients and talk about many things—such as children, family, cooking, and weekend activities—before getting to the task at hand. She found this process difficult to teach to Caucasian supervisees, who wanted to approach clients in a linear, task-oriented fashion. In addition, she needed to help her supervisees negotiate with managed care companies, who demand documentation of work as related to specific treatment goals.

Pheng, a Hmong supervisee, described a dilemma in his agency, which had a very strict rule about serving only those who lived in a particular area. In addition, clients were expected to make appointments for service. This requirement created several problems. The concept of a calendar is foreign to the Hmong people, whose culture is very present-oriented and has only recently adopted much widespread use of the written word. Therefore people expect to receive help the day they ask for it. In addition, in the Hmong culture, face-to-face contact is greatly valued. People would assume they would not be well attended to if they called by telephone rather than coming in person. Finally, the Hmong live in very small communities rather than in large cities. Someone in need of help will be noticed and helped by the community. The Hmong therefore have little sense of a large system geared at serving large numbers of anonymous people. Pheng's concern was that if he turned away people who simply arrived at the agency for service, they would experience great rejection and would not return for further help. He was able to convince his supervisor to bend the rules a bit, so that people could be served first and then could have some time to learn the rules of the system.

In this next example, Diane, an African American supervisee, did not get the support from her supervisor to do her job the way she believed she needed to in order to be effective.

> I was hired to do outreach to African Americans. To be effective I needed to visit other community agencies. I knew if they didn't know me, didn't have a personal connection with our agency, they wouldn't refer clients. But my supervisor objected to my being "away from my job" too much. She acted as if I were visiting friends or something, rather than doing my job.
>
> Once I was able to convince her to let me go into the community, I wanted to do an open house. I was really particular about how our agency would look. I brought in flowers from home, baskets for literature and snacks; because in our community when you invite someone in, if you don't have the place looking right, they think you think less of them. If I didn't make an effort, that would be obvious to them and would reflect poorly on me and on the agency. I knew it was important. My supervisor's reaction was to be sarcastic, and call me a neatnick. When I talked to her about it, she said she didn't mean it that way, but she would say things like that to me all the time.

In this situation, the supervisor failed to honor what seems clearly to be both a question of style and a question of what constitutes effective service. Diane's approach was grounded in her knowledge of what was needed to gain credibility and trust with the African Americans in the community. Rather than facilitate Diane's effort, the supervisor stood in her way. Diane had to fight her supervisor and tolerate sarcastic and insensitive comments in order to perform her job effectively. In addition, when Diane tried to bring the issue to the table, the supervisor dismissed it rather than attempting to reach a deeper understanding of the differences between them.

Tom, a Caucasian supervisor in an agency that serves unemployed fathers, also was at odds with his supervisees' approach. Many of the clients and staff members were African American.

> We don't do a lot of job development for our clients until they are ready to look for their second or third job. Normally they have to start low on the ladder to begin to develop work habits and start dealing with multicultural issues that come up in the workplace. They can do that in a lot of warehouse, factory, and temporary situations. They need to have a hands-on learning experience, and that is where the case manager can help coach them and be available. Once they see the financial rewards, they are better risks in terms of going to school or job training. That is related to cultural poverty rather than to race issues.

> Many of the African American male staff members don't have confidence in their clients or in themselves or in the system. There is a feeling of empowerment and advocacy that I see lacking in the black male staff. They don't work as hard to advocate for their clients in terms of making referrals, going with people to first job sessions to facilitate, lending their competence to clients to help them feel a sense of their own effectiveness.

> Our philosophy is that we have to work from the bottom up, in terms of empowering clients, as well as from the top down, in terms of influencing companies to provide job opportunities for our clients. These particular workers seemed to want only to push for affirmative action measures in the companies that collaborated with us, without working with the clients to help them function effectively on the job.

> When I was in my 20s and worked with African American families, what was emphasized was personal responsibility. They didn't want any white worker coming in and enabling their kids or feeling sorry for them. I came to this agency with that attitude and found an attitude of blame toward society and excusing the client. I think this is unfair to clients because it doesn't hold them accountable.

In contrast to Diane's supervisor, Tom's response to his supervisees was, in my opinion, based on a valid concern about whether the clients were being served well. Tom viewed his workers' attitude of blame and hopelessness as an impediment to their ability to work effectively. Recall the concept of destructive entitlement discussed in Chapter 2.

From Tom's description, his supervisees appear to assume that the world owes both them and their clients something and that they have no responsibility to take action on their own behalf. Perhaps Tom's supervisees would take the position that Tom is prone to blaming the victim and acknowledges neither the role of larger society in causing the problem nor society's obligation to contribute to curing the problem.

Another supervisor might interpret Tom's supervisees' actions in a completely different light, seeing them as trying to provide the support they needed by putting pressure on organizations to provide affirmative action job opportunities. Lorraine, also a Caucasian supervisor, observed that many of her African American supervisees tended to want to give their clients food, clothing, and other necessary items. She attributed this desire to a cultural value that states that you help someone in need by giving them what you can. Her own value, which she taught her supervisees, is one of empowering people to help themselves. It is important to note, however, that although Lorraine attributed her supervisees' actions to a different concept of help and Tom attributed his supervisees' actions to a feeling of hopelessness, both supervisors operated from a core value of personal responsibility and hoped to teach their supervisees to do the same.

Anger

A significant issue in cross-cultural supervision relates to the deep feeling of anger characteristic of many people who have been oppressed for generations. This feeling is experienced by both many practitioners and many clients of color. How this is approached and how it is interpreted varies significantly among practitioners and supervisors. Sam, a Caucasian supervisee with a Latina supervisor, characterized himself as someone who was task-oriented and reluctant to take the time to allow his clients to express their feelings, particularly those of anger and mistrust. He explained his reluctance in part by his upbringing as a Caucasian male, many of whom are taught to value thinking over feeling. He also had difficulty identifying with the strength of his clients' feelings. His supervisor talked with him at length about the deep level of his clients' feelings and the cultural history behind them. Sam began to understand the source of their pain and that the opportunity to express that pain and to be emphatically heard was an important aspect of the recovery process. Until this understanding occurred, his clients could not move on to accomplish the tasks at hand. With the aid of his supervisor, Sam's ability to help his clients grow improved.

Nancy, an African American supervisee, spoke about her work with many clients of color—African American and Hispanic as well as Native American. She discovered a theme of deep anger and mistrust due to generations of oppression as well as experiences in their own lives. In contrast to Sam, Nancy, because of her personal experience with oppression, was able not only to understand the anger but also to tolerate its intensity and to stay present for her clients while they expressed it. As a result, she had enormous success with clients whom others had considered untreatable.

> One of my clients, a Native American man, had enormous anger. He came one day and raged. He said awful things, screamed, called people names. He told me he had never said such things before. It was scary for me, but I just stayed with him. I could relate to his anger, and I didn't take it on as being about me in some way. He came in after that and said things were much better. He had never felt safe like that before. Since then he has changed a lot. Before this he saw himself only as a victim. Now his goal is to go to college. Being a good father is very important to him, and he wants to teach other Native American men about fathering and about not being a victim. I find that after I can stay with the pain, my clients' trust is higher. Then I can challenge their belief systems and help them become more functional and productive.

To be effective, Nancy needed to give her clients room to come to sessions sporadically and to miss many scheduled appointments. Her observation was that, until they could see some real value in the treatment, they would not make it a priority to overcome obstacles such as lack of transportation and child care and the enormous effort it takes simply to survive. Once Nancy was able to gain their trust, clients came regularly. Although she was able to document her success, she often received feedback from her supervisor that she was not performing adequately. She did not get the raises others received, and the reason offered was that her statistics were low. Low statistics are a result of having clients who fail to keep appointments. In addition, Nancy was questioned about the validity of seeing her clients on a more long-term basis, although from her point of view, it was necessary in order to gain hard-earned trust. In this situation, the supervisor appeared to be judging Nancy's work by external standards that were not clearly relevant to the treatment needs of this population.

The example of Tom and his supervisees, discussed above, can also be explored in light of the question of anger. Tom's supervisees tended to blame society for the problems their clients experienced, rather than holding them accountable for their own behavior. This blame, no doubt, emerged from the same very understandable and legitimate feelings of anger Nancy and Sam described. However, unlike Nancy and Sam, Tom's supervisees related to their own and their clients' anger in a manner that seemed to reinforce powerlessness and hopelessness rather than productivity and growth.

Establishing Professional Boundaries

As stated earlier, the very notion of counseling or mental health treatment is primarily a Western, Euro-American idea. Therefore the guidelines for what constitutes professional behavior are grounded in North American and European values. In Laos, for example, there is no such thing as the profession of social work, either in the narrow sense of counseling or in the broader sense of intervention on a macro level. Many supervisors and supervisees of color speak about challenging the dominant cultural norm for appropriate boundaries, stating that it does not fit or work either for them or for clients of color. Rebecca, an Hispanic supervisor, made the following statement.

> I try to minimize the boundaries between me and my workers. I make it a point just to go and sit with them and talk about whatever they are talking about. I make a point not to keep myself separated. We go to lunch a lot together. We celebrate special occasions together. We try to go to one of each other's homes periodically so we can get to know one another better in our own settings.
>
> I went to several supervision conferences where the clear message was, "You don't do that." You don't invite a staff person to lunch or to your house. You don't become his or her friend, because that is a boundary violation. At first I thought that was true, but I don't think so any more.
>
> It wasn't natural to me to keep myself separated from people I work with. It didn't feel good. It didn't make me feel any more connected if we had a difficult case to talk about and I had to empathize with them. It doesn't feel right to empathize for fifteen minutes. As I went to more conferences where diversity was talked about, people of color were coming together and saying, "Wait a minute. That doesn't fit because we didn't grow up that way. We are not like that. It's not our way of doing things." Or someone would be brave enough to say, "I don't do that and nothing horrible has happened to me." It gave the rest of us courage to do things in a way that works better for us, even if it goes against the norm.

This same idea was expressed by Joe, an African American supervisee who commented that "when you work with people of color, the boundaries are different." This applies both to sharing more personal information than he would with many Caucasian clients and to actions he might take with clients, such as spending time in their homes, chatting, and helping with household chores. Although he is experimenting with how this could work, he feels unable to talk about it with his Caucasian supervisor, who Joe thinks will not understand the merit in or the rationale behind what he is doing.

Indeed, some Caucasian supervisors do express concern over what they consider poor boundaries on the part of their supervisees. Glenda described the following situation with a Cambodian supervisee.

She didn't have any background on professional methods, behavior, or her role going into a family. We found out that she was assisting a lot of her relatives. Soon we realized that the majority of her caseload consisted of relatives. The community perceived that she was there only to help those who were related to her. It was an accessibility issue for us. Secondly, it was a boundary issue. She was getting paid for something that was her role in the family, and she was personally unable to be objective. Her uncles were coming in and demanding that she help them in her role as a woman in the family setting. It was difficult for her to understand why this was hard for the agency.

These examples again call into question the distinction between a conflict in shared meaning and a need for limit setting. The important factor is not whether those from other cultures establish boundaries that resemble what is typically recommended. Boundaries are created to keep the professional and the client, as well as the supervisor and the supervisee, clear about the purpose of the relationship. Boundaries function to contain the power of the professional or supervisor so that it is used only to attend to the needs of the client or supervisee (Peterson, 1992). To develop and maintain effective boundaries and help their supervisees do the same, supervisors must understand both the cultural context of supervisees and their clients and the function of boundaries, rather than specific rules about how to establish them (Peterson, personal communication, 1995).

If a supervisor like Rebecca or a practitioner like Joe identifies the need to make more personal connections with their supervisees or clients in order to do effective work, then they should do so. At the same time, however, they must remember to maintain clarity about the impact of the power differential in the relationship. Rebecca, for example, needs to remember that while she works to minimize the boundaries between herself and her workers, she still has the responsibility to hold them accountable. The impact on her relationship with her supervisees of her power to evaluate will not evaporate in the social situation.

Glenda's concern was that her supervisee had lost sight of the difference between herself and her clients created by her role as professional. As a result, her ability to serve them in a competent manner was compromised. She was denying service to clients in the community who were not in her family, and she was unable to help her family members in an objective and fair manner.

Importance of Understanding the Culture

As we saw in the discussions of approach to clients and biculturalism, supervisees benefit from help in blending their own cultural backgrounds with that of their clients as well as with that of their supervisors. Donna, a Native American supervisee, spoke about the help she received from her supervisor, Mike. He would help her think through how, as a Native American, she would work with a Vietnamese family, for example. She was able to identify both the assumptions she might bring to the work and what she might need to know to be more effective. She could compare, for example, the way she was raised to value and discipline children with the way in which her clients would do so, and she could talk about how she might constructively work with differences between herself and her clients. She found Mike's approach more helpful than Lew's. Lew seemed to want to compare each of their cultural backgrounds in a more theoretical way. Lew avoided connections to Donna's personal experience as well as to Donna's actual clients.

Marie Jose, a Latina supervisee, has a Caucasian supervisor whom she considers an excellent clinician who is effective at helping her work with the interface between her background and her work. However, although she considers this supervision extremely useful, she would find it even more so if her supervisor understood more about her own culture. A similar sentiment was expressed by Sophia, a Cambodian supervisee whose Caucasian supervisor had years of experience as a social worker in a mainstream agency and knew little about Southeast Asian cultures. Sophia was struck by the number of times her supervisor would make a general statement about Southeast Asians or be unable to distinguish between Laotian, Cambodian, and Vietnamese customs and values. She could understand this failing because she herself would have difficulty distinguishing among Caucasians from German, Danish, or French backgrounds. However, the supervisor's lack of more refined knowledge lessened the value of her feedback. It may also have contributed to Sophia's sense of being discounted by her supervisor, in that the inability to distinguish carried a subtle message of "you're all alike."

On the other hand, it is important that clinicians and supervisors avoid the assumption that people whose cultural backgrounds are different from one's own do not have similar human concerns and needs (Pederson, 1991; Fouad, 1995). Tanya, an African American supervisee, gave the following account.

> One time I was telling my supervisor about a child who came from a family in which the dynamics were very abusive. The child was 12 years old and pregnant. My supervisor said to me, "Well, she must be in the life." I asked her what she meant by that, and she said, "Drugs and prostitution." When I asked her where she got that from, her reply was, "She's African American, she's 12, and she's pregnant." I told her it was the dynamics in the family—not being loved—that led her to getting pregnant.

Tanya's point was simply that this child, like any other, needs a loving and supportive family. Her supervisor would not necessarily assume that a Caucasian 12-year-old who was pregnant was also on drugs or into prostitution; rather, she would assume that the girl's family had not provided her with the care she needed.

One way to address the question of the importance of understanding another's culture is to recognize that the experience and communication of empathy is a profound way to create shared meaning. That is, people feel understood by those who fully feel and communicate empathy for them. I believe there are three types of empathy, all of which are equally valuable. The first type comes from being an insider, giving us the ability to know about another's experience because of our own, very similar one. People in the same cultural group, or people in groups who have a great deal of commonality with one another, can share this type of empathy. The second type of empathy comes from being an outsider who is able to feel the human experience of another person. By listening carefully to someone, we can come to understand both cognitively and emotionally what the other person might be experiencing. This kind of empathy can be shared between any two human beings who are deeply sensitive to one another. The third type of empathy comes from the accumulation of knowledge gained through the first two types. We can listen intently to many people who have had a similar experience, whether it be dealing with incest, depression, childbirth, parenting, growing up African American in New Orleans, or immigrating from Laos. In time, we begin to understand aspects of that experience in a more general way. That is, we can begin to make some intuitive guesses about how the person in front of us might be responding. That person can perceive our communication of this understanding as empathy. For all three types of empathy, two things must occur: (1) We must feel and share the empathic response, and (2) we must pay attention to whether our response is indeed an accurate reflection of the particular individual with whom we are talking.

As was mentioned in Chapter 2, valuable knowledge on the part of the supervisor is an essential ingredient in effective supervision. This unarguable fact is complicated by the reality that what may be ideal is often also unrealistic. The increase of diversity both in agencies and in clientele is a relatively recent phenomenon. Many supervisors and supervisees lack the experience and skills necessary to communicate the third type of empathy in cross-cultural supervisory relationships. An authentic dialogue and mutual education process appears to be the most useful way to gain those skills. Paul, a Caucasian supervisee who worked in an agency with a very diverse staff, described a model for this process. Paul's African American supervisor suggested a format whereby staff members shared their own cultural history and experiences with one another. This sharing provided all practitioners with both a knowledge base and an environment of safety from which they could begin to learn from one another.

Chau (1990) suggested that society needs to move to a position of cultural pluralism instead of maintaining the current common stance that the dominant culture is superior. Although this seems to be the obvious and most effective direction to take, the actual achievement of authentic cultural pluralism requires a challenge to values so deep and dear that many are reluctant to attempt it. And, indeed, one may ask whether to operate under an assumption that all approaches are equally viable is in fact practical. We come back again to the overlap between shared meaning and limit setting, balancing the need to understand, affirm, and promote differences with the need to define—to the best of our ability—the parameters of competent service to clients.

I had the good fortune of being able to speak to Liz, whose story opened this chapter, almost 2 years after our initial contact. She stated that she had grown immensely in the past 2 years and was feeling much more comfortable with the task of cross-cultural supervision. She made the following comment:

> I had to go through the pain of the difference between us before I could recognize the similarities. For a while, I didn't know if I knew anything. It shook me up totally. I was a jumble of raw, inadequate feelings. After I learned more about their customs and how to do things, I got my own self-esteem back. After that, the differentness was more of a plus than a threat.

Liz described herself as a "fuller person," more deeply aware and appreciative of the different possibilities for doing and being. At the same time, she was more grounded in her own professional values, recognizing both her need and her right to stand behind them. Faced with the same dilemma today, she would take longer to make her decision, discussing all sides of the issue and working harder to understand and be understood by all participants. Although the final decision would probably be quite similar to the one she had made originally, her process would be one that was more fully informed by the cultural contexts of her supervisee and the clients.

DEFINITION OF RACISM

An important area to address is how one defines racism. As discussed in Chapter 2, it is often difficult to determine whether a particular action taken by a supervisor or a supervisee has an underlying element of racism. In Chapter 2, we saw an example of a supervisee receiving lower evaluations than he thought he deserved without what he considered a reasonable explanation. Another supervisee was assigned fewer clients than were other comparable workers and sensed that she was being treated as less competent than she actually was because of her race. Many supervisees and supervisors of color have spoken about the need to "prove" themselves more than have their Caucasian counterparts. Although these actions were interpreted as racist by the supervisees, in all probability the supervisors and agency administrators in these stories would not agree with this interpretation.

Part of the difficulty stems from the fact that a lot of racism is subtly expressed, and many people do not either recognize or acknowledge the possibility that racism may be influencing their reactions or behaviors. Part of the difficulty also arises because of a lack of shared meaning regarding what constitutes racism. Holly, a Caucasian supervisor, recounted an interaction she had with Gloria, an African American supervisee.

> I work on the floor a lot, putting my papers in piles in order to keep them organized. I was teaching an African American woman about the paperwork connected to our program, and I was throwing it out on the floor. She took that as an insult. In her mind that meant that I was treating her as low. She felt that by throwing papers on the floor, I was treating her like a slave. I have trouble sometimes sorting out what is a racial issue from what is a power issue.

As Holly mentioned here, it can be difficult to distinguish between race and other issues. A white worker might also have taken offense to her behavior; another African American might not have minded it. Holly sensed that Gloria had other emotional difficulties that influenced the way she interpreted and responded to things. Therefore she suspected that Gloria would be more likely to interpret an insignificant gesture as demeaning. Her experience with Gloria, furthermore, indicated that Gloria tended to label actions as racist instead of considering other possible interpretations. Holly has many other African American supervisees, including Marianna, whom she regards as a highly competent employee. Holly trusts Marianna to make sound and thoughtful judgments. If Marianna were to consider an action racist, Holly would believe her, because Marianna's interpretations of others are rarely clouded by her own personal difficulties.

Emma, an African American supervisee, makes the important point that although she assumes that race may be a factor in almost any interaction, this does not mean she assumes that the participants are racist. Rather, her belief is that people must be willing to identify and discuss race as a part of understanding what is occurring, but many people are hesitant to do so. She defines this reluctance itself as racist because it creates a situation in which important issues are avoided *because* of someone's race. Emma described an example of a black coworker who was not performing well. People talked about it to one another, but no one—including the supervisor—addressed the worker directly. Emma thought that by avoiding the problem, the supervisor was setting the worker up for failure, because the worker had no opportunity to learn of her problems and try to improve. Furthermore, if the supervisor could not demonstrate that he had tried to work with his supervisee, he could not defend himself from an accusation of racism by the worker in the future, should he decide to set limits with her later.

One of the variables that defines an attitude or action as racist is the attendant belief that one racial group is inherently superior to another. Even if unintentional, a lack of awareness and certainly a lack of interest in those who are different from oneself can communicate a message that the "other" is not valuable enough to be noticed. I mentioned earlier that many practitioners of color feel called upon to adapt to the values and norms of the dominant culture. Although there is practical value in that adaptation, when it is one-way, it may well be experienced as racism.

This is a particularly thorny problem because it naturally carries enormous emotional charge. People who feel mistreated because of racism and people who feel unjustly accused of being racist both have strong responses to these experiences, which then create deep mistrust. In my opinion it is not useful to assume that because someone defines an action as racist, it is; nor is it useful to assume that because someone's behavior is not consciously intended to be racist, it isn't. Webster's dictionary defines racism in the following manner:

> 1: a doctrine, or teaching, without scientific support that claims to find racial differences in character, intelligence, etc., that asserts the superiority of one race over another or others, and that seeks to maintain the supposed purity of a race or the races.
> 2: any program or practice of racial discrimination, segregation, etc., based on such beliefs. (Neufeldt & Guralnik, 1988, p. 1106)

This definition serves as a useful guideline for deciding whether racism is occurring. However, the definition also requires that we closely and honestly examine ourselves to determine whether those beliefs are operating. I agree with Emma's statement that in cross-cultural relationships where there are racial differences, there is probably always an element of race that deserves attention. To not address this element increases the danger that particular actions or attitudes will be interpreted as racist whether they really are or not. As I have stated previously, probably the most important ingredient in cross-cultural supervision is the creation of an ongoing and authentic conversation about the differences between supervisor and supervisee. This does not imply that the participants need to be focused solely on this issue; rather, the discussion can happen in a natural way when appropriate. Because of the sensitivity of the issues involved, this discussion often does not occur. In the next chapter, on trust, we will explore this dynamic as well as the creation of an environment that encourages the dialogue.

SUMMARY

The concept of shared meaning in supervision relates to a mutual understanding and, ideally, a mutual agreement in two primary arenas. The first arena is the contract, which delineates what will happen in supervision. Although contracting is a mutual process, it is important to remember that ultimately the supervisor has the power to set expectations for the supervisee's performance. Issues to be covered in the contract include the structure of supervisory sessions, expectations of the supervisee, standards for evaluation, types of information that will be shared in supervision and how that information will be used, and the focus of a particular session.

The second major issue that requires shared meaning is that of approaches to treatment. Sometimes it is quite useful for supervisees to be challenged to learn new ideas, even if those ideas contradict previous learning. Sometimes supervisees need more depth in the approaches with which they are familiar. In either case, the most effective approach is for the participants to have a basic agreement regarding what is helpful to clients. A lack of compatibility in this area can cause tension in the relationship and has implications related to the power dynamics discussed in the previous two chapters. If supervisees don't value their supervisor's approach, they will be less open to becoming learners. In addition, when there is a conflict about approach, the supervisor must determine whether the conflict reflects simply a difference in philosophy or whether there is cause for concern about the quality of the supervisee's practice.

The context has an impact on both contract and approach to treatment. The philosophy of treatment espoused by the organization is generally connected to the population being served. Another significant contextual influence is that of funding sources, which often dictate types and length of treatment. Part of the supervisor's job is to mediate between the demands of the agency and the beliefs of the staff regarding effective treatment. The context influences contracting regarding the nature of the supervisee's job and standards for evaluation. It may also influence the degree of availability of the supervisor.

Many of the challenges in cross-cultural supervision can be defined as issues pertaining to shared meaning. Arriving at a mutual understanding requires clear communication. In addition, our beliefs about what is helpful to clients are formed by our particular backgrounds, values, and experiences. Although the complexities of this process occur in any relationship, supervisors and supervisees from very diverse backgrounds are more likely to encounter barriers to understanding and agreement than are those whose backgrounds are similar.

There are a number of important issues to consider in cross-cultural supervision. People from a minority culture living in the dominant culture are dealing with issues related to biculturalism. Understanding supervisees' relationships to these issues is valuable for helping them work with clients. There are enormous differences in style of communication, dress, tone of voice, formality, and so on, among cultural groups that can potentially lead to misunderstanding and mistrust. Awareness of the differences and of one's own impact helps mitigate against unintentional hurt or insult.

One's ideas about what constitutes effective treatment is greatly affected by one's personal and professional experiences. The cultural background of the clients being served also influences decision making in this area. A challenge in cross-cultural supervision is to blend the values and norms of all the cultures involved. Determining whether a conflict regarding treatment is a shared meaning or a limit-setting issue becomes increasingly complicated in cross-cultural situations. The more supervisors and supervisees understand about one another's cultures, the more effectively they can negotiate this terrain. However, this is not an easy task, given the rapidly rising degree of diversity among both staff and clientele.

Finally, a sensitive and important issue in cross-cultural supervision is that of defining racism. Part of the challenge is arriving at a shared meaning regarding what actually constitutes racist actions and attitudes. Like so many of the dynamics between supervisor and supervisee, this definition often appears to depend on "the eye of the beholder." Probably the most effective way to handle this issue and other issues pertaining to shared meaning is to closely examine one's own attitudes and to discuss them, in an authentic manner, in the relationship. The next chapter will focus on the creation of a trusting environment in which this can occur.

QUESTIONS TO PROMOTE CRITICAL THINKING

1. A supervisee is hired with the understanding that part of her job entails supervising all foster home placements. Among those who do foster home placements is her own supervisor, who likes to keep a finger in direct practice in order to be more sensitive to staff concerns. Discuss this arrangement in terms of the principles of contracting. What kinds of expectations need to be clarified for this arrangement to work effectively? What are the connections here between power issues and those of shared meaning?

2. A supervisee who is a lesbian believes it is important for her clients to know her sexual preference. Her supervisor is not comfortable with this practice. What are the possible factors that contribute to their differences? Develop arguments for this situation as a shared meaning question about philosophy and as a power issue about limit setting.

3. Using the story of Liz that opened this chapter, discuss your beliefs concerning questions about determining the child's best interests in this context. What other courses of action might Liz have taken, and what would be the implications of those choices?

4. Using the examples of Ron, Adriana, Jon, Doris, and Wes (pp. 109–113), discuss guidelines you would use for distinguishing between stylistic differences and inappropriate behavior. Talk about your own style with regard to your impact on others. Describe a situation you have encountered in which you interacted with someone whose style was different from yours and was difficult for you to handle. How did you interpret their actions, and what did you do in the situation?

5. Imagine Doris's (pp. 111 and 115) response to a Caucasian supervisee in a family practice agency who is reluctant to meet with family members together, believing that each individual will not be able to talk freely about the problems. What variables should Doris take into consideration? How does the cultural issue affect her response? Is she in danger of missing something important, in either scenario, by making allowances for cultural differences?

6. Create a scenario in which Tom (p. 117) talks with his supervisees about his concerns. What does he gain and what does he lose by discussing the issue in light of the concepts of destructive entitlement and personal responsibility? What other approach might he take? What kinds of responses is he likely to receive from his supervisees, and how can he best address those responses?

7. Describe your reaction to the approach to boundaries taken by Rebecca and Joe (p. 120). How do your cultural background and your professional training affect your responses?

8. Discuss the mechanisms by which you determine whether your own or others' attitudes and behaviors are colored by racism.

Chapter Five

Trust

Marilyn had been working for about 3 years in a mental health clinic that served a variety of individuals, families, and couples, and she had a good relationship with George, her supervisor. At that point, George was promoted and the job of supervisor became available. Among those who applied was Tim, a colleague of Marilyn's. Marilyn had mixed feelings about Tim. She vacillated between feeling close to him and impressed by his enormous capacity for insight, to feeling uncomfortable with what she experienced as intrusiveness and a lack of professional boundaries in their relationship. She was somewhat concerned, as well, that he seemed to encourage excessive dependency in his female clients. In spite of the fact that she expressed her concerns to George, Tim was hired for the position. Marilyn felt betrayed by George and fearful of potential problems in her relationship with Tim as her new supervisor.

At the beginning, things seemed to be working out. Although Tim had some weaknesses as an administrative supervisor, he enjoyed clinical supervision. He was well versed in a psychodynamic approach to treatment, which led him to interpret interactions primarily in light of the dynamics of transference and countertransference. Marilyn's style as a supervisee had always been to share openly her concerns, questions, and vulnerabilities. She approached her work with Tim in the same manner. The combination of both Marilyn's and Tim's intense styles of interaction lead them quickly to the identification and exploration of Marilyn's personal issues.

Although Marilyn was an open and eager learner, she was young and had several unresolved issues in her own life. Most significantly, she was easily intimidated by her highly critical parents and was only beginning to notice and object to the disrespectful and critical attitude of her husband. She struggled with a lack of belief in her abilities and tended to emphasize her flaws. Although her work performance was more than adequate for someone with her level of experience, she had great difficulty viewing herself as a competent clinician.

In time, she began to experience Tim as critical of her as well. He seemed satisfied with her work in supervision only if she was talking about her doubts. He believed that this approach was superior to others in its focus. When Marilyn objected, Tim interpreted her objection as evoked by transference. Marilyn was left in a state of confusion. She believed that she should acknowledge personal problems that could interfere with her work and that she should represent herself honestly. Although she felt threatened by Tim's approach, she also recognized the kernel of truth in much of his feedback, and she believed that her defensive response derived partly from her resistance to acknowledging the accuracy of his observations. In addition, she knew she expected criticism from authority figures and from men, and therefore she could be projecting that expectation onto Tim. However, she suspected, but could not substantiate, that Tim was using the focus on her to avoid acknowledging his part in the escalating struggle between them.

After many months, Marilyn began talking to her peers about the problems she was having with Tim and discovered that they were also dissatisfied. They perceived Tim as using his position as administrative supervisor to make decisions about such things as support for outside training based on how he felt about the supervisee who was making the request. In clinical supervision, they experienced him as arrogant and disrespectful. Tim continued to see the problem as one that he did not create. He believed deeply in his approach to supervision and the validity of identifying issues related to transference and countertransference. He noted, for example, that there were strong gender and developmental dynamics at play. All the staff members, including Tim, were approximately the same age—late twenties to early thirties. All the practitioners except one were women. Several practitioners, including by this time Marilyn, were in the process of divorcing. Tim postulated that, as a single man, he was the object of much of their collective anger toward the men in their lives.

George met complaints by the staff with what the staff experienced as a defensive reaction; one that supported Tim and did not acknowledge his possible contribution to the difficulties. Although George shared his concerns privately with Tim, he wanted to avoid undermining Tim's authority as supervisor. In addition, he thought many of the staff's complaints were not accurate. A deep division between staff and administration began to develop, open communication virtually stopped, and secretive closed-door conversations increased. Eventually the tension became so great that an outside consultant was hired. The result of that process was a structural decision that Tim would no longer offer clinical supervision to the staff but would continue in his position as administrative supervisor. Staff members were free to seek outside consultation if they needed direction on their clinical practice, but Tim would still be responsible for evaluating them on their performance. Although this action reduced some of the difficulties, tensions and mistrust in the agency continued. The staff felt discounted because Tim was not more severely reprimanded and because he was now in the position of evaluating the staff's work without actually being exposed to it in the course of supervision. The administrators felt discounted because the staff did not appear to appreciate their efforts at resolution and continued to maintain an adversarial stance.

Marilyn proceeded to seek consultation, which led to an expansion in her skills and confidence. At the same time, she felt exhilarated by newly found freedom, both from her oppressive marriage and from the oppression of her relationship with Tim. Her anger toward and mistrust of Tim continued, however, and she began to treat him with open disrespect. In response to the fact that staff relationships were not improving, Tim and George decided to add a section to the yearly evaluation that included a ranking on the degree of effort each employee was putting into resolving the ongoing conflict. Marilyn was not surprised that her own "grade" in this area was low. However, she was dismayed by the fact that Tim singled her out as being the least cooperative staff member. She was even more devastated by the fact that he framed her new learning as a clinician as having harmed rather than improved the quality of her work. He believed that the psychodynamic approach was superior to others in its focus on unconscious motivations and its goal of deep structural change. Many other approaches, in his eyes, were superficial in nature and did not address underlying causes and cures for clients' problems. Although she acknowledged that she had been inappropriate in her treatment of him, she thought the criticism of her work was designed to punish her by undermining her confidence.

This story illustrates a strong connection between the dynamics of the power differential, the creation of shared meaning, and the development of trust in the supervisory relationship. Marilyn experienced Tim as abusing his supervisory power. Tim perceived Marilyn as projecting her other experiences with authority figures onto him and therefore as unable or unwilling to see or respond to him clearly.

The lack of shared meaning evident here is intricately connected to notions about the use of power and the development of trust. Marilyn did not disagree in principle with the psychodynamic approach to treatment or supervision. However, she did disagree with Tim's particular use of the approach because she thought he used it to justify excessive intrusiveness and to blame her and others for problems in the relationship. In addition, she identified his lack of support for the new approaches she brought to her work as a punitive power play rather than as a philosophical difference between them. Tim was quite committed to the psychodynamic approach and believed it was clearly the most effective way to get at deeper meanings and motivations for both supervisees and clients. He was genuinely concerned that Marilyn's move in other directions was a reflection of her reluctance both to face more challenging work with clients and to confront those personal issues that kept her from being the most effective worker she could be. Tim's concern about Marilyn's resistance was supported by her blatantly disrespectful treatment of him and her refusal to accept any of his input.

We also see in this story the influence of the larger context, the agency, on this struggle. George attempted to support his supervisee, Tim, while at the same time negotiating a reasonable compromise with the staff. From George's point of view, the staff was unwilling to appreciate this effort. The staff members saw George as biased toward Tim and unwilling to respond to their concerns. Marilyn received support from her peers, which both affirmed her own reality and fueled the intensity of her struggle with Tim. No doubt there was a great deal of truth in the perception of each of the participants involved. However, they had neither mutual understanding nor agreement on the problem or the solution. The result was a deepening mistrust between Marilyn and Tim.

The supervisory literature and individual supervisors and supervisees are quick to point out that a trusting relationship is essential for effective supervision. Often, however, the statement is made without further elaboration about what actually creates trust or mistrust. Given the intricate relationship, particularly between the dynamics of trust, shared meaning, and power, it is often difficult to sort out which is operating. Frequently two or three are operating simultaneously. In this chapter, I will attempt to single out those elements of the relationship that seem primarily related to the development of trust. The following issues will be addressed: the dynamics of shame, honesty, cross-cultural issues, and trust; the connection between context and the development of trust; and the communication of compassion.

DYNAMICS OF SHAME
IN SUPERVISION

Shame can be defined as an inner feeling of being diminished or insufficient as a person (Fossom & Mason, 1986). Individuals who feel shameful experience a sense of being exposed, and they judge themselves as personally inadequate. Because of the personal vulnerability inherent in clinical practice, supervisees are susceptible to feelings of shame (Berger & Dammann, 1982; Liddle & Schwartz, 1983; Alonso & Rutan, 1988; Jacobs, 1991). The question is not whether shame will surface in supervision. Rather, the question is whether it will be handled effectively. The assumption is that unless shame is adequately addressed, it will compromise the well-being of the supervisee (Alonso & Rutan, 1988). Although some supervisors believe any occurrence of shame is negative and should be avoided as much as possible, others believe that shame handled productively can potentially improve the supervisee's work with clients. There is no one correct way to approach a supervisee's shame because, as has been repeatedly illustrated, one must take into account the particular needs and styles of both supervisee and supervisor. However, there does appear to be a strong connection between how each experiences the treatment of this issue and whether the relationship is characterized as trusting.

Sources of Shame

Several factors can lead to a supervisee's feelings of shame. Among these factors are the vulnerability of being a novice, the impact of the intense pain presented by clients, and the impact of transference and countertransference phenomena on the supervisee (Alonso & Rutan, 1988). Both developmentally young and more professionally mature practitioners are susceptible to feelings of vulnerability, which can potentially lead to shame. Beginning supervisees often experience the "impostor syndrome," as they take on the role of clinician with little confidence that they know what they are supposed to do. No matter what the field, it is often difficult for an adult to be a beginner, and putting oneself in that position often evokes the sensation of feeling like a child again. This is probably related to a larger cultural myth that once one reaches adulthood, one has "arrived" at a place of permanent security and confidence. In addition, when cast in the role of professional and of expert, it is easy to assume you are supposed to know the answers. As a result, new clinicians often feel as if they are misleading their clients, whom the clinicians believe expect and deserve better help than they can offer.

In addition to the typical self-doubt of the beginning supervisee, because of the complex and personal nature of the treatment process, all clinicians sometimes feel confused, stuck, or ashamed of something they have done with a client. In my earlier discussion of the ethical ideal (Noddings, 1984), I stated that any clinician could land in a position in which there seems no alternative but to compromise that ideal. This situation occurs in part because of the phenomena of transference and countertransference, which evoke strong reactions from both client and practitioner. All of us have had experiences such as getting too angry with a client, not setting a clear enough limit, avoiding a confrontation, disclosing too much personal information, or making a poor decision on a client's behalf. Depending on our tendency toward self-deprecation and on the degree of severity of our mistake, such actions may well result in our feeling shame.

A significant source of shame for many supervisees derives from the similarities between their life experiences and their clients'. Rosa, a Latina supervisee, told the following story.

Our agency has a whole department that deals with women and prostitution, and in my family one person was murdered in prostitution and
another has been missing for 20 years. I just found out recently that she
is alive. There is rampant alcoholism in my family as well. We get a lot
of referrals from this department, and I felt very uncomfortable about the
way people were talking about the clients. One day I just exploded and
started sobbing. I said that we were all talking about these people like
they were someone else, and they are like my family.

It is not unusual for practitioners to assume a "we/they" posture
with regard to clients. This posture is reinforced by the medical model
approach to treatment, which implies that clients are sick and come to
practitioners to be cured. It is also reinforced by the practitioner's
desire for self-protection from two major sources of discomfort. First,
when one faces intense personal pain on a daily basis, it begins to feel
necessary to steel oneself from being personally affected by its enormity. Second, it is inevitable that such pain will remind workers of
similar struggles in their own lives. As stated above, the role of expert
creates an expectation, for both practitioner and client, that the practitioner has some wisdom about life that the client wants to learn.
Although there is validity in this expectation, it does not imply that
practitioners have somehow solved all of life's problems and therefore
easily move through the dilemmas with which we are all faced. Rosa's
shame came both from her own feeling that her family is inadequate
and from her belief, reinforced by the attitude she perceived in her colleagues, that as a professional she should be apart from and superior
to her clients.

Rosa's analysis of her own shame included a racial element as well.
She is biracial and bicultural (Latina and Caucasian) and, as a child,
faced both subtle and blatant discrimination. In her opinion her father,
who is Mexican, had a great deal of pain about his family and his race.
He worked in factories that habitually laid off the Mexican workers
first, and he spent most of his life in poverty and in alcoholic shame
and rage. In reaction, Rosa denied the Mexican part of herself, which,
in part because of her current work, she is only now beginning to fully
acknowledge. That acknowledgment includes attention to both the
pain and the beauty of her heritage.

Avoiding Shame

As stated above, many supervisors believe that any feeling of shame
supervisees experience is negative because it reinforces their deficiencies and vulnerabilities rather than their strengths. Because others
believe that some shame, effectively handled, can in fact be useful,
they do not go out of their way to avoid its occurrence. However, this

does not mean they believe that supervisors should purposely shame supervisees. Therefore, many supervisors attempt to create an atmosphere that minimizes its occurrence and negative impact. Two effective mechanisms for accomplishing this are communicating a message of respect for the supervisee, and creating an environment of safety in which supervisees feel free to expose their work without fear of unduly harsh or unfair criticism. Mark, a supervisor in a large county agency, made strong connections among the need to create a safe and respectful atmosphere, his supervisees' willingness to tell their stories, and his ability to effectively perform the limit-setting function.

> Accountability in supervision is about helping people take responsibility for paying attention to their own competencies and to where they need to improve their competencies. It also has to do with being accountable for making ethical decisions about how cases are handled. I've given them guidelines for all of these things.
>
> In a way, it's a scary thing. Each of my staff has an average of 70 open cases. I supervise up to 12 people, which means I'm responsible for about a thousand cases. I can't possibly know what's going on in each of those cases in order to maintain full supervisory accountability for them.
>
> It's kind of a leap of faith. I try to promote openness and self-disclosure by paying attention directly to their abilities. My hope is that then if people have ethical concerns or need help with cases where they are stuck, they will feel safe to talk about it rather than covering it up.

Sasha, who has been a supervisor and a supervisee, elaborated on the creation and effect of a supervisory environment that is conducive to talking about one's work.

> I think the goal of supervision is to provide a safe environment for professionals to grow on many levels. It's a place to look at your relationship with clients, your philosophy of treatment, and your relationship to your own ghosts. Supervision is safe when you feel the support of someone who believes in you and in your work. This helps you to be willing to ask for assistance when you're stuck.
>
> It's easier to work with challenging clients when you have good supervision, because when you are with the client, you feel that you are not alone. I find when I have that kind of support I do better work, because I have a place to take it. When this is possible, the places where any of us can get stuck change dramatically, because you can look at your work, learn from it, and go back in and do something different.

Both examples illustrate the connection between respect and safety. Mark stated that he encourages his staff to be open with him by paying attention to their abilities. Sasha stated that when she has the support of people who believe in her work, she feels safe both to look at it more closely and to take risks in treatment. People usually feel freer to expose their vulnerabilities to those who communicate a fundamental belief in them.

Among the ways that supervisors can create a safe environment is to give overt permission to make mistakes. This has the effect of saying (1) it is expected, acceptable, and in fact important to make mistakes in order to learn; and (2) supervisees should talk about mistakes when they occur. The following statement, offered by Judy, a supervisor, illustrates this message.

> I think supervisors, particularly those who wear two hats like I do (administrative and clinical), can give a tacit message that "If you tell me where you're screwing up, it's going to show up in your evaluation." That means "Only tell me about what you are doing well." I think that's an unethical position for a supervisor to take.
>
> When I begin my work with people, I say, "How many mistakes will you be willing to allow yourself? One or two or ten or twelve? I believe the more mistakes you're willing to allow yourself, the more you're going to learn here."

Other supervisors might not overtly encourage mistakes but will still work to minimize the possibility that supervisees will feel shame when mistakes occur. Sidney tries to express the attitude that "Your mistake wasn't a big deal. It was unfortunate, but now what you need to do is try to recoup it." Myra gives feedback about mistakes almost as an afterthought as a way to minimize a possible shameful reaction. A possible disadvantage of this approach is the unintended message that mistakes are indeed cause for shame and therefore should be glossed over as quickly as possible. In contrast to the first examples, this attitude could lessen the supervisee's learning opportunity.

An important mechanism for communicating respect is the manner in which feedback is offered. Diana, the supervisor in the following example, talked about her approach to intervention in live supervision, developed out of a desire to avoid shaming her supervisees.

> I never interrupt a live supervision session to give feedback without invitation. I have worked with so many supervisees who had very negative experiences with the intrusion. Of course, it's always a matter of how the feedback is given. I know there are multiple views, but over the years, I've worked with so many people who have had such bad experiences, that they were afraid to use themselves in their work. They would feel demeaned, intimidated, shamed, and they would ultimately get more anxious.

Live supervision is widely discussed, especially in the marriage and family therapy literature. For many years it was seen as the most effective form of supervision, particularly by those in the profession of marriage and family therapy. Live supervision enables the supervisor to actually see a supervisee's actions, rather than simply hearing the supervisee's impressions of what occurred. In addition, live supervision provides the opportunity to teach supervisees new interventions in the immediate context of the session (Boscolo & Cecchin, 1982; Byng-Hall, 1982; Ganahl, Fergeson, & L'Abate, 1985; Schwartz, 1988). Diana's comments allude to one of the potential pitfalls of this method—namely, that a supervisor's on-the-spot interruption of a session can easily be experienced as a shaming criticism of the supervisee's actions. This is especially true if the supervisee already feels exposed and vulnerable simply by virtue of being observed. If the interruption is not done with care, the possibility of harm to the supervisee is increased. Diana accurately pointed out that whether or not one intrudes in live supervision is less important than how one does so. Shoshanna, a supervisee, described an incident in live supervision in which her supervisor made a significant effort toward creating a nonshaming environment.

> Once I really botched an interview that my supervisor, Sandy, was observing. I was very withholding and was projecting my own issues onto the clients. Later, Sandy said, "Okay, we have to talk about this." First she said all the things that she saw that were helpful, and then she said, "Okay, now we need to look at what else was going on in the interview."
>
> She started identifying what she saw me doing. As she did that, she asked in a really supportive way, "What was going on for you there? That was obviously not the kind of work I've seen you do before." It became an opportunity for me to identify what I was projecting in the interview. Sandy talked with me about how I can know when I am hooked with clients.
>
> Her particular manner is one of great support, and acknowledgment for all the skills that I have. Then in a direct but not confronting way, she has me look at myself. Her attitude is that if she can keep the experience as nonshaming and nonthreatening as possible, the supervisee will be more open to hearing what she has to say.

Shoshanna described Sandy's approach as a careful one. Sandy went out of her way to place her criticism in a larger context that included Shoshanna's strength as a clinician and that was worded in a gentle and supportive manner. Both supervisors and supervisees experience respectful treatment as sending the message that the supervisee's ideas are valuable and will not be dismissed in a judgmental fashion. Within that framework, it is easier to accept constructive criticism. Sometimes, however, even if the supervisor is careful to communicate in a balanced manner, the supervisee responds with shame. Shirley's story illustrates such a situation.

> I worked with a man who was just too helpful and too talkative. I started off by framing his behavior positively. "I like the energy you bring to

these sessions, Kim." He smiled. I kept going that route, but also began dropping in some suggestions that maybe we still didn't know what the clients needed because of all the energy that he brought. They were just sort of sitting back and basking in his energy.

I said, "You might want to, as a therapeutic technique, kind of underfunction and let them see what they do with it." He couldn't do that. I thought, "Okay, this is much more than just new-worker anxiety. This is more about his personal traits." Then I suggested more firmly that this is what he do. I said, "We don't know what's going on in this family. I don't think you've given them a lot of time to talk about it, yet."

He sat there, getting defensive and quiet, then defensive, then quiet. He came to our next session without a tape of an interview and didn't have much to talk about. I decided not to let it go, so I said, "I was harder on you last session than I have been before. I'm wondering if you are reacting to that." He hemmed and hawed and said, "Yeah, I think I am." He told me I really blindsided him. After being so positive, what was I doing? Setting him up? I tried to explain to him what I was doing with him, but he still felt blindsided.

I said, " I think we can work on this. There are some specific things I want you to do differently and I think you can do them. You certainly have shown the capacity to create an environment in which people continue to want to come back and see you. I think if you can do that, then you can do this."

With a lot of pushing and prodding, he did get better. But there was reserve that entered into our relationship. I had injured him. I kept bringing it up. I would ask, "How are you feeling? Are you feeling hurt by me? Do you think I'm being honest in this feedback?" He would say he did, and that it felt better, but I still felt some reserve.

Shirley attempted to avoid a shameful response by communicating respect for Kim's strengths and by framing his problematic behavior in the most positive manner she could and suggesting alternative approaches that might help the situation. When this failed to produce the desired change, she became more direct. In spite of her careful efforts, Kim felt so stunned by the criticism that he never fully regained trust in the relationship. From his point of view, Shirley's care amounted to a lack of initial honesty. Shirley again worked hard to mend the breach in the relationship, an attempt at which she felt only partially successful. We may wonder whether Kim would have responded more favorably to a more direct and less careful approach. He appears to be a man who would react strongly to anything perceived as negative feedback.

It is not uncommon for a supervisee to feel shamed because of a lack of direct feedback, either positive or negative, from the supervisor, as Jerry's story illustrates:

I practiced a technique that I was not really comfortable with, and I was concerned that I might have harmed my clients. During my discussion with Fred, my supervisor, I felt extremely vulnerable. I did not receive affirmation of myself as a person or as a practitioner. He also never really said, "I don't agree with that technique," or "I think that was a mistake." It was more like I always sensed by his lack of support that he thought it was a mistake, but he didn't clearly say that. Instead, I felt that he let me fry in my own shame, or my own uncertainty. Part of me believed that what I did was right, and part of me was really disturbed at the consequences that occurred.

It is possible to understand this encounter as one in which Fred abandoned his limit-setting function by not stating a clear parameter regarding Jerry's practice. The resulting feeling for Jerry was that it compounded his shame. In Chapter 3, I offered an illustration of abandonment of the limit-setting function that occurred because of an unspoken "secret pact" between a supervisee and her supervisor. They simply did not discuss issues that could lead to feelings of discomfort or shame. The avoidance of shame becomes problematic when important issues are neglected in favor of the personal comfort of both supervisor and supervisee. Not only might the supervision be less effective because the learning is not as great, there is a danger, as we see in Jerry's story, that the avoidance itself can lead to shame and mistrust.

Direct Approaches to Shame

In part because of the above concerns, some supervisors, although not intentionally shaming, will talk directly about the supervisee's feelings of shame when necessary rather than attempt to avoid its occurrence. They believe that simply normalizing supervisees' feelings of insecurity can send the message that because they are normal, there is no reason to explore them further. This encourages the supervisee to hide these feelings when they arise (Jacobs, 1991). Shoshanna, who, in an earlier example, described her supervisor Sandy's gentle and respectful approach, gave this account of a different supervisor who was quite direct and powerful in the manner with which she confronted shame.

Margaret is a very challenging, confronting person. Her attitude is that she won't avoid saying things because someone might be upset. She just says what she needs to say and then if the other person reacts negatively, she'll deal with them about it. When I was first getting to know her I questioned whether or not I could tolerate her straightness, her directness, and her challenges. Then I realized that this was exactly what I needed. I needed someone to challenge me.

She challenged me on something I did with a client. I immediately felt some shame. I don't think I told her right at that point, but I know we talked about it later. She said to me, "Your shame really gets in the way, sometimes, of my being able to say stuff to you." She could tell that I would start feeling that way, and then I would back off. At that point, I wasn't able to hear what she had to say.

She confronted my pulling away from the situation and using it as a way to put myself down rather than using it as a way to be curious about myself. "Why am I responding this way? What's going on with me that I can't hear what she's saying to me? What am I afraid to look at?"

Until we had that conversation, I didn't start asking myself those questions. Within a year, we had explored questions such as, "What am I afraid will happen if I expose this part of myself or my work to her? Am I afraid that she won't want to do supervision with me anymore?" All of my worries came out on the table. We were able to talk about every one of them.

I learned that nothing I was thinking was going to happen. I began to see that it was my own withholding that was getting in the way both in supervision and with my clients, not my skill or my lack of skill as a practitioner.

This is an example of shame evoked by the interaction between supervisor and supervisee. Margaret approached it first as an issue in their relationship and ultimately as an issue that was potentially getting in the way of Shoshanna's work. Shoshanna found this approach quite useful because she had not been challenged so deeply before. It allowed her to face her fear that Margaret would disapprove of her and reject her as a supervisee. Convinced that she was safe from rejection, Shoshanna was able to operate with more courage both in supervision and in her work. Although another interpretation of this interaction is entirely possible, both concluded that Shoshanna's fear of Margaret's rejection was a function of Shoshanna's shame alone rather than of Margaret's style. Shoshanna said she found both her relationship with Margaret and that with Sandy ultimately very safe and very valuable. Her first supervisory experience was with Margaret, and only later did she encounter Sandy. Shoshanna wondered whether, had she experienced Sandy's gentle approach first, it would have diminished the impact and perhaps the necessity of Margaret's approach. She concluded, however, that the bind she put herself in with her shame was so powerful that it required a powerful style to break through it.

I've craved that kind of challenge in my life for a very long time. I welcomed it and I was scared of it. If I would have had her second, I know that it still would have been very intriguing. The way she worked with me helped me break through the shame bind that I'd never been able to break through in therapy. And I had had two years of therapy in preparation both for my profession and my life. I don't think Sandy could have broken through the bind in the same kind of way.

This is another example of the notion of courage (Doherty, 1995), in that Margaret challenged Shoshanna to push herself past her usual level of comfort in order to face herself fully and move past the powerful block of her shame. This also supports Peterson's contention (1984) that trust in the relationship will increase if the supervisee has confidence that the supervisor will go as far as necessary to understand the supervisee's work. Shoshanna was clearly saying that Margaret's was an important intervention, without which she would have neither felt safe with Margaret nor felt deeply confident about her work.

Another example of a direct approach to shame was shared by Rosa, the Latina supervisee mentioned earlier, whose shame about her family was evoked by the clients with whom she worked. In her opinion, her shame was exacerbated by her supervisor's reluctance to encourage conversations about issues related to race. When she finally did begin to share her pain, she was met with silence, left exposed in a nonresponsive group. Her supervisor did nothing to facilitate the discussion, and, as a result, Rosa was left with a sense of personal vulnerability and mistrust. In this situation, trust was diminished by the supervisor's lack of willingness or ability to talk about Rosa's shame directly. In contrast to this experience, in which her pain fell on unresponsive ears, Rosa told the following story about exploring the same issue with Nancy, from whom she sought outside consultation.

> I told her about the prostitution stuff. I always get scared when I talk about that subject because it just feels so loaded. People have opinions about it. I was talking about it and crying and so full of shame. I didn't say anything about it, and Nancy said, "You look like you are in such shame," and asked me to talk about it. She kept bringing me back to it and back to it and finally I said to her, "I just feel that people expect that from us." I think if someone has a sister who is a prostitute, it is because she is mentally ill. If my sister is, it's because she is Mexican. That helped me understand why it bothers me so much, and Nancy encouraged me to keep talking about that and to try to figure out what it means. That was really helpful. She said that if I get to the root of the shame, I won't keep reacting to it so much.

Deflection of Shame

In the preceding two stories, the supervisees reported that they found the direct focus helpful. However, a supervisee could also experience this degree of personal examination as crossing the line from supervision into therapy. Furthermore, many people argue that this type of focus can potentially reinforce the shame rather than reinforce the supervisee's sense of being a competent clinician. Lee, a supervisor, described his approach, which he characterized as one of deflection.

If a supervisee feels shame, I wouldn't ask about it. The first thing I would do would be to probably deflect it, because I think shame is that sense of having the bottom disappear out from under you. If I say, "Wow, it looks like the bottom has disappeared," I am affirming the supervisee's sense of weakness, rather than that of strength. I wouldn't do that. Instead, I would say, "So you feel like the bottom disappeared. I don't believe it did. So, let's go on with our work."

I know that as a supervisee from the perspective of feeling shameful, it looks like it's just splattered all over the wall. I would be more likely to go over and look at a different wall, and say, "Look at this wall here. I know you've got all that over there, but let's do some supervision." My contract is to help the supervisee be a strong practitioner.

Ian, the supervisor in the next example, also acknowledged the vulnerability inherent in exposing one's work. His bias was clearly that attention to those feelings are not appropriate in supervision, and that to attend to them would reinforce weakness rather than strength. This notion is similar to that expressed in Lee's statement above. However, whereas Lee tended to redirect the supervisee in a supportive fashion, Ian would be highly confrontive of the supervisee.

Presumably, the supervisee is exposing something that is as close to him as anything. His effort's to change somebody. It's his whole profession. So, the whole thing is vulnerable. Anybody would be strange not to feel vulnerable. But, for change to occur with clients, the worker needs to be able to foster his ability to influence others and change, and the client has to have this belief in the worker. Supervision can be a place to practice convincing other people that you are competent.

If you allow yourself to be overcome by your sense of vulnerability, and if you allow yourself to respond in a shameful manner, that is going to work against you in your effort to foster a belief about yourself. You need to be able to conduct yourself as a competent practitioner.

A supervision group is not a place to come and get taken care of. For me, it isn't a place for that kind of support. I think shame puts responsibility on the other. If you're feeling shameful, then of course everyone should rush to your rescue.

If shame is an internal anger, an anger directed at self, let's get that anger directed outward. So, I might say, "Why are you getting angry internally? This is a reaction to something here, so react to it out here. Get mad. Who are you going to get mad at? Are you mad at me because of what I said?" Some of my implied messages are: "Are you a baby? Are you waiting for us all to take care of you? Are you such a person that you come into professional groups and show your vulnerability to get people to care for you?" That isn't what is expected.

One might perceive Ian's approach as actively shaming the supervisee for expressing vulnerability. Clearly Ian's philosophy is that to be competent, one must not expose personal vulnerability. Indeed, many supervisees would feel belittled, demeaned, and discounted by his attitude and would no doubt respond to him with mistrust. Ian later added that his choice of approach is influenced by an important variable—namely, the context in which his supervisees are working. The client population consists of poor families living in the inner city. His assessment was that the cultural norms of many of these families dictate that members relate to one another through conflict. He maintained that the norms about "nice," nonconfrontational behavior may be appropriate for white, middle-class clinicians but entirely inappropriate for effective interaction with these particular families. To be effective with these families, in his opinion, the practitioner needs to be able to be comfortable with a more conflictual and confrontational type of interaction. The supervision group becomes a training ground for learning how to do that. Assuming Ian was accurate in his assessment of the situation, the question about what creates trust and safety becomes more complicated. Ian appeared to be saying that supervisees who would feel unsafe because of his approach may in fact be inappropriate for the job. He could argue that to deal with shame in a nurturing manner would make him untrustworthy because it would create a false sense of safety that could backfire if he did not adequately prepare his supervisees to deal with the clients.

In addition to considering the client population, Ian believed he should focus on the clients in supervision. By contrast, Margaret, Sandy, and Nancy tended to focus more on the practitioner's use of self. Often those supervisors who discourage the direct discussion of shame tend to regard supervision as more client- or case-focused. Those who approach shame directly usually regard supervision as a practitioner-focused process. My own observation is that, depending on the needs of the supervisee, both types of approach can be quite useful. Carole, a supervisee, illustrated this point in the following story.

> One time I was talking about a woman client who was keeping a significant secret from her husband. I thought the woman needed to tell her husband. My supervisor challenged me pretty strongly about what made me think that she had to tell. As we processed it, I began to think it might not be cut and dried. Maybe all the secrets don't have to be out there, at least not right away. At first I felt like I was being told that I was thinking wrong. I felt ashamed and that I needed to defend myself. But we didn't stop there and discuss my feelings. I realized she was not really talking about me. She was just talking about the facts of the case. I began to think, "Maybe I can adjust what I'm thinking here. I still think that secrets are damaging, but maybe there's a time and a place."
>
> We kept going and eventually I started feeling better. Something in me shifted and I no longer felt like a bad person. I think part of what made it shift was I couldn't just get up and leave, in my shame, so I kept

asking her to explain what she meant. On the other hand, I like to figure out how I am getting hooked. If she had gone this way, she would have asked me something like, "Where are you going away from yourself with this now?" This would have shifted the focus from the case to me. When I look at the ways that I abandon myself in shame, I am able to be more effective as a practitioner and as a supervisee. However, if I get too caught up in my own feelings, I can lose a sense of my competence. I can see value in either approach, because I'm in danger of going too far in either direction.

HONESTY

As many of the stories in the previous section indicated, the way in which shame is addressed in supervision has a significant impact on the supervisee's feeling of safety, and therefore of trust, in the supervisory relationship. Equally important for the establishment of trust is whether both supervisor and supervisee experience the other as honest. Honesty is closely tied to the concept of accountability, which was defined in Chapter 1 as the act of taking responsibility both for one's behavior and for the impact of that behavior on self and on others. It is the commitment to tell the truth about oneself to the best of one's ability and a commitment to take responsible action. Accountability is discussed in this book primarily in the context of the supervisee's accountability to the supervisor. However, a trusting relationship requires that supervisors hold themselves accountable to their supervisees as well.

Honesty of the Supervisee

Because of the power differential that exists, it is the supervisor's behavior that generally sets the tone for the relationship. However, if the supervisee is not honest, the relationship cannot be characterized as trusting. As mentioned before, supervisees frequently withhold parts of their story, often as a form of self-protection. A supervisee who feels a need for self-protection, by definition, does not trust the supervisor. We cannot know, without examining a specific situation, whether it is the supervisor or the supervisee whose trustworthiness is questionable. However, a supervisor who interprets the withholding as an attempt to hide something or to avoid an important issue is likely to think the supervisee is being dishonest, as Jamal did in the following example.

I lost confidence in him as a practitioner. What I saw was more of his weakness and his inability to deal with me or to cope with the stress of the confrontation about it. So while he was talking about his work, I felt that he wasn't being honest with me.

It is important to recognize that what seems to be dishonesty may actually be a problem of lack of shared meaning—for example, in the case of a supervisee whose culture views admitting your problems as an indication of lack of control (Ryan & Hendricks, 1989). Sometimes, however, the distinction between honesty and shared meaning is difficult to make, and trust issues emerge. Janet told the following story about a supervision group for student interns, of which she was the leader.

> The group comprised four Caucasian students and one from Laos. She was unable to attend the first meeting, so when the second one began, I asked her if she had any discomfort with entering the group late. I was trying to help her become integrated into a group whose members had already started to connect with each other. Her response to me seemed extreme. She stated, "We do not talk about feelings in my culture," and that to be asked to do so was to place her in a very uncomfortable position. In addition, my pointing out that she was late was humiliating to her. This seemed to become the foundation for a great deal of mistrust in this group. The other members all supported her and saw me as an inappropriately intrusive and culturally insensitive supervisor. All attempts I made to resolve the issue were met with hostility.

Although it is likely that the supervisees would add another dimension to this story, Janet concluded that the group members were using the cultural conflict as a way to mask other issues they did not want to face. She did not think their concern was authentic, but she was unable find a way to address what she considered to be the real issues. The result for her was that she did not trust her supervisees.

Honesty of the Supervisor

Often an indication of the supervisor's honesty is whether the supervisee feels free to challenge the supervisor. This is a power issue, because the challenge can be seen as bringing the supervisor's authority into question. It is a trust and specifically an honesty issue in that permission to challenge is ultimately communicated by supervisors' willingness both to listen to the feedback and to acknowledge their part in an interaction. Angie made a connection between her own personal development, her willingness to accept challenge from her supervisees, and her concurrent ability to let go of control.

> Earlier in my career, I might have noted that someone was upset with me and not talked about it. I was being more careful. This was probably because I wasn't ready to meet more of myself. Today, if I see something going on between us, I'll ask about it. I will comment more on my own

reality, my own experience in the supervisory process. I will also give them more permission to give me feedback. I was more controlling earlier on of what they did, what I did, and how much feedback anyone got. I was probably trying to stay in shallower water.

Supervisees receive a range of messages from their supervisors regarding permission to challenge. On one end of the continuum are those who, in the supervisee's experience, respond well to negative feedback.

I thought my supervisor was giving different attention to the men in the group than to the women in the group. She gave more positive affirmation for their work, acquiescing sometimes to what they were saying and doing, and just heaping them with praise for how wonderful they were, as male clinicians, to be so sensitive.

I got to a point where I was tired of it, so one day I decided I needed to say something about it. We talked about it at length. Her reaction was surprise and I think a little hurt about what I was saying, because she doesn't see herself that way at all. Her comment was something like, "I'll give some thought to that. I'll do some of my own self-observation." It was left at that and I have seen a shift in her behavior since then.

Frequently the message is more mixed. Brad, another supervisee, described his supervisor's behavior in the following manner.

She says that she welcomes disagreement, but at times I'm not sure if she really means it. I gave her some feedback on something I didn't think was right. There was a pause where we both stared at each other for a second, as if to say, "Now, what do we do?" I think she likes to have people agree with her. When she is challenged, there's a change in the dynamic of the relationship, so people are on new footing.

She doesn't get defensive or angry. It's more as if she is saying, "Gee, things were working so well when you saw it my way." She has made sarcastic comments, like, "It's so nice we have an agency that is willing to listen to new ideas." This is what I get. It's kind of a double message. However, in spite of this, I trust her. She genuinely respects me and demonstrates a lot of concern for the well-being of our relationship. This makes me think that, even though she is uncomfortable with challenge, she is basically an honest person.

Challenge can be on either the relationship level, if the supervisee talks about something that has occurred between them, or on the professional level, if the supervisee questions the supervisor's directives or ideas. Sometimes, as in the following example, the supervisor may accept challenge on one level but not the other. In this account, the supervisee stated that the supervisor was rigid and closed to being questioned on clinical approaches. However, the supervisee trusted him anyway because of his honesty on a relationship level.

Geoff always seemed to need to be right. I remember a client whose behavior clearly indicated to me that he was sexually abused. Geoff wouldn't see it that way. He tried to take me in the direction of a more psychoanalytic interpretation. I remember he was very upset and angry with me because I wasn't agreeing with him and I was challenging him.

However, once another colleague was very hurt by Geoff and by other members of the staff. One day, she got mad and said, "I have had it with all of you. I'm treated like a nonentity, and I don't like it." Geoff was taken aback. He had a big, soft heart. He apologized and said, "Now that you're saying that, I can see that it's true." He owned his part and things changed. I liked and trusted him because of his ability to do this.

At the other end of the continuum are those relationships in which the supervisee feels a total lack of permission to challenge. In the following situation, the supervisor participated in staff consultation meetings. The overt message was that the supervisor was acting like a colleague who valued input from the others on the quality of his practice. However, Grant, one of the other staff members, did not view him as genuinely open to that input.

He presents cases in a complicated and intellectual manner that is difficult to follow. It takes so much time to understand exactly where he's coming from that it's hard to give feedback. He tends to present in such an engaging sort of way that I often feel there is nothing to critique. If I do find an area that he may not be as well-versed in and try to say, "Hey, wait a minute; there is another side of this story or another way to handle it," he diverts the discussion in a way that communicates that he is not open to really hearing it. In addition, he tends to present ideal cases, rather than the more typical clients we work with.

Both in this example and in the one that follows, the underlying theme is the supervisor's dishonesty. The supervisor responded to the feedback, in the first example, by deflecting it and, in the next, by defensively criticizing the supervisee for bringing up the concern. This type of reaction gives the message that the supervisor is not willing either to take an honest look at his own behavior or to acknowledge that behavior to the supervisee.

I confronted him about his accepting phone calls during our supervision. He was very angry with me. He said something like that he was real concerned about me. That I was going to have more difficulty dealing with my colleagues. I shouldn't have challenged him about that. His message was clearly, "It's your problem." I think he was too wrapped up in his own business, had never done his own work, to be able to adequately supervise someone doing this work.

The supervisee's final statement is reminiscent of the comment made by Angie, who spoke of the connection between her willingness to "meet more of herself" and her ability to be open to her supervisees' feedback. The premise here is that both supervisors and their supervisees need a great deal of personal skill in order to be honest in their dealings with one another. As in the practitioner/client relationship, supervisors who have not grappled with their own issues will play them out in the supervisory relationship.

Although the focus here is primarily on the supervisor's communication of permission, it is also important to note that the supervisee might be reluctant to challenge the supervisor. Kendra, who supervises Vietnamese workers, notes that they would be quite hesitant to voice any dissatisfaction with her. She works to create an environment in which they feel safe to do so. However, she never feels sure that she has all the information she needs about how they are experiencing her.

As noted in the discussions on limit setting and on shame, the manner in which both the supervisor offers feedback and evaluations and the supervisee receives them is an important dimension in the relationship. No matter how it is presented, supervisees usually value honest feedback and have more trust for supervisors who are willing to give it. The following is an example in which a supervisor gave positive feedback that did not seem genuine.

> He would make comments about me, like that he thought I had a certain kind of wisdom, and inside I laughed about that. I thought, "What does he know about that? How does he know me? He must just be saying stuff." If my supervisors never see anything but positive things about my work, I start to wonder about their credibility.

Here we see a connection between power and trust. If supervisors are not believable, supervisees will neither trust them nor ascribe to them the power to teach. In addition, the impact may be even more serious, leaving the supervisee feeling betrayed or otherwise deeply hurt by the interaction. Monica, a supervisee, talked about a workplace in which one of the unspoken rules was that the sharing of personal vulnerability was seen as a weakness.

> I am someone who can be quite emotional, and I cry quite easily. Sometimes I cry with my clients when they are in deep pain. I found out that my colleagues were seeing this as a real weakness on my part, talking behind my back about how poorly I was doing. Before I learned this, I was feeling really crazy. I could tell that people were treating me differently than they had been before, but I didn't know what was happening. I would go to talk to my supervisor, and say, "I don't know what's going on. I just am feeling crazy and overwhelmed." She was very sympathetic and very nice, and she told me I was doing well and that she supported my work.
>
> I didn't know my supervisor shared the larger agency belief about personal vulnerability. I went away on vacation, and when I came back

she'd been fired. She was gone. At that point people started telling me what was going on behind my back. I found out that she was one of the people talking about me. She had been telling other people, "Yes, isn't it terrible what's going on with Monica? She certainly does seem upset a lot." But she wasn't talking to me about it. All I knew was that I was feeling crazy and that I thought that she was my ally.

Clearly, this story indicates some serious systemic problems in the agency, which are affecting the supervisory relationship. We will discuss the impact of the agency context in more detail below. In addition, Monica's supervisor is actually lying either to Monica or to others about her view of the situation. Although this appears to be an extreme example, this level of dysfunction is certainly not unique, and the impact on the supervisory relationship is devastating.

Sharing of Personal Information

One way trust can be enhanced is for supervisors to share their own emotional responses (Shulman, 1982, 1993; Alonso & Rutan, 1988; Fox, 1989). If supervisors present themselves as human beings whose external behavior is congruent with inner feelings, supervisees can more easily relate to them and therefore trust them with their own vulnerabilities. Larry, who had a great deal of admiration for his supervisor, Matt, offered the following story.

One time I had a terrible session with a client. I felt knifed all over the place. I wasn't prepared for it. I left a note for Matt, saying that I wanted a friendly ear. I just wanted to connect with him. Sometime later that day, Matt came into my office. He said, "I want you to know I got your note. There is nothing I can give you. I cannot be here for you because I've had a very bad day, too. In fact, I just canceled my last session, and I'm going home."

My first reaction was to be really angry and to say, "How dare you do that to me! Where are you when I need you?" But I knew he didn't do it on purpose. He was just a basket case that day, like I was. It ended up having a great positive effect on me. First of all, I told him how angry I was. He acknowledged that he probably would have been angry, too. But, as angry as I was, something changed for me. I understood my own limitations and I understood his. Somehow, I thought he never had any limitations. That day he became a real person to me. Sometimes you don't have milk to breast-feed because you haven't eaten anything yourself. I also realized that I had seen other clients that day and I had survived, and that I could count on myself.

Since that time two things happened for me. I trusted myself more, and I also trusted Matt. Although I had always felt pretty free to tell Matt what was happening for me, after that it became even easier. I guess that was because I knew I didn't have problems because I was inexperienced or just somehow inadequate. I had them because I'm human. And I knew that he understood that, since he was willing to talk about his own limitations.

We saw in Chapter 3 that sometimes supervisors' sharing of personal vulnerabilities can be experienced as a burden. Clearly, in this situation Matt's actions were quite positive. Matt showed himself to be a trustworthy individual, both in his authenticity and in his willingness to accept responsibility for the impact of his behavior.

Support of the Supervisee's Work

There is a strong connection between power and trust in the question of whether supervisees feel supported by their supervisors. There are certainly times when the supervisor does not and perhaps should not back the supervisee's clinical practice. In Jamal's account, the supervisor did not trust the supervisee as clinician because of that individual's dishonesty. However, there are other situations in which the supervisee deserves that backing but cannot count on the supervisor to provide it. This lack of support is generally perceived as a misuse of the supervisor's power, which creates mistrust in the relationship. April, a supervisee in a large outpatient clinic, told the following story.

I saw an adolescent girl one time, and met with her mother on that same occasion. It was clear, both from my conversations with the mother on the phone and from my interactions with her, that she was a very angry woman who distorted a lot. I had a productive session with the daughter, but they did not return. Later she called my supervisor, Ellie, to complain about me. Our agency serves a rather difficult population, and many people receive occasional complaints from clients. Ellie assumed that the client's complaint was accurate and that the problem was mine. She told me that "We keep careful records of complaints about supervisees." I felt intimidated by this comment, since it seemed as if she would hold this complaint against me in some way.

Later, I was talking with a group of colleagues about the fact that our clientele seems to be one that doesn't stick in treatment. We get a lot of people who don't show for appointments. I commented that this was different from my experience at other agencies in other communities. One of the others said I should mention this to Ellie, who didn't seem to believe this was the case. I did so, innocently. Later that day, Ellie brought me into her office and said that because of my problem connecting with clients, I would need more regular supervision. I didn't mind that, since I liked the person she assigned me to, and the supervision was very good. But I was shaken, in both of these situations. I was scared that if someone decided to sue me, the agency would not support me.

In this example, the client was treated as a "customer" who is "always right" and the supervisee was treated as a poor salesperson who has not done the job of selling her services. Although it is certainly important to take client dissatisfaction very seriously, it is equally important to support supervisees who have acted capably and with integrity. The goal is competent service to clients, which, as discussed earlier, often requires courage on the part of the practitioner to say or do things that may evoke a negative response from the client. If supervisees cannot trust their supervisors to back them up, they may lose the courage to take challenging steps with their clients.

TRUST IN CROSS-CULTURAL RELATIONSHIPS

An important variable affecting trust in cross-cultural relationships is the effect of the historical relationship between ethnic groups. Chad, an African American, talked about the same issue of trust and power illustrated in April's account, adding the dimension of racial tension in his positions as supervisee and supervisor.

> In any supervisory relationship, there is a power differential. Therefore the supervisee is always afraid that the supervisor could use that power indiscriminately. So there is always an issue of trust. How will they use their power over me? Can I trust them with how I am? Do they trust me in terms of how I do my work? I think especially between blacks and whites, you have the history of slavery, segregation, and de facto integration.
>
> Being a person of color as a supervisor, there are a lot of people looking at you, wondering whether you are capable of doing the job. You are sort of in this no-person's land, in that historically you have not had power in this society and suddenly you are in a position of power. People wonder, more than they would with a Caucasian, about whether you will be able to handle it.

Rita, a Native American supervisee, postulated that historical tension between African Americans and Native Americans contributes to the mistrust she feels toward her African American supervisor. This feeling is compounded by a shared-meaning difference—namely, her supervisor's more aggressive style versus her own more quiet one. She assumed, however, that her interpretation of her supervisor's approach as hostile had to do in part with her own built-in assumption about African Americans.

> I think it was easier for me to have supervisory relationships with my European and Indian supervisors than with my African American one. I think the American Indian and African American cultures are so very

different in terms of the makeup of families, how kids interact, and the rhythm of the people that it makes it more difficult to overcome history. That history includes the fact that when the American Indian tribes were imprisoned, the African Americans often were the jailers. Generations later, the tension about this is still there. In addition, the people are very different. American Indian people tend to be very quiet, into themselves, and not real busy. African American people are very loud, vocal, and into who they are, which is a beautiful part of their culture. But when you combine these differences with history, it does not make for an easy interaction.

In Chapter 4, I discussed the problem of defining racism. Racism is rarely blatantly expressed, particularly in a human services agency, where people are conscious of political correctness and of professional values and ethics that oppose discrimination and oppression and honor diversity. Below the surface, however, is frequently a deep mistrust that complicates interactions and interpretations of behavior. This mistrust is fueled by feelings of rage, guilt, defensiveness, hurt, and fear, which have developed as a result of generations of racial tension.

Both supervisors and supervisees have experienced a feeling of intimidation regarding race issues, which blocks honest communication and deepens the feeling of mistrust. Carol, an African American supervisee, told the following story.

> I was angry with my supervisor, and I let her know that. Later she would walk by me in the hall and not look at me, just avoid me. I knew I had been angry, but I didn't threaten her or hit her. I just looked angry and talked in a loud voice, because my voice *is* loud. I know the American culture is very threatened by African American anger, but she wouldn't talk to me about it. Even when I tried to bring it up, she would just change the subject.

As Carol mentioned, part of the difficulty here is connected to style. However, the difference in style is compounded by anger and fear on both sides and by the supervisor's unwillingness to discuss the issue honestly. Dana, another African American supervisee, described a dynamic that she observed between Caucasian and African American people at her agency.

> If I go to my white supervisor or co-worker and say this issue has racial aspects to it, their antennas go up because they don't know if I'm calling them racist. If we were both white, it would be easy to have the conversation. But since I'm black, they feel like or act as if they aren't qualified to talk about racial issues. I think if they don't think it is racial, they should challenge me on it. If they don't, I can intimidate them. I can always holler racism and they can't back up their position, because they've never called me on my behavior. If I know I can intimidate them

when there isn't really a racial issue, and they can't challenge me on it, it's institutional racism, because they are afraid of me calling them racist. That goes on daily here.

As this example illustrates, this dynamic is a complex one. Like Carol, Dana made a case for an honest dialogue in which the question of race is really placed on the table to be discussed. Like many other practitioners of color, she has experienced the sense of being stone-walled by colleagues, supervisors, and supervisees when questions arise that are related to race. We are reminded of Rosa, the Latina supervisee who described the pain of being met with unresponsive silence when she dared discuss her own feelings about race. Matts (1995) noted that a large majority of the participants in her study perceived a lack of initiative on the part of supervisors and colleagues regarding this issue. Attempting to be color-blind as well as being ignorant, feeling awkward, holding negative stereotypes about those who are different, and having fears about how to proceed often lead to adopting a rule of silence regarding racial tension. In addition, people in the majority of any group may make assumptions in the course of conversation that presume common experience. Those whose circumstances are different often react by feeling discounted and invisible. Many practitioners of color state that the fact that they are often the only one of color in their agency creates a feeling of isolation and a sense that there is no one with whom they can validate their own perceptions.

However, the intimidation Dana referred to is also real. In the litigious atmosphere of today's society, agencies and supervisors are quite sensitive to the need to avoid possible lawsuits for discrimination. Although discrimination still occurs and the need for legal protection against it is large and justified, the increased fear of lawsuits probably has done as much harm as good toward the goal of more respectful and equal treatment in the workplace. In Chapter 3, I spoke about the concept of destructive entitlement. There are those who, out of rage about their own oppression or a cultural heritage of oppression, take advantage of the power to intimidate and place those around them in a bind, in which any action or inaction is defined as racist.

In Chapter 4, I discussed questions regarding the need for the supervisor to understand the supervisee's culture. Clearly, the greater understanding the supervisor has about that culture, the better. However, to some extent a barrier may remain, even in the best of circumstances. Tanya, an African American practitioner, stated that Denise, her Caucasian supervisor, is an excellent clinician. However, Tanya often does not completely trust Denise's advice about African American clients because she cannot be sure that her supervisor understands the subtleties of those clients' needs and issues. This concern, however, does not affect the overall trust she feels for Denise because Denise has obvious genuine concern for Tanya and for their relationship. It is almost a truism to state that, for most supervisory relationships—cross-cultural or otherwise—authenticity of the participants is key to the feeling of trust. However, whereas Tanya is able to put her hesitance regarding Denise's credibility into a larger context, another supervisee might simply discount Denise as unable to be helpful. That supervisee might believe that Denise has no right to comment on the reality of her African American clients because of Denise's own very different background. If Denise attempted to do so in this scenario, she could be met with hostility from her supervisee.

Judy, a Native American supervisee, told the following story.

> In our agency, a biracial (Latino/Caucasian) worker and a Caucasian worker were doing cotherapy with an African American family. Lee, a worker on the staff, also African American, started confronting them about whether they could work with this family, given that they were not African American themselves. Even though both of them are quite competent with clients from a variety of backgrounds, they seemed unable to defend themselves. The rest of the staff was quiet, I think because the issue was race and they were afraid to challenge Lee's position. Our supervisor did nothing to intervene. Nothing happened until I finally brought the issue up both to Lee and to the rest of the staff, and we all talked about it. My supervisor gave us no guidance, however. He simply let us go where we wanted with it.

The question about whether a practitioner has to "be one" to "work with one" is not unique to racial or cultural issues. The chemical dependency field, for example, has a long tradition of hiring recovering addicts to help others. There are convincing arguments for the advantages and disadvantages of having experience that is similar to or different from that of one's clients. It is a shared-meaning question, as it points to a philosophy about what constitutes effective treatment. It becomes a trust issue when people are afraid to address the question because of underlying racial tension. Judy was disturbed, and rightly so, at her supervisor's lack of direction on this question. She believed strongly that Lee's challenge was unwarranted, particularly given the skills and awareness of the two clinicians involved in the case. Judy believed, further, that it was the supervisor's job to facilitate an honest discussion. However, the supervisor seemed unwilling to take Lee on, partly because to do so could evoke a conflict about race. We might also discover, upon further investigation, that this particular supervisor is reluctant to evoke conflict in any arena and is in general a weak leader. The reality remains, however, that racial tension often blocks genuine exchange for all participants in the process. In this situation, for example, it is possible that Judy's ability to effectively raise the issue was precisely because she is herself a person of color and therefore less vulnerable to the accusation that she can't have a credible position on the topic.

CONTEXTUAL ISSUES AND TRUST

The context within which supervision occurs may or may not affect the development of trust in the relationship. The story of Marilyn and Tim, with which this chapter began, is an example of this dynamic. It is interesting to note that although all the other participants—Marilyn's colleagues, George, and the outside consultant—affected the situation in different ways, none were able to enhance the trust between Marilyn and Tim. The support Marilyn felt from her colleagues helped empower her to take a stand vis-à-vis Tim and may also have fueled the tension. To the extent that Marilyn felt unsupported by George, she felt mistrustful not only of Tim but of the agency as a whole. The consultant provided a solution that diminished the day-to-day intensity of the problem, but it did not improve the supervisory relationship. This story suggests that, although the context has an influence, frequently the specific behavior of supervisor and supervisee toward one another has a bigger impact on the development of trust than does the context per se.

As an illustration of this phenomenon, both supervisors and supervisees question whether a supervisee is wise to share very vulnerable information with a supervisor to whom the hierarchical structure of the context has ascribed positional power. One might postulate that Monica, the supervisee whose supervisor spoke behind her back, ran into difficulties because she failed to recognize that this person was also her boss and that she should monitor her degree of sharing accordingly. One might further argue that the culture of the entire agency was one in which messages were confusing, people were frequently dishonest, and the general feeling was one of a lack of safety. However, it is also possible that Monica's supervisor herself is a fundamentally untrustworthy person. In contrast, Monica talked about another supervisor, also a boss in an agency setting, who was very safe and trustworthy because of her nonshaming attitude.

> I took the same risks with her as I take with anybody else. I can remember working with a family with a kid who just scared the daylights out of me because she was so rageful. One day, I went into my supervisor's office and I just cried and I said, "This is just awful. I don't know what to do." And she was wonderful. She was very affirming and supportive, and she gave me some ways to think about it. So, I was very vulnerable with her and got good stuff from her. My reviews from her were always good. I don't think I thought about what she was going to write down about my performance.

In this situation, the context was one in which honest and nonshaming interactions were promoted. Often there is a lack of congruity between the larger context and the supervisory relationship. Sometimes the context is trustworthy but the supervisory relationship is not. In the following case, the supervisee was able to gain support from faculty in her academic setting for difficulties she was experiencing in her field placement.

> I had the support of several people who knew this particular man, knew he was not ethical and was being very unprofessional, and just challenged him along with me. I did my piece as the student, and they did their piece as the advisors in the process.

As in the case of Marilyn and Tim, the context in this example neither enhanced nor diminished the trust between supervisor and supervisee. Rather, the supervisee was able to get support from the school to challenge her supervisor. The field placement situation is a common one in which students and their supervisors run into conflicts with one another. The role of faculty liaison is to support that relationship, acting as a facilitator to both during a conflict. Part of the challenge of the liaison role is sorting out whether the problem lies with the supervisor, the student, or both. In the example just cited, the faculty liaison determined that the supervisor's behavior was the problem. In that case, the student was helped both to challenge and to protect herself from harm from him.

Sometimes the context is perceived as untrustworthy, but the supervisor is trusted. The deciding factor seems to be how the supervisor is perceived in relationship to the environment. Roberto, a Latino supervisee, gave the following account.

> I had a white boss who was excellent. We worked in a church agency, and he knew the church inside and out. They had just started a unit to work with Latinos and hired me. It was even harder there because there were three cultures: white, church, and me, working in a Latino community. There was no one else for me to talk to. The people in the community were saying, "We don't trust the church. We used to trust you, but we don't anymore because you work for the church." So, here I am trying to build up trust with them. However, I had the sense that the church was only serving Latinos because of outside pressure to do so, not because they really wanted to. I felt there was no support in any place. That was hard because I had to question what I was doing there and why, and how I could bring these two groups together.
>
> A very classic thing happened, in which I would ask for resources for the Latinos and the agency would refuse, saying that it would not be fair to give special treatment to this particular clientele. A few years later, they built a whole new division for women and children, and no one said anything about that unit getting special resources.
>
> I felt stuck in the middle, between the Latino community, who were angry at the church, and the agency, which was not supporting me. My supervisor was very helpful. He would tell me what the church was about and tell me how to work with it. He was open to hearing from me

about what I thought would work in the community. He would advocate on their behalf in the agency. I never doubted his commitment to me and my work.

This example is particularly significant given the racial issues involved. The level of mistrust was high between clients and church, and the church seemed to be serving this particular clientele only in response to outside pressure. Roberto was in the awkward position of trying to advocate to his clients, who viewed him as having betrayed their trust by working for the church. The potential for racial tension between Roberto and his supervisor was high, given that his supervisor was white. However, his supervisor appears to have been extremely effective in his role of mediator between practitioner and agency. Although the job remained difficult, Roberto trusted his supervisor because he made an effort to advocate for his supervisee, as well as to help him understand and deal with the agency context.

In another example of a trustworthy supervisor in an untrustworthy context, Pat aligned closely with his supervisee:

The culture in this agency was traditional, psychoanalytic, and staid. I was regarded as kind of a heroic exception because I wasn't as stiff and staid or reliant on that kind of formality. I gave more feedback. I had an alliance with my supervisee in helping him to be an effective clinician in the way that system operated. He felt affirmed and empowered by the process.

If I had been in the role where I was so identified with the system and felt like I had to impart to him the culture of the system, I don't think he would have felt very empowered. He would have felt that he was being indoctrinated or something. And he would not have felt very affirmed.

In Pat's opinion, the alignment enhanced his supervisee's trust in him. A simple human fact is that people tend to trust those whom they experience as being more "on their side." However, a supervisor will not and should not always be on the "side" of the supervisee. In fact, although a short-term trust might develop by taking this position, the long-term consequences of deepening a "we versus they" dichotomy between supervisee and agency may be quite serious. George, in our opening story, was caught in a bind familiar to many supervisors. He made what he would define as a genuine attempt to validate Tim's supervisees' concerns, support Tim, hold all participants accountable, and try to reach a viable solution for the agency as a whole. Naturally, this process required disappointing some of the very people he was trying to help. Marilyn, for example, felt betrayed by George's support of Tim, seeing it as discounting her own experience and concern. This feeling was exacerbated by the fact that, out of respect for Tim's confidentiality, George could not clearly tell her what he was doing with Tim. Therefore Marilyn trusted neither George nor

Tim. In the discussion in Chapter 3 about information sharing, a significant variable was the supervisee's perception of the supervisor's motivation. Of course, that very perception is colored by the supervisee's own motivations and desires.

Although trust is generally affected most by the specific relationship between supervisor and supervisee, there are certainly times when it can be greatly enhanced by intervention from someone in the larger context. In my role as faculty liaison, I have observed that, every year, one or two students quickly decide they are unhappy with their placements and want to change. Frequently the source of the difficulty is the student's anxiety coupled with a misunderstanding between supervisor and supervisee. The student then becomes scared and concludes that the supervisory relationship is not a safe one. I find that if I can help students sort out the issues, they almost inevitably feel both calmer and empowered to address concerns more directly with their supervisors. Although I always offer to talk to the supervisor or come to the agency and talk to both of them, this rarely becomes necessary. The student and supervisor usually go on to develop a trusting and effective relationship.

Blocks to the Establishment of Trust Created by Context

There are occasions when conditions within the context block the supervisor's ability to create trust, and the supervisor feels powerless to counteract the conditions. Beth described a situation in which she was hired as a supervisor and given the mandate to weed out some ineffective employees. She soon realized that, although these people were indeed ineffective, part of the responsibility lay with the agency. People had been hired who were not well suited for the job and were not offered the support they needed in order to learn. The agency, therefore, was potentially liable because it could not document a good-faith effort. To protect the agency, Beth thought, she could neither be completely honest with her supervisees nor help them deal with the shame they felt about their own failure because she was unable to acknowledge the agency's failure to support them.

In another example, Jayaratne and associates (1992) measured the perception of African American practitioners of their supervisors with regard to emotional support, social undermining, and criticism. In this study, the workers in public agencies perceived a higher level of criticism and less emotional support from their African American female supervisors than from either their African American male or their white male or female supervisors. By contrast, the white male supervisors were perceived this way in private agencies. The authors postulated that because of affirmative action, African American women had a great deal of opportunity in the public agencies, leading to envy and hence mistrust of those supervisors by others in the organization. In private agencies, the authors suggest, the white male still had the advantage, thus evoking a similar response of envy from others.

It is interesting to note that in their analysis of the results, the researchers assumed that the supervisees were misperceiving their supervisors' actions. As we have seen in the examples reported throughout this book, that is entirely possible. On the other hand, perhaps those perceptions were accurate. Another explanation for these results is that the African American female supervisors and the white male supervisors are in fact more critical and less supportive precisely because, in their agency contexts, each of those groups has special privilege. The assumption behind this explanation is that any group that is given advantage because of race and gender rather than competence is in danger of including in its ranks those who are not optimally suited for the job and who therefore may not be trusted as colleagues or as supervisors.

COMMUNICATION OF COMPASSION

Boszormenyi-Nagy developed the concept of *multidirected partiality* to describe the attitude that he believes should guide the practitioner's stance. Practitioners must work to see things from the perspective of everyone involved, even those who are not present. Practitioners need to have compassion for the pain each family member has experienced and must make an effort to understand the impact of that pain on the individual's current psychological state. In addition, practitioners must hold each member accountable for his or her current behavior. In other words, compassion does not excuse destructive behavior. Multidirected partiality is distinguished from neutrality, or avoiding siding with anyone, and from unidirected partiality, or siding with one member of the family against the others (Boszormenyi-Nagy & Spark, 1984; Boszormenyi-Nagy & Krasner, 1986; Boszormenyi-Nagy, 1988; Goldenthal, 1993).

In supervision, adoption of this stance has several effects. First, if supervisors model compassion for every family member's very human condition, supervisees will be challenged to do the same. In addition, supervisees will indirectly receive the message that their own condition is equally deserving of such treatment. Supervisors can communicate this message directly to supervisees as well, by demonstrating compassion for them as they encounter painful personal issues in supervision and by communicating an attitude of acceptance for the supervisees' natural fears and feelings of inadequacy as they risk new behaviors in their work. Finally, this compassion is authentic and realistic, as it includes an expectation that the supervisee will act with integrity. As I have demonstrated in this chapter, the creation of a safe, accepting (nonshaming) environment as well as one in which participants can count on the honesty of the others is the foundation for trust between supervisor and supervisee. A supervisor whose actions are guided by the principle of multidirected partiality will contribute greatly to the enhancement of trust in the relationship.

SUMMARY

The establishment of trust in the supervisory relationship is crucial to its well-being. Although many would state that this point is obvious and "goes without saying," we rarely talk about what actually enhances or diminishes that trust. In my opinion, two basic elements contribute to the development of a trusting relationship: honesty and the supervisor's attention to the supervisee's shame. For a variety of reasons, shame seems to arise almost inevitably at some point during practitioners' work and, therefore, during their supervision. It is therefore incumbent on supervisors to recognize this inevitability and make some decisions about how they want to deal with it when it occurs. Supervisors and supervisees alike hold a variety of opinions about what sort of approach is most effective. Some supervisors go out of their way to avoid a shameful response from their supervisees. Others rely on the relational process to deal with those feelings when they arise, believing that the direct acknowledgment and discussion of shame is a useful part of the supervisory process. Still others believe just the opposite—namely, if those feelings are present, they should be minimized and deflected; talking about them directly would do the supervisee a great disservice. By the same token, some supervisees would prefer to talk directly about their own vulnerability, whereas others would find that process demeaning. Furthermore, some supervisees are less prone to shame and more able to work it through than others are. The important message here is not that there is a "right" way to handle shame or that the supervisor has necessarily made a mistake if the supervisee feels shame. The message is rather that if trust is a problem in the supervision, shame might be the issue.

The second major element, honesty, is related to the concept of accountability, defined in Chapter 2 as telling the truth about oneself and taking responsible action. Although the supervisor bears the primary responsibility for setting the tone in the relationship, clearly both participants need to approach one another with authenticity if the relationship is to succeed.

As stated repeatedly throughout this book, both supervisor and supervisee bring their personal histories into the relationship, and those histories affect the way they view one another. Racial tensions, which permeate society both currently and historically, add stress to cross-cultural supervisory relationships and can contribute to mistrust between supervisors and supervisees. This mistrust is sometimes deepened by problems in shared meaning, which lead to hurt, insult, and fear.

The final section of this chapter consisted of a discussion about the relationship between the context and the development of trust. Certainly the dynamics in the larger agency add complications to the supervisory relationship that can either enhance or diminish trust between supervisor and supervisee. Ultimately, however, it is the behavior between supervisor and supervisee that determines whether or not that relationship itself is considered trustworthy.

QUESTIONS TO PROMOTE CRITICAL THINKING

1. Compare the approaches to shame illustrated by Sandy (p. 138), Margaret (pp. 140–141), and Lee (pp. 142–143). Discuss what is gained and what is lost with each approach. Which approach would you find most effective as a supervisor and as a supervisee, and why?

2. Kim (pp. 138–139) is a supervisee who seems quite sensitive to criticism. From Shirley's point of view, this sensitivity was getting in the way of Kim's learning. Speculate as to how Kim would explain the situation. Analyze the approach Shirley took to address the problem. What are some other options Shirley might have chosen?

3. Ian (pp. 143–144) made a powerful argument for the need to discourage a supervisee's expression of shame in the context of supervision. Defend and challenge his argument.

4. Larry's trust of his supervisor (pp. 150–151) was clearly enhanced by Matt's sharing of his own vulnerability. Imagine a scenario in which his action had the opposite effect. Create a role play in which Matt and Larry talk about Larry's negative response.

5. Identify some things that tend to keep you from discussing uncomfortable differences between you and your supervisor. Talk about both your own issues and those things you think have more to do with your supervisor's qualities.

6. Using the examples of Carol and Dana (pp. 153–154) as a basis for discussion, identify your own concerns about confronting racial and cultural differences.

7. Many of the stories in this chapter illustrate the connection between power, shared meaning, and trust (for example, Marilyn and Tim, pp. 130–131; Monica, pp. 149–150; April, p. 151; and Chad, p. 152). Discuss a supervisory relationship you have experienced or know about that you would characterize as untrustworthy. How did the use of power and the degree of shared meaning contribute to the lack of trust? What impact did the context have on the situation?

Epilogue

The stories and discussions in this text have demonstrated that the supervisory process is as complicated and challenging as the people who are engaged in it and the environments in which they are working. My hope is that supervisors and supervisees alike will understand more deeply the complex dynamics that occur in their relationships and use this understanding to enhance the quality of their experience in supervision. The stories shared by both supervisors and supervisees in this book range from very positive to very negative. Although there is no one right and one wrong way to do supervision, it is possible to identify some features that characterize poor, average, and highly successful supervisory relationships.

Poor relationships are characterized by deep feelings of mistrust on the part of either the supervisors, the supervisees, or both. Often supervisors are seen as abusive of their power, using it to punish their supervisees or to serve their own needs in some way. Supervisees experience these supervisors as being dishonest, as sometimes giving mixed messages, or as becoming quite defensive or closed in response to a challenge. They often characterize these supervisors as shaming and the relationships as very unsafe. Supervisors characterize supervisees in these relationships as being withholding, unwilling to open themselves to feedback, and dishonest in their accounts of their work. Occasionally they characterize their supervisees as having too much shame to be able to make effective use of supervision. Poor relationships, therefore, are those in which there is an absence of trust and shared meaning and where the power and authority is often handled in an abusive manner.

Average relationships are those in which little is happening in the supervision. The supervisors are frequently seen as not having anything especially valuable to teach. However, this is not always the case. In some situations, the supervisors may be perceived as knowledgeable but, because of a lack of another element in the relationship, the supervisees are unable to fully benefit from the knowledge. For example, a supervisor could be a well-respected expert but be unable to arrive at a satisfactory contract with a supervisee regarding frequency of sessions.

Supervisors in these relationships are often viewed as not particularly in charge of the process. If supervisees feel safe, it is most often because they know nothing real will be discussed; therefore they have no reason to feel threatened. These relationships are average rather than overtly negative because the supervisors are often experienced as benign. A good example of this type of relationship is the supervisee who experienced her relationship with her supervisor as one of mutual growth and one in which she had a great deal of respect and fondness for her supervisor, who was a friend and colleague as well. However, she did not perceive this as excellent supervision because he lacked the ability to teach her and to challenge her in a deeply honest way.

Therefore average experiences are those in which some but not all the elements of relationship presented in the model are in place. There could be an adequate knowledge differential but a lack of shared meaning, or a sense of trust in the relationship but a lack of feeling that the supervisor was in charge or had something valuable to teach.

Some of the general features of good supervisory relationships include the following. The supervisors are seen as having an approach to treatment the supervisees consider effective and about which the supervisors are perceived to have greater knowledge. The supervisors are willing and able to set limits when necessary. The supervisees have a clear sense that the supervisors are in charge of the relationship and will use that power fairly. Supervisees are clear as well, about what is expected of them and what they can expect from the process. They also know they have the power to ask for what they want and need. In addition, they are respectfully acknowledged if they challenge their supervisors on either clinical or relationship issues. The supervisors are experienced as safe—that is, not shaming—although the approach to shame may differ dramatically among them. In the language of the conceptual model, these relationships are characterized by a high degree of trust and shared meaning and an effective use of power and authority.

References

Abroms, G. M. (1978). Supervision as metatherapy. In F. Kaslow (Ed.), *Supervision, consultation and staff training in the helping professions* (pp. 81–99). San Francisco: Jossey-Bass.

Alexander, J., Barton, C., Schiavo, R., & Parsons, B. (1976). Systems-behavioral intervention with families of delinquents: Therapist characteristics, family behavior, and outcome. *Journal of Consulting and Clinical Psychology, 44,* 656–664.

Alonso, A., & Rutan, J. (1988). Shame and guilt in psychotherapy supervision. *Psychotherapy, 25*(4), 576–581.

Alpher, V. (1991). Interdependence and parallel processes: A case study of structured analysis of social behavior in supervision and short-term dynamic psychotherapy. *Psychotherapy, 28*(2), 218–231.

American Association for Marriage and Family Therapy. (1991). *Code of ethics.* Washington, DC: AAMFT.

Asante, M. (1987). *The Afrocentric idea.* Philadelphia: Temple University Press.

Ault-Riche, M. (1987). Teaching an integrated model of family therapy: Women as students, women as supervisors. *Journal of Psychotherapy and the Family, 3*(4), 175–192.

Barnard, J., & Goodyear, R. (1992). *Fundamentals of clinical supervision.* Boston: Allyn & Bacon.

Bartlett, W. (1983). A multidimensional framework for the analysis of supervision of counseling. *The Counseling Psychologist, 11*(1), 9–20.

Beck, A., & Emmery, G. (1985). *Anxiety disorders and phobias: A cognitive perspective.* New York: Basic Books.

Berger, M., & Damman, G. (1982). Live supervision as context, treatment and training. *Family Process, 21,* 337–344.

Bernal, M. E., Saenz, D. S., & Knight, G. P. (1991). Ethnic identity and adaptation of Mexican American youth in school settings. *Hispanic Journal of Behavioral Sciences, 13*(2), 135–154.

Boscolo, L., & Cecchin, G. (1982). Training on systemic therapy at the Milan Centre. In R. Wiffen & J. Byng-Hall (Eds.), *Family therapy supervision: Recent developments in practice.* London: Academic Press.

Boszormenyi-Nagy, I. (1988). *Foundations of contextual therapy: Collected papers of Ivan Boszormenyi-Nagy.* New York: Brunner/Mazel.

Boszormenyi-Nagy, I., & Krasner, B. R. (1986). *Between give and take: A clinical guide to contextual therapy.* New York: Brunner/Mazel.

Boszormenyi-Nagy, I., & Spark, G. (1984). *Invisible loyalties: Reciprocity in intergenerational family therapy.* New York: Brunner/Mazel.

Boyd-Franklin, N. (1989). *Black families in therapy.* New York: Guilford.

Broome, B. (1991). Building a shared meaning: Implications of a relational approach of empathy for teaching intercultural communication. *Communication Education, 40*(3), 235–249.

Burton, A. (Ed.). (1970). *Encounter.* San Francisco: Jossey-Bass.

Byng-Hall, J. (1982). The use of the earphone in supervision. In R. Wiffen & J. Byng-Hall (Eds.), *Family therapy supervision: Recent developments in practice.* London: Academic Press.

Cade, B. W., & Seligman, P. M. (1982). Teaching a strategic approach. In R. Wiffen & J. Byng-Hall (Eds.), *Family therapy supervision: Recent developments in practice* (pp. 167–180). London: Academic Press.

Caust, B. L., Libow, J. A., & Raskin, P. A. (1981). Challenges and promises of training women as family systems therapists. *Family Process, 20*, 439–447.

Chau, K. (1990). A model for teaching cross cultural practice in social work. *Journal of Social Work Education, 2*, 124–133.

Cheung, F. K. (1994). Asian American and Pacific Islanders' mental health issues: A historical perspective. *Asian American and Pacific Islander Journal of Health (2)*, 94–107.

Connell, G. (1984). An approach to supervision of symbolic-experiential psychotherapy. *Journal of Marital and Family Therapy, 10*, 273–280.

Cohen, B. (1987). The ethics of social work supervision revisited. *Social Work, 32*(3), 194–196.

Cook, D., & Helms, J. (1988). Visible racial/ethnic group supervisees' satisfaction with cultural supervision as predicted by relationship characteristics. *Journal of Counseling Psychology, 35*(3), 268–274.

Corsini, R., & Wedding, D. (1995). *Current psychotherapies* (5th ed.). Itasca, IL: F. E. Peacock.

Cromwell, R. E., & Ruiz, R. A. (1979). The myth of macho dominance in decision making within Mexican and Chicano families. *Hispanic Journal of Behavioral Sciences, 1*, 355–373.

Cross, W. E., (1991). *Shades of black: Diversity in African American identity.* Philadelphia: Temple University Press.

Dean, R. (1984). The role of empathy in supervision. *Clinical Social Work Journal, 12*(2), 129–139.

Denton, N. A., & Massey, D. S. (1989). Racial identity among Caribbean Hispanics: The effect of double minority status on residential segregation. *American Sociological Review, 54*, 790–808.

Doehrman, M. J. G. (1976). Parallel processes in supervision and psychotherapy. *Bulletin of the Menninger Clinic, 40*(1), 3–104.

Doherty, W. (1995). *Soul searching: Why psychotherapy must promote moral responsibility.* New York: Basic Books.

Doherty, W., & Boss, P. (1991). Values and ethics in family therapy. In A. S. Gurman & D. P. Kniskern (Eds.), *Handbook of family therapy* (2nd. ed.). New York: Brunner/Mazel.

Eckstein, R., & Wallerstein, R. (1958). *The teaching and earning of psychother-apy.* New York: Basic Books.

Fantz, R., (1996). A case approach to gestalt therapy. In . Corey (Ed.), *A case approach to counseling and psychotherapy.* Pacific Gro , CA: Brooks/Cole.

Farmer, S. (1987). Conflict management and clinical sup vision. *The Clinical Supervisor, 5*(3), 5–28.

Felix-Ortiz, M., Newcomb, M. D., & Myers, H. (1994). A mu idimensional mea-sure of cultural identity for Latino and Latina adolesce ts. *Hispanic Jour-nal of Behavioral Sciences, 16*(2), 99–115.

Fouad, N. (1995). Balancing client and cultural specificity. *The Counseling Psy-chologist, 23*(1), 63–67.

Fossom, M., & Mason, M. (1986). *Facing shame: Families in recovery.* New York: Norton.

Fox, R. (1989). Relationship: The cornerstone of clinical supervision. *Social Casework, 70*(3), 1946–1952.

Frankel, B. R., & Piercy, F. P. (1990). The relationship among selected supervi-sor, therapist, and client behaviors. *Journal of Marital and Family Therapy, 16*(4), 404–421.

French, J., & Raven, B. (1960). The bases of social power. In D. Cartwright & A. Zander, (Eds.), *Group dynamics.* Evanston, IL: Row, Peterson.

Ganahl, G. F., Fergeson, L. R. R., & L'Abate, L. (1985). Training in family ther-apy. In L. L'Abate (Ed.), *Handbook of family psychology* (pp. 1281–1308). Homewood, IL: Dorsey Press.

Garrett, K., & Barretta-Herman, A. (1995). Missing links: Professional devel-opment in school social work. *Journal of Social Work Education, 17*(4), 235–243.

Gartrell, N. (Ed.). (1994). *Bringing ethics alive.* New York: Harrington Park Press.

Goldberg, J. (1993). Exploring the murky world of dual relationships. *Family Therapy News, 24*(3), 24–25.

Goldenthal, P. (1993). *Contextual family therapy: Assessment and intervention procedures.* Sarasota, FL: Resource Press.

Green, R., & Kolvezon, M. (1982). Three approaches to family therapy: A study in convergence and divergence. *Journal of Marital and Family Therapy, 5*, 39–50.

Gurman, A., Kniskern, D., & Pinsoff, W. (1986). Research on the process and outcome of marital and family therapy. In S. Garfield & A. Bergin (Eds.), *Handbook of psychotherapy and behavior change: An empirical analysis* (3rd ed.). New York: Wiley.

Haley, J. (1988). Reflections on supervision. In H. Liddle, D. C. Breunlin, & R. C. Schwartz (Eds.), *Handbook of family therapy training and supervision* (pp. 358–367). New York: Guilford.

Hass, L. J., Alexander J. F., & Mas, C., (1988). Functional family therapy: Basic concepts and training program. In H. Liddle, D. C. Breunlin, & R. C. Schwartz (Eds.), *Handbook of Family Therapy Training and Supervision* (pp. 128–148). New York: Guilford.

Heath, A. (1982). Team family therapy training: Conceptual and pragmatic considerations. *Family Process, 21*, 187–194.

Horner, A. (1988). Developmental aspects of psychodynamic supervision:

Parallel process of separation and individuation. *The Clinical Supervisor,* 6(2), 3–12.

Jacobs, C. (1991). Violations of the supervisory relationship: An ethical and educational blind spot. *Social Work, 36*(2), 97–192.

Jayaratne, S., Barbs, H., Gannet, L., Nagoya, B., Sing, B., & Chess, W. (1992). African American practitioners' perceptions of their supervisors: Emotional support, social undermining, and criticism. *Administration in Social Work, 16*(2), 27–43.

Jones, R. L. (Ed.). (1972). *Black psychology.* New York: Harper & Row.

Kadushin, A. (1974). Supervisor-supervisee: A survey. *Social Work, 19,* 288–298.

Kadushin, A. (1992). *Supervision in social work* (3rd ed.). New York: Columbia University Press.

Kahn, E. M. (1979). Parallel process in social work treatment and supervision. *Social Casework: The Journal of Contemporary Social Work, 60*(9), 520–528.

Kaiser, T. (1992). The supervisory relationship: An identification of the primary elements in the relationship and an application of two theories of ethical relationships. *Journal of Marital and Family Therapy, 18*(3), 283–296.

Kiev, A. (Ed.). (1964). *Magic, faith and healing.* New York: Free Press.

Kinzie, J. D. (1989). Therapeutic approaches to traumatized Cambodian refugees. *Journal of Traumatic Stress, (2),* 266–275.

LaFromboise, T. D. (1983). *Assertion training with American Indians: Cultural/behavioral issues for training.* Las Cruces, NM: Educational Resources Information Center Clearinghouse on Rural Education and Small Schools.

LaFromboise, T. D. (1989). *Circles of women: Professional skills training with American Indian women.* Newton, MA: Women's Educational Equity Act Publishing Center.

Leong, F. T. L. (1993). History of Asian American Psychology. *Monograph Series, Asian American Psychological Association.*

Leong, F. T. L., & Whitfield, J. R. (Eds.). (1992). *Asians in the United States: Abstracts of the psychological and behavioral literature, 1967–1991.* (Bibliographies in Psychology, no. 11.) Washington, DC: American Psychological Association.

Levy, C. S. (1973). The ethics of supervision. *Social Work, 18,* 14–21.

Levy, C. S. (1982). *A guide to ethical decisions and action for social science administrators—A handbook for managerial personnel.* New York: Haworth Press.

Liddle, H. A. (1988). Systemic supervision: Conceptual overlays and pragmatic guidelines. In H. A. Liddle, D. C. Breunlin, & R. C. Schwartz (Eds.), *Handbook of family therapy training and supervision* (pp. 153–171). New York: Guilford.

Liddle, H., Breunlin, D. C., & Schwartz, R. C. (Eds.), (1988). *Handbook of family therapy training and supervision.* New York: Guilford.

Liddle, H. A., Davidson, G. S., & Barrett, M. (1988). Outcomes of live supervision: Trainee perspectives. In H. A. Liddle, D. C. Breunlin, & R. C. Schwartz (Eds.), *Handbook of family therapy training and supervision* (pp. 386–398). New York: Guilford.

Liddle, H., & Schwartz, R. C. (1983). Live supervision and consultation: Conceptual and pragmatic guidelines for family therapy trainers. *Family Process, 22,* 477–480.

Loganbill, C., Hardy, E., & Delworth, U. (1982). Supervision: A conceptual model. *The Counseling Psychologist, 10*(1), 3–41.

Lowenstein, S., Reder, P., & Clark, A. (1982). The consumers' response: Trainees' discussion of the experience of live supervision. In R. Wiffen & J. Byng-Hall (Eds.), *Family therapy supervision: Recent developments in practice* (pp. 115–130). London: Academic Press.

Ly, P. (1996). *Rearing children in America: Nurturing program for Hmong parents and adolescents.* Paper presented for the Second Annual Hmong National Development Education Conference, Sacramento, California, April 4–6.

Martinez, K. (1994). Cultural sensitivity in family therapy gone awry. *Hispanic Journal of Behavioral Sciences, 16*(1), 75–89.

Marsella, A. J., & Pedersen, P. B. (Eds.). (1981). *Cross cultural counseling and psychotherapy.* New York: Pergamon Press.

Matts, K. (1995). *Communication in Cross Cultural Supervision.* MSW Clinical Research Paper, College of St. Catherine/University of St. Thomas, St. Paul, MN.

Mazza, J. (1988). Training strategic therapists: The use of indirect techniques. In H. A. Liddle, R. C. Breunlin, & R. C. Schwartz (Eds.), *Handbook of family therapy training and supervision* (pp. 93–109). New York: Guilford.

McDaniel, S. H., Webber, T., & McKeever, J. (1983). Multiple theoretical approaches to supervision: Choices in family therapy training. *Family Process, 22,* 291–300.

McRoy, R., Freeman, E., Logagan, S., & Blackmon, B. (1986). Cross-cultural field supervision: Implications for social work education. *Journal of Social Work Education, 22*(1), 50–56.

Miller, P. (1990). Covenant model for professional relationships: An alternate to the contract model. *Social Work, 35*(2), 121–125.

Minnesota Statutes. §148B.07(4) (1992).

Montalvo, B. (1973). Aspects of live supervision. *Family Process, 12*(4), 343–359.

Munson, C. (1989). Trends of significance for clinical supervision. *The Clinical Supervisor, 7*(4), 1–8.

Munson, C. (1993). *Clinical social work supervision* (2nd ed.). New York: Haworth Press.

NASW Council on the Practice of Clinical Social Work. (1994). *Guidelines for Clinical Social Work Supervision.* Washington, DC: NASW.

Nelson, T. (1991). Gender in family therapy supervision. *Contemporary Family Therapy, 13*(4), 357–367.

Neufeldt, V., & Guralnik, D. B. (Eds.). (1988). *Webster's New World Dictionary of American English* (3rd ed.). New York: Simon & Shuster.

Nichols, W. (1988). An integrative psychodynamic and systems approach. In H. A. Liddle, D. C. Breunlin, & R. C. Schwartz (Eds.), *Handbook of family therapy training and supervision* (pp. 110–127). New York: Guilford.

Nichols, M., & Schwartz, R. (1995). *Family therapy* (3rd ed.). Boston: Allyn & Bacon.

Noddings, N. (1984). *Caring: A feminine approach to ethics and moral education.* Berkeley: University of California Press.

Northern, H. (1989). *The expanded definition of clinical social work.* National Council on the Practice of Clinical Social Work.

Olson, J., & Pegg, P. (1979). Direct open supervision: A team approach. *Family Process, 8,* 463–469.

Papero, D. (1988). Training in Bowen theory. In H. A. Liddle, D. C. Breunlin, & R. C. Schwartz (Eds.), *Handbook of family therapy training and supervision* (pp. 62–77). New York: Guilford.

Pederson, P. (1991). Multiculturalism as a generic approach to counseling. *Journal of Counseling and Development, 70,* 6–12.

Pederson, P. B. (1994a). *A handbook for developing multicultural awareness* (2nd ed.). Alexandria VA: American Counseling Association.

Pederson, P. B. (1994b). *Culture-centered counseling: A search for accuracy.* Newbury Park, CA: Sage.

Pederson, P. B., & Ivey, A. (1993). *Culture-centered counseling and interviewing skills: A practical guide.* Westport, CT: Praeger.

Pederson, P. B., Sartorius, N., & Marsella, A. (Eds.). (1984). *Mental health services: The cross cultural context.* Newbury Park, CA: Sage.

Perlman, H. (1979). *Relationship: The heart of helping people.* Chicago: University of Chicago Press.

Peterson, M. (1984). *Clinical supervision.* Paper presented at the University of Minnesota School of Social Work, Minneapolis, MN.

Peterson, M. (1986). *The parallel process.* Paper presented at the University of Minnesota School of Social Work, Minneapolis, MN.

Peterson, M. (1992). *At personal risk: Boundary violations in professional-client relationships.* New York: Norton.

Peterson, M. (1993a). Covert agendas in supervision. In C. Storm (Ed.), *Supervision bulletin, VI*(1). Washington, DC: American Association of Marriage and Family Therapy.

Peterson, M. (1993b). Speak out. *Family Therapy News, 24*(3), 2.

Pirotta, S., & Cecchin, G. (1988). The Milan training program. In H. A. Liddle, D. C. Breunlin, & R. C. Schwartz (Eds.), *Handbook of family therapy training and supervision* (pp. 38–61). New York: Guilford.

Rabanowitz, J. (1987). Why ongoing supervision in social work: An historical analysis. *Clinical Supervisor, 5*(3), 79–90.

Reid, E., McDaniel, S., Donaldson, C., & Tollers, M. (1987). Taking it personally: Issues of personal authority and competence for the female in family therapy training. *Journal of Marital and Family Therapy, 13*(2), 157–165.

Rubinstein, G. (1992). Supervision and psychotherapy: Toward redefining the differences. *The Clinical Supervisor, 10*(2), 97–115.

Ryan, A., & Hendricks, C. (1989). Culture and communication: Supervising the Asian and Hispanic social worker. *The Clinical Supervisor, 7*(1), 27–40.

Ryder, R., & Hepworth, J. (1990). AAMFT Ethical Code: "Dual Relationships." *Journal of Marital and Family Therapy, 16*(2), 127–132.

Schneider, S. (1992). Transference, counter-transference, projective identification and role responsiveness in the supervisory process. *The Clinical Supervisor, 10*(2), 71–84.

Schwartz, R. C. (1988). The trainer-trainee relationship in family therapy training. In H. A. Liddle, D. C. Breunlin, & R. C. Schwartz (Eds.), *Handbook of family therapy training and supervision* (pp. 172–182). New York: Guilford.

Sherry, P. (1991). Ethical issues in the conduct of supervision. *The Counseling Psychologist, 19*(4), 566–584.

Shulman, L. (1982). *Skills of supervision and staff management*. Itasca, IL: F. E. Peacock.

Shulman, L. (1993). *Interactional supervision*. Washington, DC: NASW Press.

Sigman, M. (1989). Parallel process at case conferences. *Bulletin of the Menninger Clinic, 53*(4), 340–349.

Springman, R. (1989). Reflections on the role of the supervisor. *British Journal of Medical Psychology, 69*(3), 217–228.

Stoltenberg, C., & Delworth, R. (1987). *Supervising counselors and therapists: A developmental approach*. San Francisco: Jossey-Bass.

Storm, C. (1993). Dual relationships: Broadening our understanding. In C. Storm (Ed.), *Supervision Bulletin, VI*(1). Washington, DC: American Association of Marriage and Family Therapy.

Storm, C., Peterson, M., & Tomm, K. (1997). Multiple relationships: Stepping up to complexity. In T. Todd and C. Storm, (Eds.), *The complete systemic supervisor: Context, philosophy and pragmatics*. Boston: Allyn & Bacon.

Sue, D. W., Allen, E., & Pederson, P. (1996). *A theory of multicultural counseling and therapy*. Pacific Grove, CA: Brooks/Cole.

Sue, D. W., & Kirk, B. A. (1972). Psychological characteristics of Chinese-American students. *Journal of Counseling Psychology*, (19), 471–478.

Sue, D. W., & Kirk, B. A. (1973). Differential characteristics of Japanese-American college students. *Journal of Counseling Psychology*, (20), 142–148.

Sue, D. W., & Sue, D. (1990). *Counseling the culturally different* (2nd ed.). New York: Wiley.

Sue, S., & Morishima, J. (1982). *The mental health of Asian Americans*. San Francisco: Jossey-Bass.

Swinomish Tribal Community. (1991). *A gathering of wisdoms. Tribal mental health: A cultural perspective*. LaConner, WA: Swinomish Tribal Mental Health Project.

Tannen, D. (1990). *You just don't understand: Women and men in conversation*. New York: Ballantine.

Thompson, P., Shapiro, M., Nielson, L., & Peterson, M. (1989). Supervision strategies to prevent sexual abuse by therapists and counselors. In B. Sanderson (Ed.), *It's never O.K.: A handbook for professionals on sexual exploitation by counselors and therapists* (pp. 19–26). Minneapolis: Task Force on Sexual Exploitation by Counselors and Therapists, Minnesota Program for Victims of Sexual Assault, Department of Corrections.

Tomm, K., & Wright, L. (1979). Training in family therapy: Perceptual, conceptual and executive skills. *Family Process, 18*, 227–250.

Tomm, K. (1993). Defining supervision and therapy: A fuzzy boundary? In C. Storm (Ed.), *The Supervision Bulletin VI*(1) Washington, DC: American Association of Marriage and Family Therapy.

Trafzer, C. E. (Ed.). (1985). *American Indian identity: Today's changing perspectives*. Sacramento: Sierra Oaks.

Toupin, E. S. W. A. (1980). Counseling Asians: Psychotherapy in the context of racism and Asian-American history. *American Journal of Orthopsychiatry*, (50), 76–86.

Turner, F. J. (1986). *Social work treatment: Interlocking theoretical approaches* (3rd ed.). New York: Free Press.

Uba, L. (1994). *Asian Americans: Personality patterns, identity and mental health.* New York: Guilford.

Upchurch, D. (1985). Ethical standards and the supervisory process. *Counselor Education and Supervision,* (December), 90–99.

Van Heusden, A., & Van den Eerenbeembt, E. (1987). *Balance in motion: Ivan Boszormenyi-Nagy and his vision of individual and family therapy.* New York: Brunner/Mazel.

Van Kessel, L., & Haan, D. (1993). The Dutch concept of supervision: Its essential characteristics as a conceptual framework. *The Clinical Supervisor,* 1(4), 5–27.

Weinbach, R. (1994). *The social worker as manager: Theory and practice* (2nd ed.). Boston: Allyn & Bacon.

Wetchler, J. (1989). Supervisors' and supervisees' perceptions of the effectiveness of family therapy supervisor interpersonal skills. *American Journal of Family Therapy, 17*(3), 244–256.

Wheeler, D., Avis, J., Miller, L., & Chaney, S. (1986). Rethinking family therapy education and supervision: A feminist model. *Journal of Psychotherapy and the Family, 1*(4), 53–71.

Wiffen, R., & Byng-Hall, J. (Eds.). (1982). *Family therapy supervision: Recent developments in practice.* London: Academic Press.

Woods, M., & Hollis, F. (1990). *Casework: A psychosocial therapy* (4th ed.). New York: McGraw-Hill.

Yepez, E., Reeser, L., & Wertkin, R. (1994). A model policy on sharing information with field instructors. Unpublished paper, presented at the Council on Social Work Education Annual Program Meeting, Atlanta, GA.

Index